NFT™

Not For Tourists Guide to
PHILADELPHIA

Get more on
notfortourists.com

Keep connected with:
Twitter:
twitter/notfortourists

Facebook:
facebook/notfortourists

iPhone App:
nftiphone.com

P9-CEU-894

Skyhorse Publishing

designed by:
Not For Tourists, Inc
NFT™—Not For Tourists™ Guide to Philadelphia
www.notfortourists.com

| **Publisher** | **Production Manager** | **Research** |
| Skyhorse Publishing | Aaron Schielke | Jess Bender |

Creative Direction & **Writing and Editing** **Graphic Design and**
Information Design Donna Blicharz **Production**
Jane Pirone Emily Doutre Aaron Schielke
Patricia Glowinski Katherine Yaksich
Craig Nelson
Director Scott Sendrow **Information Systems**
Stuart Farr **Manager**
City Editor Juan Molinari
Managing Editor Emily Doutre
Scott Sendrow

Printed in China
ISBN# 978-1-62636-054-9 $16.95
ISSN 2163-9175
Copyright © 2014 by Not For Tourists, Inc.
8th Edition

Every effort has been made to ensure that the information in this book is as up-to-date as possible at press time. However, many details are liable to change—as we have learned.
Not For Tourists cannot accept responsibility for any consequences arising from the use of this book.

Not For Tourists does not solicit individuals, organizations, or businesses for listings inclusion in guides, nor do we accept payment for inclusion into the editorial portion of our book; the adve__ sections, however, are exempt from this policy. We always welcome communications from anyone regarding ANYTHING having to do with our books; please visit us on our website at ww__ notfortourists.com for appropriate contact information.

www.skyhorsepublishing.com

10 9 8 7 6 5 4 3 2 1

Dear NFT User,

We never get tired of saying "Philadelphia: City of Winners." Sure, the Fightins have mostly underperformed this decade. And of course the schools are woefully underfunded and in danger of going into receivership. But at least we have a world-class newspaper to cut through it all…oh wait. But in point of fact, the truth is we're all really geeked about our chances at these schmancy new casinos popping up everywhere. Yessir, we're feeling luckier and luckier 'round these parts. Besides, mindless boosterism is for lesser cities—Boston, for instance. Kidding! (Well, sort of.)

Of course, Philadelphia is much more than just sports fans, street parties, and municipal sclerosis, and we here at NFT have worked hard to tell you about it. In this book you'll find hard facts, honest opinions, and decent advice on everything from where to get drunk on the cheap to which museum is best to take parents to. If you're new to the city, we'll help you get acquainted. If you've been here a while, hopefully we can point out some places you've never been to, but should definitely check out.

The new edition is full of hundreds of new listings and updates, but if there's still something amiss or missing, by all means let us know. Your feedback is essential in helping us make this the ultimate guide to Philly. Dig www.notfortourists.com to give us pro or con feedback. We can take it! And check out our nifty mobile app, for the latest up-to-date information on the go.

Cheers,
—Jane, Scott, Emily, et al.

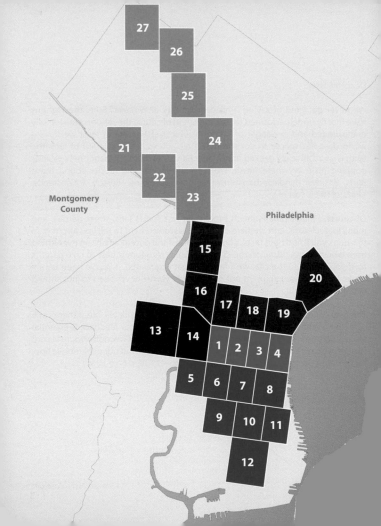

Table of Contents

Map 1 · **Center City West**

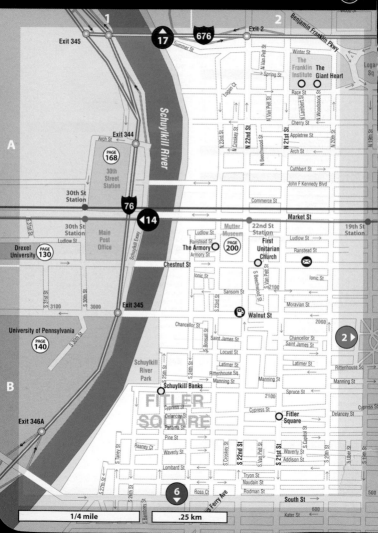

Map 1

Not quite University City and not quite Rittenhouse, Center City West straddles a strange area of Philadelphia. But it also holds some of our best gems: The **Mutter Museum** and **Franklin Institute** are two of the most interesting museums in Philly (beware: the Institute's giant heart smells), and you can always take in an indie rock show at the **First Unitarian Church**.

O Landmarks

- **The Armory** • 22 S 23rd St
  215-564-1488
  Gorgeous building hosting events like antique fairs and roller derby. Cool.
- **First Unitarian Church** • 2125 Chestnut St
  215-563-3980
  Frequent indie rock shows in the basement. Seriously.
- **Fitler Square** • Locust St & S 21st St
  Quakers are why Philly is so green, so pay respects.
- **The Franklin Institute** • 222 N 20th St
  215-448-1200
  IMAX, Planetarium and lots of kiddie-fare.
- **The Giant Heart** • 222 N 20th St
  Oversized human heart model enthralling generations of Philly-area youth.
- **Schuylkill Banks** • 2500 Spruce St
  215-222-6030
  Running, biking, roller blading, hanging (out).

Coffee

- **Almaz Cafe** • 140 S 20th St
  215-557-0108
  Cute! Like, seriously.
- **Good Karma Café** • 331 S 22nd St
  215-546-1479
  Decent coffee shop with a Philosophy.

Farmers Markets

- **Fitler Square** • S 23rd St & Pine St
  Saturdays, 10 am-2 pm, year-round.
- **The Porch Farmers' Market** •
  N 30th St & Market St
  Wednesdays, 11 am-2 pm, May-Sept.
- **Schuylkill River Park Farmers' Market** •
  25th St & Spruce St
  Wednesdays, 3 pm-7 pm, in season.

Nightlife

- **The Bards** • 2013 Walnut St
  215-569-9585
  Laid-back watering hole.
- **Doobies** • 2201 Lombard St
  215-546-0316
  You'll quickly become fast friends with everyone in the place.
- **Helium Comedy Club** • 2031 Sansom St
  215-496-9001
  Top-rated comics haggle for laughs in an uninspired, basement-like room.
- **Irish Pub** • 2007 Walnut St
  215-568 5603
  Rowdy student hang-out unsafe for morally mature.
- **Medusa** • 27 S 21st St
  215-557-1981
  A "write your name on the ceiling when the bartender's not looking", kind of place.
- **Mix Brick Oven Pizza** • 2101 Chestnut St
  215-568-3355
  Beer. And pretty decent pizza.
- **Ranstead Room** • 2013 Ranstead St
  Cool speakeasy. Look for the double R's on the door.
- **Roosevelt Pub** • 2220 Walnut St
  215-569-8879
  Penn fave and with good reason: best drink deals in the city.
- **Tank Bar** • 261 S 21st St
  215-546-4232
  Giant fish tank highlights this sultry joint.
- **World Cafe Live** • 3025 Walnut St
  215-222-1400
  Awesome live shows, but not much else.

Map 1

Center City West

Restaurants

- **Agno Grill** • 2104 Chestnut St
  267-858-4590 • $
  Build your own Mediterranean noms.
- **Audrey Claire** • 290 S 20th St
  215-731-1222 • $$$$
  Simple, classic dishes done with suitable aplomb.
- **The Bards** • 2013 Walnut St
  215-569-9585 • $$
  Fries and curry sauce are a must.
- **Bistro St. Tropez** •
  2400 Market StMarketplace Design Center
  215-569-9269 • $$$$
  Way-upscale French bistro has style to spare.
- **Café Lutecia** • 2301 Lombard St
  215-790-9557 • $
  Baguette or croissant sandwiches, simple, delicious soup, and the best lemonade in the city.
- **Dmtri's** • 2227 Pine St
  215-985-3680 • $$
  Great for small dishes with big drinks.
- **El Rey** • 2013 Chestnut St
  215-563-3330 • $$
  Mexico, brought to you by Stephen Starr.
- **Erawan Thai Cuisine** • 123 S 23rd St
  215-567-2542 • $$
  Not a looker, but the dishes (esp. the glass noodles) are solid.
- **Fitler Dining Room** • 2201 Spruce St
  215-732-3331 • $$$
  Charming French bistro by way of Pub & Kitchen.
- **Friday Saturday Sunday** • 261 S 21st St
  215-546-4232 • $$$$
  The Tank Bar on the second floor is a great place to get lit.
- **Fuji Mountain** • 2030 Chestnut St
  215-751-0939 • $$$
  Thoughtful and cozy, belly up to the sushi bar and do a shot of fish.
- **Gavin's Cafe** • 2536 Pine St
  267-519-2494 • $
  Grab some empanadas to-go for a Schuylkill side picnic!
- **Mama Palma's** • 2229 Spruce St
  215-735-7357 • $
  Wood-fired, thin-crust pie in variations unthinkable—so you thought.
- **Mama's Vegetarian** • 18 S 20th St
  215-751-0477 • $
  Cheap, tasty, healthy, and they'll even deliver. Try the falafel.
- **Melograno** • 2012 Sansom St
  215-875-8116 • $$$$
  Sophisticated yet unpretentious Italian joint packs 'em in.
- **Meritage** • 500 S 20th St
  215-985-1922 • $$$
  Former snob stop has been transformed into a lively bistro.
- **Noble: An American Cookery** •
  2025 Sansom St
  215-568-7000 • $$$
  Pretentious in name, but the food and drink holds up.
- **Porcini** • 2048 Sansom St
  215-751-1175 • $$$
  Tiny but amazingly endearing. The ravishing food helps.
- **Primo Hoagies** • 2043 Chestnut St
  215-496-0540 • $
  One of the premier hoagie experiences in the city.
- **Pub & Kitchen** • 1946 Lombard St
  215-545-0350 • $$
  Pub food deserving of a better moniker.
- **Pure Fare** • 119 S 21st St
  267-318-7441 • $
  Great lunch option when you feel guilty about skipping the gym.
- **Roosevelt Pub** • 2220 Walnut St
  215-569-8879 • $
  Have some fine pub fare in an FDR-inspired setting.
- **Tampopo** • 104 S 21st St
  215-557-9593 • $
  Inexpensive and speedy sushi, with lots of veggie options.
- **Thai Singha House to Go** • 106 S 20th St
  215-568-2390 • $
  Tasty Thai food to-go in a tiny space.
- **Tinto** • 114 S 20th St
  215-665-9150 • $$$$
  Every decadent thing you could think of is on the menu.
- **Twenty Manning** • 261 S 20th St
  215-731-0900 • $$$$
  Hipster haute with a solid bar scene.
- **Vernick** • 2031 Walnut St
  267-639-6644 • $$$
  Simple and inventive. One of Philly's best restaurants.
- **Vic Sushi Bar** • 2035 Sansom St
  215-564-4339 • $$
  Get down and dirty with the cheap and fresh.
- **Village Whiskey** • 118 S 20th St
  215-665-1088 • $$
  Garces forgoes small plates for big burgers.

Catch a stand up comedy show at **Helium** (and don't miss the rousing combination of crazies and legitimately good comics on open mic night), discover how hair care can be kind of scary at **Julius Scissor**, and make sure you're ready for nausea if you take in a not-made-for-IMAX film at the **Franklin Institute**'s IMAX theater.

Shopping

- **Bilt-Well Furniture Showroom** •
  2317 Chestnut St
  215-568-4600
  You hope there merchendize is beter then there speling.
- **Bulb** • 2056 Locust St
  215-732-2224
  Light up your life.
- **Capogiro** • 117 S 20th St
  215-636-9250
  Artisanal gelato and sorbetto.
- **Classical Guitar Store** • 2038 Sansom St
  215-567-2972
  Dude, where do you keep your Strats?
- **Dahlia's** • 2003 Walnut St
  215-568-6878
  Unique jewelry pieces in a refreshingly Israeli atmosphere.
- **Darling's Coffeehouse & Famous Cheesecakes** •
  2100 Spring St
  215-496-9611
  They make a nice pumpkin cheesecake.
- **Dollar General** • 520 S 23rd St
  215-732-3079
  Save Time. Save Money.

- **Home Sweet Homebrew** • 2008 Sansom St
  215-569-9469
  Friendly folks & brew supplies galore.
- **Julius Scissor** • 2045 Locust St
  215-567-7222
  A hair artiste, with various hair-crafted sculptures on display.
- **Long In The Tooth** • 2027 Sansom St
  215-569-1994
  Big space selling cds, records, and movies into late-nite when you're drunk and ready.
- **Nook Bakery & Coffee Bar** • 15 S 20th St
  215-496-9033
  Small-batch baking and coffee.
- **Pleasure Chest** • 2039 Walnut St
  215-561-7480
  Honey, where are my dang nipple clips?
- **Rejuvalux Body Klinic Day Spa** •
  2012 Walnut St
  215-563-8888
  Enjoy all their various transdermal services.
- **Springboard Media** • 121 S 13th St
  215-988-7777
  Best Mac store in the city.
- **Trader Joe's** • 2121 Market St
  215-569-9282
  It's not just for cheap yuppies anymore.
- **Wonderland** • 2037 Walnut St
  215-561-1071
  Pipes, bongs, hookahs—strangely, all just for tobacco!

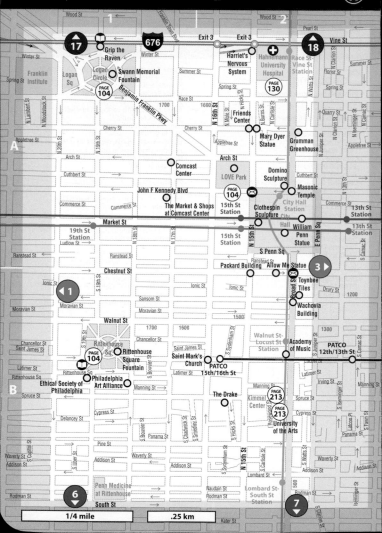

Map 2 · Rittenhouse / Logan Circle

Map 2

Walnut Street is where the decadent shop and later eat at an array of look-at-me restaurants. Rittenhouse Square sits at the center of the universe, filled with crusty punks, moms, and rich old ladies who refuse to pick up their dog shit. Too crowded? Go take a look at the fountain in Logan Square.

O Landmarks

- **Academy of Music** • 1 S Broad St
  215-893-1999
  Scorsese shot the opening to *The Age of Innocence* here.
- **Allow Me Statue** • 1412 Chestnut St
  Biz-dude holding umbrella is always creepy.
- **City Hall** • JFK Blvd & Market St
  Its the largest municipal building in the world.
- **Clothespin Sculpture** • Market St & N 15th St
  Obviously, a take on the ills of modern society. Or something.
- **Comcast Center** • 1701 Arch St
  Tallest green building in the nation.
- **Domino Sculpture** •
  1401 John F Kennedy Blvd
  Stand under a giant domino for a great photo op.
- **The Drake** • 1512 Spruce St
  866-963-3058
  Historic, elegant 32 story art deco building—that you can live in!
- **Ethical Society of Philadelphia** •
  1906 Rittenhouse Sq
  215-735-3456
  [Tape] deck the halls!
- **Friends Center** • 1501 Cherry St
  Check out the helicopters landing and taking off.
- **Grip the Raven** • 1901 Vine St
  Inspiration to Poe and Dickens, at the Free Library.
- **Grumman Greenhouse** •
  N Broad St & Cherry St
  Former US military plane molded into a greenhouse—in crash position.
- **Harriet's Nervous System** •
  Vine St & N 15th St
  Medical college entrance still displays her—since 1888.
- **LOVE Park** • Kennedy Blvd & N 15th St
  The skater Mecca of the world, if only it were legal.
- **The Market & Shops at Comcast Center** •
  1701 JFK Blvd
  215-496-1810
  Food court for office slaves.
- **Mary Dyer Statue** • N 15th St & Cherry St
  Hanged Quaker martyr makes for moving piece.
- **The Masonic Temple** • 1 N Broad St
  215-988-1900
  Giant staircases and oak appointments.
- **Packard Building** • Chestnut St & S 15th St
  Shyamalanadingdong turned it into a train station for *Unbreakable*. Meh.
- **Philadelphia Art Alliance** • 251 S 18th St
  215-545-4302
  Multidisciplinary arts center; great concerts, too.
- **Rittenhouse Square Fountain** •
  Walnut St & S 18th St
  The perfect wade-to-your-pant-cuffs pool to take the edge off the summer.
- **Saint Mark's Church** • 1625 Locust St
  215-735-1416
  Scenes from *Fallen* were shot here. Too bad no one saw the movie.
- **Swann Memorial Fountain** •
  Logan Sq & N 19th St
  Summertime, kids swim for free.
- **Toynbee Tiles** • S Broad St & Sansom St
  Mysterious tiles all over the city.
- **Wachovia Building** • S Broad St & Sansom St
  Parts of *Trading Places* were shot here. Wowee.
- **William Penn Statue** •
  W Broad St & W Market St
  We will never dress him in Flyers' gear again.

Coffee

- **Capriccio Café** • 110 N 16th St
  215-735-9797
  Feels more Eurpoean than Philadelphian.
- **Flixir Coffee** • 207 S Sydenham St
  Pour-overs and distressed wood.
- **La Citadelle** • 1600 Pine St
  215-546-0820
  Understated coffee house worth your afternoon.
- **La Colombe** • 130 S 19th St
  215-563-0860
  The bitter Philly favorite.
- **La Colombe Torrefaction** • 1414 S Penn Sq
  215-977-7770
  One of the city's best brews, with beans to go.

Map 2

Rittenhouse / Logan Circle

🍎 Farmers Markets

- **Rittenhouse Farmers' Market** •
S 18th St & Walnut St
Saturdays, 10 am-3 pm (year-round);
Tuesdays, 10 am-1 pm (May-Sept).
- **Suburban Station Farmers' Market** •
N 16th St & John F. Kennedy Blvd
Thursdays, 12 noon-6:30 pm, year-round.

🍸 Nightlife

- **Ashton Cigar Bar** • 1522 Walnut St
267-350-0000
The cigar bar returns to Philly.
- **The Black Sheep Pub** • 247 S 17th St
215-545-9473
Pricey but authentic English pub atmosphere
rules.
- **The Corner Foodery** • 1710 Sansom St
215-567-1500
Featuring two of Philly's great loves: beer and
sandwiches.
- **Devil's Alley** • 1907 Chesnut St
215-751-0707
Something for everyone in a spacious, relaxed
gastropub.
- **Drinker's Pub** • 1903 Chestnut St
215-564-0914
At the door you'll find Weaver—the best
bouncer in Philly.
- **The Franklin Mortgage & Investment Co.** •
112 S 18th St
267-467-3277
A bit pretentious, but totally amazing
cocktails.
- **Good Dog** • 224 S 15th St
215-985-9600
Yumalicious local brews are featured in their
draught pulls.
- **The Happy Rooster** • 118 S 16th St
215-963-9311
The Passion of the Cristal: Mel's fave bar in
Philly.
- **Mace's Crossing** • 1714 Cherry St
215-564-5203
Where Tad and Kitty unwind from grueling
regatta-cheering.
- **McGlinchey's** • 259 S 15th St
215-735-1259
Brilliantly low-end Uarts joint has cheap pints
and Ms. Pac Man.

- **Misconduct Tavern** • 1511 Locust St
215-732-5797
Giant flatscreens make for some excellent
sports watching.
- **Monk's Café** • 264 S 16th St
215-545-7005
Possibly the best beer list in the city. Long
wait, though.
- **Noche** • 1901 Chestnut St
215-568-0551
Is cowprint fur on the walls sassy? Or just
weird?
- **Nodding Head Brewery & Restaurant** •
1516 Sansom St
215-569-9525
Monk's much-less-annoying alter ego has
good home brew.
- **Oscar's Tavern** • 1524 Sansom St
215-972-9938
Beers so big you need two hands to hold 'em.
- **Philadelphia Art Alliance** • 251 S 18th St
215-545-4302
Challenging concert series in lovely old
Rittenhouse mansion.
- **PHS Pop Up Garden** • 313 S Broad St
215-988-8800
Why can't every vacant lot in Philly turn into
a beer garden?
- **Raven Lounge** • 1718 Sansom St
215-840-3577
It's all fun and games at this funky hot spot.
- **Ritz-Carlton Rotunda** • 10 Avenue of the Arts
215-523-8000
They say your first million is the hardest. Well
worth a toast.
- **Rouge** • 205 S 18th St
215-732-6622
Rittenhouse fave.
- **Stir** • 1705 Chancellor St
215-732-2700
Fun gay friendly dance club. With cheap
drinks!
- **Tangier Café** • 1801 Lombard St
215-732-5006
Sparkling little oasis reaches back to North
Africa, circa 1932.
- **Tavern on Broad** • 200 S Broad St
215-546-2290
- **Tequilas** • 1602 Locust St
215-546-0181
When you want to sober up, there's also
decent, upscale Mex waiting for you.

Although ridiculously cheap lager can be had at **Oscar's**, you'll appreciate **Monk's** expansive beer menu. Sure, the Ritz-Carlton Rotunda is the end-all-be-all of places to be seen, but fine cocktails are also crafted at Franklin **Mortage & Investment Co.** Meanwhile, **The Black Sheep** will help you wind down in style.

- **Time Restaurant** • 1315 Sansom St
215-985-4800
Did someone say Absinthe?
- **Tir Na Nog** • 1600 Arch St
267-514-1700
Sports-themed Irish bar panders to the City Hall set.

🍴 Restaurants

- **10 Arts Bistro and Lounge** • 10 S Broad St
215-523-8273 • $$$
Upscale local fare at The Ritz.
- **a.kitchen** • 135 S 18th St
215-825-7030 • $$$
Delicate dining and people watching among the Rittenhouse elite.
- **Alfa** • 1709 Walnut St
215-751-0201 • $$$
Betas, get the f*** out.
- **Alma de Cuba** • 1623 Walnut St
215-988-1799 • $$$$
Cuban soul food without all that annoying Communism.
- **Barclay Prime** • 237 S 18th St
215-732-7560 • $$$$$
Starr, well done.
- **Bellini Grill** • 220 S 16th St
215-545-1191 • $$
Pricey, mediocre Italian.
- **Bistro La Baia** • 1700 Lombard St
215-546-0496 • $$
If you're craving Italian and don't feel like waiting.
- **Bliss** • 220 S Broad St
215-731-1100 • $$$
Unpronounceably delicious dishes, but don't let the chef's yelling get to you.
- **Branzino Italian Ristorante** • 261 S 17th St
215-790-0103 • $$$
Go alfresco if you can.
- **Butcher and Singer** • 1500 Walnut St
215-732-4444 • $$$$
Steakhouse for the sophisticated set.
- **Byblos** • 114 S 18th St
215-568-3050 • $$$
Hookahs and a euro-sheik menu, with the collared-shirt, gold-chain crowd to match.
- **Cafe L'Aube** • 222 W Rittenhouse Sq
215-772-3051 • $$
Great crepes to go along with their own coffee.

- **The Capital Grille** • 1338 Chestnut St
215-545-9588 • $$$$
Steakhouse for the Masters of the Expense Account.
- **Chez Collette** • 120 S 17th St
215-569-8300 • $$$$
The Sofitel Hotel's unflinching French, the brunch is very fluent.
- **Chima** • 1901 JFK Blvd
215-525-3233 • $$$
How much is too much meat?
- **Chris' Jazz Café** • 1421 Sansom St
215-569-3131 • $$$
Where Jimmy Bruno and other jazz allstars play.
- **Continental Mid-Town** • 1801 Chestnut St
215-567-1800 • $$
With such cool design, it's a shame such uninspired preps attend.
- **The Corner Foodery** • 1710 Sansom St
215-567-1500 • $$
Featuring two of Philly's great loves: beer and sandwiches.
- **D'Angelo's Ristorante Italiano** • 256 S 20th St
215-546-3935 • $$
Old school Italian just outside the Square.
- **The Dandelion** • 124 S 18th St
215-558-2500 • $$
Stephen Starr goes to England.
- **Davio's** • 111 S 17th St
215-563-4810 • $$$$
The calamari, for one, is pretty special.
- **Del Frisco's Double Eagle Steak House** •
1426 Chestnut St
215-246-0533 • $$$
High end steakhouse with somewhat lacking service.
- **Devil's Alley** • 1907 Chesnut St
215-751-0707 • $$
Something for everyone in a spacious, relaxed gastropub.
- **Devon Seafood Grill** • 225 S 18th St
215-546-5940 • $$$$
Swanky, but you definitely pay the price.
- **Di Bruno Brothers** • 1730 Chestnut St
215-665-9220 • $
Pricey gourmet to go—or stay and eat in the freon.
- **Dolce Carini** • 1929 Chestnut St
215-567-8892 • $
Unadulterated NY-style pies.

Map 2

Rittenhouse / Logan Circle

- **Estia** • 1405 Locust St
215-735-7700 • $$$
Upscale Greek: not only does it exist, but it is excellent.
- **Famous 4th Street Delicatessen** •
38 S 19th St
215-568-3271 • $$
Legit pastrami and massive sammiches fit for your bubbe.
- **Federal Donuts** • 1632 Samsom St
215-665-1101 • $
Legendary handmade donuts and Korean twice-fried chicken.
- **Fountain Restaurant** • 1 Logan Sq
215-963-1500 • $$$$$
When money is no object.
- **Good Dog** • 224 S 15th St
215-985-9600 • $$
Bark up a good dog burger (presumably still made of cow).
- **HipCity Veg** • 127 S 18th St
215-278-7605 • $
Impressive vegan salads and sammies. Try the Groothie.
- **Honeygrow** • 110 S 16th St
215-279-7724 • $$
So fresh and so local.
- **Il Pittore** • 2025 Sansom St
215-391-4900 • $$$
Upscale and delicious Italian.
- **Jane G's** • 1930 Chestnut St
215-563-8800 • $$
Underrated Szechuan.
- **Jean's Cafe** • 1334 Walnut St
215-546-5353 • $
Cheap and tasty breakfast sandwiches. All the art kids like 'em.
- **Joe's Pizza** • 122 S 16th St
215-569-0898 • $
Some of the best 'za in the city. Weird hours.
- **Jose Pistola's** • 263 S 15th St
215-564-4101 • $$
Best nachos is Philly? No doubt!
- **La Creperie Cafe** • 1722 Sansom St
215-564-6460 • $$
Pizza crepes? Believe it, pilgrim.
- **La Fontana Della Citta** • 1701 Spruce St
215-875-9990 • $$
Solid sauce joint.
- **La Viola** • 253 S 16th St
215-735-8630 • $$
Sweet, cozy BYOB; perfect for when you can't stand waiting in line at Monk's anymore.

- **La Viola Ovest** • 252 S 16th St
215-735-8631 • $$
Reliable sister to La Viola across the street.
- **Lacroix at the Rittenhouse** •
210 W Rittenhouse Sq
215-790-2533 • $$$$
Luxe out at the Rittenhouse Hotel. Make a night of it.
- **Le Castagne** • 1920 Chestnut St
215-751-9913 • $$
Lots of insalatas amidst the rain of pesces, pastas, and carnes.
- **Little Pete's** • 219 S 17th St
215-545-5508 • $$
A greasy spoon with no apologies.
- **The Lounge** • 1 Logan Sq
215-963-1500 • $$$
Get your blue-blood on and order a crustless watercress sandwich.
- **Marathon Grill** • 121 S 16th St
215-569-3278 • $$$
Amidst class-action lawsuits, the grub still has class.
- **Marathon Grill** • 1818 Market St
215-561-1818 • $$$
Amidst class-action lawsuits, the grub still has class.
- **Matyson** • 37 S 19th St
215-564-2925 • $$$$$
The food is great, but the desserts are sublime.
- **Metropolitan Bakery** • 262 S 19th St
215-545-6655 • $
The people who make bread for half the city.
- **Miel Patisserie** • 204 S 17th St
215-731-9191 • $$
Stunning French desserts and fine chocolates. Ooh la la.
- **Monk's Café** • 264 S 16th St
215-545-7005 • $$
Great beer list and monster fries, Belgian-style. Plan to wait.
- **Nodding Head Brewery & Restaurant** •
1516 Sansom St
215-569-9525 • $$
Almost as good as Monk's and no wait.
- **Nom Nom Ramen** • 20 S 18th St
$
Fatty pork broth will melt your face off.
- **Paolo's Pizza** • 1334 Pine St
215-545-2482 • $
Salty as a codfish, but a nice hand-tossed crust.

The restaurant scene around Rittenhouse Square offers some of Philly's finest culinary experiences, but a sandwich from **Good Dog** is comparable in its own way. That said, **Lacroix** provides a fine French dining experience, guests and gawkers of the Four Seasons enjoy the all encompassing luxury of **Fountain**, and the Stephen Starr's ritzy meat establishment **Barclay Prime** out-steaks the competition.

- **Parc** • 227 S 18th St
  215-545-2262 • $$$$
  Fancy French bistro. Lobster cocktails.
- **Pietro's Coal Oven Pizzeria** • 1714 Walnut St
  215-735-8090 • $$
  Delicious thin-crust pies and solid salads.
- **The Prime Rib** • 1701 Locust St
  215-772-1701 • $$$$$
  Tasteful and elegant steakhouse in the Warwick.
- **Pumpkin** • 1713 South St
  215-545-4448 • $$
  The Sunday tasting menu is "the jam."
- **Rouge** • 205 S 18th St
  215-732-6622 • $$$$
  French/Asian foo foo that will not be ignored.
- **Sahara Grill** • 1334 Walnut St
  215-985-4155 • $$
  Middle Eastern; no eye contact.
- **Sbraga** • 440 S Broad St
  215-735-1913 • $$$
  Creative fine dining.
- **Seafood Unlimited** • 270 S 20th St
  215-732-3663 • $$
  So-so frutti di mare.
- **Shake Shack** • 2000 Sansom St
  215-809-1742 • $
  Philly outpost of the excellent NYC milkshake and burger joint.
- **Shiroi Hana** • 222 S 15th St
  215-735-4444 • $$
  Contemporary sushi house caters to tuna lovers.
- **Spread Bagelry** • 262 S 20th St
  215-545-0626 • $$
  Wood fired bagels. A little pricey but good.
- **Su Xing House** • 1508 Sansom St
  215-564-1419 • $$
  Veggie Chinese food to dream about.
- **Tavern on Broad** • 200 S Broad St
  215-546-2290 • $$$
  No luck gettin' hip with any dolled-up sheik daddy at this here gin mill.
- **Tequilas** • 1602 Locust St
  215-546-0181 • $$
  Upscale Mex has beautiful, open ceilings and fine offerings.
- **Tria** • 123 S 18th St
  215-972-8742 • $$
  Artfully-appointed food tailored to fit serious wine.

- **Underdogs** • 132 S 17th St
  215-665-8080 • $
  The elitist cousin of Citizens Bank Park's Dollar Dog Night.
- **Varalli** • 231 S Broad St
  215-546-6800 • $$$$
  Soak in the atmosphere—and stick to the wine.
- **XIX (nineteen)** • 200 S Broad St
  215-790-1919 • $$$$
  19 floors up to dine on the deep.
- **Yellow Juice Bar** • 2046 Sansom St
  267-888-8368 • $
  Not all the juice is yellow, but it is quite tasty.

🛍 Shopping

- **Adresse** • 45 N 2nd St
  215-985-3161
  You know you can't afford it if they only have three items for sale.
- **Anthropologie** • 1801 Walnut St
  215-568-2114
  UO-owned, but this one's for the ladies and femmes.
- **Apple Store** • 1607 Walnut St
  215-861-6400
  For all your iNeeds.
- **Athleta** • 1722 Walnut St
  215-732-1983
  Threads for the yoga set. Free classes.
- **Barnes & Noble** • 1805 Walnut St
  215-665-0716
  Ho-hum, just another behemoth of a bookstore with all the usual trimmings.
- **Benjamin Lovell Shoes** • 119 S 18th St
  215-564-4655
  Tasteful Euro-wear with a conservative bent.
- **Boyd's** • 1818 Chestnut St
  215-564-9000
  Where visiting NBA players score sweet suits.
- **Buffalo Exchange** • 1713 Chestnut St
  215-557-9850
  On a good day, some great finds.
- **Bundy** • 1809 Chestnut St
  215-567-2500
  Mac specialists have somewhat limited selection but solid service.
- **City Sports** • 1608 Walnut St
  215-985-5860
  Full-service from sneaks to parkas.

Map 2

Rittenhouse / Logan Circle

- **Coach** • 1703 Walnut St
215-564-4558
I surrender, here's the deed to my house.
- **Crumbs Bake Shop** • 133 S 18th St
215-523-9800
The NYC cupcake craze has finally arrived in Philly.
- **David Michie Violins** • 1714 Locust St
215-545-5006
Exquisite, tuneful, and strung with cat guts.
- **Destination Maternity** • 1615 Walnut St
215-567-1425
Casual, comfy clothes for moms-to-be.
- **Di Bruno Brothers** • 1730 Chestnut St
215-665-9220
Say cheese.
- **Di Bruno Brothers** •
1701 John F Kennedy Blvd
215-531-5666
Say cheese.
- **Food & Friends** • 1933 Spruce St
215-545-1722
By "friends," they mean beer.
- **Frankinstien Bike Worx** • 1529 Spruce St
215-893-0415
If you're really lucky, one of the Dead Milkmen will stop by.
- **Gap Outlet** • 1912-18 Chestnut St
215-564-4094
Hidden gem for the trendy…or the cheap.
- **Giovanni & Pileggi** • 258 S 11th St
215-568-3040
Fancy-pants folks love to have their follicle paradigm shifts here.
- **Greenhouse Market** • 1324 Chestnut St
215-545-2306
Ultra-fresh salad bar.
- **H&M** • 1725 Walnut St
215-563-2221
Urban Outfitters is shaking in its purple cowboy boots.

- **Halloween** • 1329 Pine St
215-732-7711
Gothic jewelry but really tasteful.
- **Head Start Shoes** • 126 S 17th St
215-567-3247
If you can't afford anything, treat it like a musuem of hip.
- **Hello World** • 257 S 20th St
215-545-5207
Gifts for the whole fam damnly.
- **Henry A. Davidsen** • 1701 Spruce St
215-253-5905
Like Build-a-Bear, but with men's suits.
- **Holt's Cigar Company** • 1522 Walnut St
215-732-8500
Excellent stogie shop for novices to aficionados alike.
- **Immortal Uncommon** • 125 S 18th St
215-563-2344
High end consignment for the sophisticated lady.
- **Insomnia Cookies** • 108 S 16th St
877-632-6654
Delivers cookies until 3 am. We're not kidding.
- **International Salon** • 1714 Sansom St
215-563-1141
Smileless Slavs give good, cheap spa treatments.
- **Jacob's Music** • 1718 Chestnut St
215-568-7800
If you ask, they'll play you "Piano Man" on any of their models. Please don't ask.
- **Jos. A. Bank Clothiers** • 1650 Market St
215-563-5990
High-end Tory-wear for today's neoconservatives.
- **Joseph Fox Bookshop** • 1724 Sansom St
215-563-4184
Strong-minded independent.

Walnut Street is Center City's main shopping artery. Much is upscale (**Coach**, **Ubiq**) but there are also a lot of affordable options (**Urban Outfitters**, **Zara**, **H&M**). And then there's the **Apple Store**, for all your iNeeds. For a change of pace, hit up **Buffalo Exchange** on Chestnut for hipster-approved used clothing.

- **Knit Wit** • 1729 Chestnut St
  215-564-4760
  Despite the awful pun, an evening wear store for 'mature' ladies.
- **Liquid Hair Salon** • 112 S 18th St
  215-564-6410
  Expect perfection from this friendly yet chic salon.
- **Lucky Brand Jeans** • 1634 Walnut St
  215-732-8934
  When $150 feels about right for a pair of miner-pants.
- **Maron Chocolates** • 1734 Chestnut St
  215-988-9992
  Candy, ice cream, chocolate—what's not to love?
- **Maxx's Produce** • 225 S 20th St
  215-735-3644
  A corner store with edible produce? For realsies?
- **Metropolitan Bakery** • 262 S 19th St
  215-545-6655
  The people who make bread for half the city.
- **Nicole Miller** • 200 S Broad St
  215-546-5007
  Manayunk's own designer gone big-time.
- **Omoi Zakka Shop** • 1608 Pine St
  215-545-0963
  Coolness from Japan and beyond.
- **Pamcakes** • 404 S 20th St
  215-546-2860
  Creative cupcakery.
- **Pearl of East** • 1720 Chestnut St
  215-563-1563
  Asian-themed furnishings; plenty of kimonos.
- **Premium Steap** • 111 S 18th St
  215-568-2920
  Get loose! (Tea, that is.)
- **Richard Nicholas Hair Studio** • 1716 Sansom St
  215-567-4790
  Hip, trendy cuts from low key stylists.

- **Salon Vanity** • 1701 Walnut St
  215-925-2211
  Not as vain as it sounds.
- **Scoop DeVille** • 1315 Walnut St
  215-988-9992
  Tasty, awe-inspiring concoctions.
- **Sophisticated Seconds** • 2019 Sansom St
  215-561-6740
  Upscale consignmentorium also has wedding dresses.
- **Stadler-Kahn** • 1724 Sansom St
  267-242-7154
  Quirky accessories and vintage curiosities.
- **Sue's Produce Market** • 114 S 18th St
  215 241-0102
  Fruits and veggies.
- **Swiss Haus** • 35 S 19th St
  215-563-0759
  Meet Philly's answer to the cronut: the Swiss Cro-crème.
- **UBIQ** • 1509 Walnut St
  215-988-0194
  Colorful whimsy that costs.
- **Urban Outfitters** • 1627 Walnut St
  215-569-3131
  Started right here and still too flashy and over-priced.
- **Vigant** • 200 S Broad St
  215-893-1234
  More cow-based products than a butcher shop.
- **VIP Food & Produce** • 1314 Walnut St
  215-735-1977
  Pretty sweet grocery spot. Lots of unique choices.
- **Zara** • 1715 Walnut St
  215-557-0911
  Business-casual. Pretty…pretty…pretty… expensive!

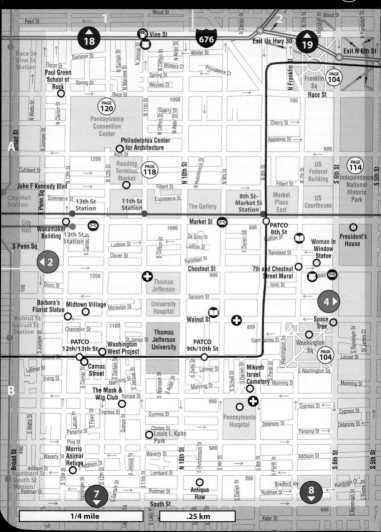

Map 3 · Center City East

Map 3

Chinatown, the Gayborhood, Independence Park—Center City East is stuffed with many tiny, distinct neighborhoods. Washington Square might not have Rittenhouse flair (although it does come close), but it does have a tree planed from a seed that was brought to the moon. Franklin Square, meanwhile, has the only mini-golf in the city.

O Landmarks

- **7th and Chestnut Street Mural** •
  Chestnut St & S 7th St
  Only tile mosaic mural in Center City.
- **Antique Row** • Pine St & S 9th St
  Furniture, books, knick-knacks of all kinds.
- **Barbara's Florist Statue** • 1300 Walnut St
  Watch him deteriorate through the seasons.
- **Camac Street** • S Camac St
  And they say the streets of Philly aren't paved in woodblocks…
- **Louis I. Kahn Park** • Pine St & S 11th St
  Named for revered Philly architect.
- **The Mask & Wig Club** • 310 S Quince St
  215-716-7378
  Penn's all-male musical comedy group.
- **Midtown Village** •
  Spruce St & Market St b/n 11th St & 13th St
  Where all the tchotchkes is.
- **Mikveh Israel Cemetary** • Spruce St & S 8th St
  Oldest Jewish cemetery in Philly, 1738.
- **Morris Animal Refuge** • 1242 Lombard St
  215-735-3256
  Children giggle more here.
- **The Oldest Photograph Sign** •
  Chestnut St & S 13th St
  It's true.
- **Pennsylvania Hospital** • 800 Spruce St
  215-829-3000
  Since 1751, the Nation's oldest. How cute.
- **Philadelphia Center for Architecture** •
  1218 Arch St
  215-569-3186
  Great exhibits and events. Black glasses required.
- **President's House** • Market St & N 6th St
  A tribute to nine presidential slaves
- **Reading Terminal Market** •
  N 12th St & Arch St
  215-922-2317
  More Amish food than you can shake a stick at.
- **Space Tree** • Walnut St & S 6th St
  Sycamore grown from a seed from space.
- **Underground Tunnel** • Locust St & Arch St
  Pedestrians can escape from the outdoor elements.
- **Wanamaker Building** • Market St & N 13th St
  The Macy's moniker now hangs in the Wanamaker Building—also home of *Mannequin* (1 and 2!)
- **Washington Square Park** •
  Walnut St & S 6th St
  Tomb of the Unknown Soldier of the Revolution.
- **Washington West Project** • 1201 Locust St
  215-985-9206
  Free HIV testing (and other health services) available to everyone.
- **Woman in Window Statue** •
  Chestnut St & S 6th St
  Eerie woman-in-white always peers out sadly.

Coffee

- **Greenland Tea House** • 210 N 9th St
  215-238-1688
  Bodacious bubble tea.
- **The Last Drop** • 1300 Pine St
  215-893-9262
  Serving La Colombe coffee.
- **Old City Coffee** • 1136 Arch St
  215-592-1897
  Awesome, awesome locally roasted coffee.
- **Ray's Café & Tea House** • 141 N 9th St
  215-922-5122
  Coffee, tea, and Chinese food.
- **Toast** • 1201 Spruce St
  215-821-1080
  Solid French press option.

Farmers Markets

- **Jefferson Farmers' Market** •
  Chestnut St & S 10th St
  Thursdays, 11 am-3:30 pm, in season.
- **Reading Terminal Market** •
  N 12th St & Arch St
  215-922-2317
  So good, but so crowded.
- **SEPTA Farm Stand** • 1234 Market St
  Wednesdays, 11 am-1:30 pm, June-Sept.

Map 3

Center City East

🍸 Nightlife

- **The Bike Stop** • 206 S Quince St
  215-627-1662
  Play pool; get ogled by gay men. Not that
  there's anything wrong with that.
- **Brü Craft & Wurst** • 1316 Chestnut
  215-800-1079
  Decent beer hall that branches beyond
  Deutschland.
- **Dirty Franks** • 347 S 13th St
  215-732-5010
  City's premier dive.
- **Drury Beer Garden** • 1311 Samsom St
  215-545-0170
  Behind Opa. A hidden gem on hot summer
  nights.
- **El Vez** • 121 S 13th St
  215-928-9800
  Features fancy, dopey cocktails but many of
  them still rock.
- **The Farmers' Cabinet** • 1113 Walnut St
  215-923-1113
  Artisan cocktails and lengthy draft list in your
  grandmother's parlor.
- **Fergie's Pub** • 1214 Sansom St
  215-928-8118
  Great pulled pints, excellent chow, and no TVs
  of any kind. Go for pub quiz night.
- **Field House** • 1150 Filbert St
  215-629-1520
  TVs at your table…you won't miss a single
  play.
- **Graffiti Bar** • 124 S 13th St
  215-732-3501
  Small, hidden bar behind an alley. Very cool.
- **Hop Sing Laundromat** • 1029 Race St
  Speakeasy. Great cocktails with a hint of
  melodrama.
- **The Irish Pub** • 1123 Walnut St
  215-925-3311
  Simple place with solid pints and great daily
  specials.
- **Las Vegas Lounge** • 704 Chestnut St
  215-592-9533
  Well, they get the seedy, paying-with-your-
  last-dollar feel right.

- **Locust Bar** • 235 S 10th St
  215-925-2191
  Not the place to go if you want to quit
  smoking; otherwise, it's fine.
- **Lucky Strikes** • 1336 Chestnut St
  215-545-2471
  The first bowling alley with a dress code, they
  keep the hoodlums out and the celebrities in.
- **McGillin's Olde Ale House** • 1310 Drury St
  215-735-5562
  One of Philly's oldest saloons has historical
  charm.
- **MilkBoy** • 1100 Chestnut St
  215-925-6455
  Cozy mix of hipsters, hospital staff, and live
  music.
- **Moriarty's** • 1116 Walnut St
  215-627-7676
  Theater crowd-pleaser has dramatic license
  to serve.
- **Sal's on 12th** • 200 S 12th St
  215-731-9930
  Tiny hipster dancing spot.
- **Strangelove's** • 216 S 11th St
  215-873-0404
  Beer geeks and vegans: together at last.
- **Tabu Lounge & Sports Bar** • 200 S 12th St
  215-964-9675
  Fun and fabulous Gayborhood staple.
- **Tavern on Camac** • 243 S Camac St
  215-545-0900
  Flaming gay piano bar cum discotheque.
- **Trocadero Theatre** • 1003 Arch St
  215-922-6888
  Former titty show palace now hosts a wild
  eclectica of music acts.
- **Vintage** • 129 S 13th St
  215-922-3095
  Being wine-giddy is more attractive than
  getting Jager-Bomb hammered.
- **Westbury** • 261 S 13th St
  215-546-5170
  Gay respite from the throbbing beats of
  surrounding clubs.
- **Woody's** • 202 S 13th St
  215-545-1893
  For nearly 30 years, a Philly gay institution.

Center City East

Map 3

Hop Sing Laundromat offers fancy, crafted cocktails. **Woody's** is a mainstay of the Gayborhood, and is large and welcoming for all. Anything goes at **Dirty Frank's**. For live music, head to **Milkboy** or the **Trocadero**. For a more Irish perspective, go to **Fergie's** but please be aware that there really is a Fergie and he is, in fact, quite Irish.

Restaurants

- **Aki** • 1210 Walnut St
215-985-1838 • $$$
Obviously get the all-you-can-eat sushi special.
- **Amis** • 412 S 13th St
215-732-2647 • $$$
Vetri's trattoria; trades tablecloth for butcher block.
- **Amuse** • 1421 Arch St
215-422-8222 • $$$
Sleek, sexy French in the Le Meridien.
- **Aqua** • 705 Chestnut St
215-928-2838 • $
Thai food and a sexy setting. Date night, anyone?
- **Banana Leaf** • 1009 Arch St
215-592-8288 • $$
New Malaysian cuisine Penang competitor; open late for no one.
- **Bassett's Ice Cream** • 45 N 12th St
215-925-4315 • $
Perfect happy ending to your Reading Terminal experience.
- **Capogiro Gelato Artisans** • 119 S 13th St
215-351-0900 • $
Some of the best gelato in the city—pricey, though.
- **Caribou Café** • 1126 Walnut St
215-625-9535 • $$$
Euroville in CC. Drink in the atmosphere.
- **Charles Plaza** • 234 N 10th St
215-829-4383 • $
Cool mood lighting sets up a fabulous veggie cornucopia of delights.
- **The Corner** • 102 S 13th St
215-735-7500 • $$
Comfort food and a rooftop bar. What's not to like?
- **Down Home Diner** • 51 N 12th St
215-627-1955 • $$
Reading's sit-down joint where Amish bumpkins in overalls serve ok stuff for cheap.
- **Dutch Eating Place** • 1136 Arch St
215-922-0425 • $
Hot turkey sandwiches smothered in gravy. And scrapple.

- **Effie's** • 1127 Pine St
215-592-8333 • $$
Simple Greek fare in an adorable setting.
- **The Farm & Fisherman** • 1120 Pine St
267-687-1555 • $$$
Ooh, it's local and organic.
- **Fat Salmon** • 719 Walnut St
215-928-8881 • $$
More like P-H-A-T, amirite?
- **Fogo De Chão** • 1337 Chestnut
215-636-9700 • $$$
If you're into meat, this is the place for you.
- **Garces Trading Company** • 1111 Locust St
215-574-1099 • $$
Philly's own Iron Chef wants to make you a sammie.
- **Green Eggs Cafe** • 212 S 13th St
267-861-0314 • $$
Light and sweet, it's time to eat.
- **IndeBlue** • 205 S 13th St
215-545-4633 • $$$
Locally sourced, organic Indian via Collingswood.
- **Imperial Inn** • 146 N 10th St
215-627-5588 • $$$
Just chow down on the dim sum. Leave the rest behind.
- **Jamonera** • 105 S 13th St
215-922-6061 • $$$
Awesome Spanish wine bar from the folks who own everything on 13th Street.
- **Jones** • 700 Chestnut St
215-223-5663 • $$$
Comfort food in a Brady Bunch-like setting.
- **Kanella** • 266 S 10th St
215-922-1773 • $$
Pricey and tasty.
- **Knock** • 225 S 12th St
215-925-1166 • $
Will Bill overcome the curse of this corner?
- **Lee How Fook** • 219 N 11th St
215-925-7266 • $$
Low-key and casual, and great hot pots.
- **Little Nonna's** • 1234 Locust St
215-546-2100 • $$
Marcie Turney and Valerie Safran continue their welcomed 13th Street takeover.

Center City East

- **Little Thai Market** • 51 N 12th St
  215-873-0231 • $
  The line wraps around the corner for a reason.
- **Lolita** • 106 S 13th St
  215-546-7100 • $$
  In this scenario, you are Humbert Humbert.
  The food is you know who.
- **Maoz** • 1115 Walnut St
  215-922-3409 • $
  Dutch falafel chain with all-u-can eat
  toppings.
- **Mercato** • 1216 Spruce St
  215-985-2962 • $$
  Don't spill the homemade pasta on the
  rosewood floor.
- **Mixto** • 1141 Pine St
  215-592-0363 • $$
  Can you say ceviche?
- **More Than Just Ice Cream** • 1119 Locust St
  215-574-0586 • $
  Succulent desserts don't overshadow the
  delectable comfort food.
- **Moriarty's** • 1116 Walnut St
  215-627-7676 • $$
  Huge theater crowd enlivens the place.
- **Morimoto** • 723 Chestnut St
  215-413-9070 • $$$
  The best shrimp tempura ever. Anywhere.
- **Nan Zhou Hand Drawn Noodle House** •
  927 Race St
  215-923-1550 • $
  Home-made noodles go into every bowl of
  delicious soup.

- **New Harmony Vegetarian Restaurant** •
  135 N 9th St
  215-627-4520 • $
  Mock if you must, but the meat here is unreal.
- **New Samosa** • 1214 Walnut St
  215-546-2009 • $$
  All-vegetarian Indian.
- **Nomad Romana** • 1305 Locust St
  215-644-9287 • $$
  Thin, Roman style pies from the always
  reliable Nomad crew.
- **Opa** • 1311 Sansom St
  215-545-0170 • $$
  Good Greek. Not to be confused with the
  Office of Property Assessment.
- **Pho Xe Lua** • 907 Race St
  215-627-8883 • $
  The fresh mango lassi should be more than
  enough inducement.
- **Prime Burger Company** • 703 Chesnut St
  267-519-0752 • $
  The poor man's Shake Shack.
- **QT Vietnamese Sandwich Co.** • 48 N 10th St
  267-639-4520 • $
  Friggin' amazing banh mi.
- **Rangoon** • 112 N 9th St
  215-829-8939 • $$
  An in-the-know Burmese spot.
- **Raw Sushi & Sake Lounge** • 1225 Samsom St
  215-238-1903 • $$$
  Hit or miss sushi.
- **Ristorante La Buca** • 711 Locust St
  215-928-0556 • $$$
  Get dressed up real nice and enjoy fine Italian
  cuisine.

Philly's food scene comes alive around here. The mega-hyped **Vetri** lives up to its reputation, while the original **Morimoto** still chugs along. And then there are several blocks of delectable Chinese, all of which **Vietnam** seems to trump (although do check out **Lee How Fook**). See also **Rangoon**'s wonderful Burmese fare. BYOB in Philadelphia is a source of civic pride and **Lolita** is one of our favorite spots, where great house-made margarita mixes are anxiously awaiting your tequila to come home.

- **Sampan** • 124 S 13th St
  215-732-3501 • $$$
  Fun Asian fusion.
- **Sang Kee Peking Duck House** • 238 N 9th St
  215-975-7532 • $$
  From obscure to titillating. And back.
- **Shiao Lan Kung** • 930 Race St
  215-928-0282 • $$
  South Cantonese joint has good veggie options.
- **Smokin' Betty's** • 116 S 11th St
  215-922-6500 • $$
  It's not every day you see turducken on a menu.
- **Spruce Rana** • 1034 Spruce St
  215-238-1223 • $
  Gourmet grub from paninis to sushi. Skinny jeans suck, anyway.
- **Strangelove's** • 216 S 11th St
  215-873-0404 • $$
  Beer geeks and vegans: together at last.
- **Tai Lake** • 134 N 10th St
  215-922-0698 • $$
  When you must have live frogs and lobster at 1 am.
- **Talula's Garden** • 210 W Washington Sq
  215-592-7787 • $$$
  City outpost of the fabled Kennett Square farm-to-table joint.
- **Toast** • 1201 Spruce St
  215-821-1080 • $$
  Super coffee, breakfast, and sammies.

- **Tria** • 1137 Spruce St
  215-629-9200 • $$$
  Get your wine and cheese on at this second location.
- **Valanni** • 1229 Spruce St
  215-790-9494 • $$
  Eclecticism with zero pretentiousness.
- **Varga Bar** • 941 Spruce St
  215-627-5200 • $$$
  Pin-up girls, burgers & beer!
- **Vedge** • 1221 Locust St
  215-320-7500 • $$$
  One of Philly's best restaurants, brought to you by vegans.
- **Venture Inn** • 255 S Camac St
  215-545-8731 • $$
  Classic American food with not so conventional clientele.
- **Vetri** • 1312 Spruce St
  215-732-3478 • $$$$
  Intimate and romantic, one of Philly's best.
- **Vietnam** • 221 N 11th St
  215-592-1163 • $
  One of the best restaurants in Philly. Be prepared to wait.
- **Vietnam Palace** • 222 N 11th St
  215-592-9596 • $
  Good, but way outclassed by Vietnam across the street.
- **Zio's Pizza** • 111 S 13th St
  215-627-1615 • $$
  Warm, cheesy, delicious.

Map 3

Center City East

🛍 Shopping

- **AIA Bookstore & Design Center** •
  1218 Arch St
  215-569-3188
  Architectural specialists have lots of amazing design books and portfolios.
- **Armand Records** • 1108 Chestnut St
  215-592-7973
  Hip-hop DJs do all their significant shopping here.
- **Bare Feet Shoes** • 1217 Chestnut St
  215-564-1686
  Fun 'n cheap threads 'n kicks.
- **Baum's** • 106 S 11th St
  215-923-2244
  Serving Philly dancers tutus and tap shoes for over a century.
- **Beaux Arts Vintage** • 1000 Spruce St
  215-923-1991
  Small, independent video rental store has helpful staff and solid picks.
- **Black Tie Formal Attire** • 1120 Walnut St
  215-925-4404
  Family-owned shop rents styles ranging from princely to Prince. Great service.
- **Bridals by Danielle** • 203 S 13th St
  215-670-9500
  Looking good on the big day ain't cheap.
- **Burlington Coat Factory** • 1027 Market St
  215-627-6933
  Seven hundred million coats and no one to help you.
- **Cella Luxuria** • 1214 Chestnut St
  215-923-0784
  Eclectic, apartment friendly furniture.
- **Chartreuse** • 1616 E Passyunk Ave
  215-545-7711
  Wanna be mom's favorite child? Shop for her here!
- **Children's Place** • Market St & S 9th St
  215-627-8187
  From infants to adolescents, plus kid beauty products.
- **Claire's** • 1001 Market St
  215-592-8507
  Accessorize, accessorize, accessorize. Quite cheaply.
- **De' Village** • N 12th St & Arch St
  215-923-9860
  African jewelry, hippo-sized.
- **DeCarlo Hair Salon** • 1210 Sansom St
  215-923-5806
  Monster assortment of hair products, including 'poos, gels and sprays.
- **Downtown Cheese Shop** • N 12th St & Arch St
  215-351-7412
  Gourmet cheese and associated accoutrements.
- **Dudes Boutique** • 646 South St
  215-928-0661
  Suede and leather shoes for the special dude in your life.
- **Duross & Langel** • 117 S 13th St
  215-592-7627
  Naked, Mojitos and Vegan…and we're talking about SOAPS.
- **Famous 4th Street Cookie Company** •
  51 N 12th St
  215-625-9870
  Embrace your inner Cookie Monster. Go for the peanut butter.
- **Garces Trading Company** • 1111 Locust St
  215-574-1099
  Philly's own Iron Chef wants to make you a sammie.
- **Giovanni's Room** • 345 S 12th St
  215-923-2960
  Gay/lesbian themed tomes, plus visiting writers and readings.
- **Greene Street Consignment Shop** •
  700 South St
  215-733-9261
  Good deals on good clothes.

Map 3

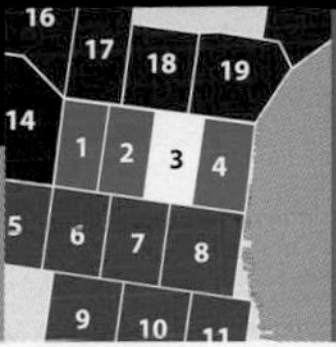

Bare Feet is a cheap, super fun adventure in kicks and threads, and **Mitchell & Ness** sells throwback jerseys that can't go out of style. If you're a student trying to fill an empty apartment, check out **Uhuru**. The delightful **PHAG** sells hip vinyl furniture, kooky martini glasses, and more. **Macy's** is Center City's only true department store; it retains some of the allure of the late, great Wanamaker's.

- **Grocery Market + Catering** • 105 S 13th St
  215-922-5252
  Premade gourmet meals for the luxurious and the lazy.
- **Hello Home** • 1004 Pine St
  215-545-7060
  Pricey furniture that spans the decades.
- **I. Goldberg Army & Navy** • 1300 Chestnut St
  215-925-9393
  Army/Navy surplus store with plenty of other goodies.
- **Insomnia Cookies** • 135 S 13th St
  877-632-6654
  Delivers cookies until 3 am. We're not kidding.
- **Lore's Chocolates** • 34 S 7th St
  215-627-3233
  This is how you get in good with your Grandma.
- **M. Finkel and Daughter** • 936 Pine St
  215-627-7797
- **Macy's** • 1300 Market St
  215-241-9000
  Apparently, all that 6th borough hype worked. Look what we got!
- **Marcie Blaine Artisanal Chocolates** •
  108 S 13th St
  215-546-8700
  Welcome to truffle town.
- **Mitchell & Ness** • 1201 Chestnut St
  267-273-7622
  Where the whole retro-Jersey craze started.
- **Old Navy** • 1001 Market St
  215-413-7012
  Fashion for overweight families, and more.
- **Old Nelson Food Company** • 701 Chestnut St
  215-627-7090
  Sandwiches and snacks not for tourists.
- **Open House** • 107 S 13th St
  215-922-1415
  Good taste spreads thick on minamilistic, funky, and modern home furnishings.

- **PHAG** • 1225 Walnut St
  215-627-0461
  Bi level, gay klitsch.
- **R.E.Load Bags** • 301 N 11th St
  215-625-2987
  Custom designed messenger bags.
- **Rustic Music** • 333 S 13th St
  215-732-7805
  Sweet little guitar shop also has a collection of CDs and vinyl.
- **Sailor Jerry** • 116 S 13th St
  215-531-6380
  Old-school tattooed t-shirts
- **SEPTA Transit Store** • 1234 Market St
  215-580-7800
  Transit junkie heaven.
- **Sound of Market Street** • 15 S 11th St
  215-925-3150
  The largest independent music store in the city. Huge amounts of jazz.
- **Spruce Street Video** • 252 S 12th St
  215-985-2955
  The largest selection of gay porn in the country.
- **Talula's Daily** • 208 W Washington Sq
  215-592-6555
  Market and cafe version of Talula's Garden.
- **Uhuru Furniture and Collectibles** •
  1220 Spruce St
  215-546-9616
  Politically minded used furniture store.
- **Wawa Food Market** • 1038 Arch St
  215-627-4121
  Common coffee stop-along for the Chinatown bus travelers.
- **Wawa Food Market** • 912 Walnut St
  215-923-1404
  For the 3 am munchie attack.
- **West Elm** • 1330 Chestnut St
  215-731-0184
  Mid-range, trendy furniture.

Map 4 · **Old City / Society Hill**

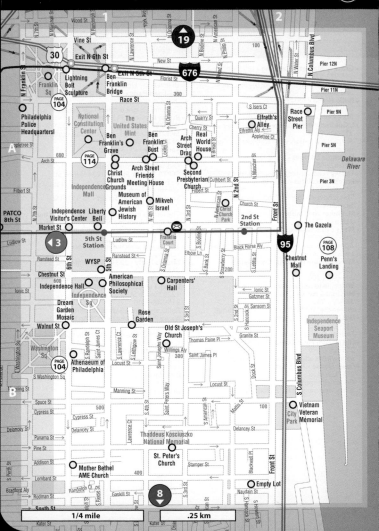

Map 4

Old City is beautiful, steeped in history, and filled with dining and nightlife. This means that while there you'll need to avoid both tourists and Jersey club-goers, but don't let that deter you. **Christ Church Park** is a quiet place to reflect, and dammit, you need to visit the **Liberty Bell** if you haven't already.

O Landmarks

- **American Philosophical Society Museum** •
104 S 5th St
215-440-3400
Kant figure out Schopenhauer? That's off the Hook.
- **Arch Street Drag** • N 3rd St & Arch St
Transformed into old-world Cinci for *Beloved*.
- **Arch Street Friends Meeting House** •
N 4th St & Arch St
Fifty plus years in the making, the thing still beats and makes kids cry.
- **Athenaeum of Philadelphia** • 219 S 6th St
215-925-2688
Beautiful, historic library and museum of antiquities and other cool stuff.
- **Ben Franklin Bridge** • Race St & N 5th St
Walk to New Jersey.
- **Ben Franklin Bust** • N 4th St & Arch St
Made from 1,000 keys donated by local school kids. No joke.
- **Ben Franklin's Grave** • N 5th St & Arch St
215-922-1695
RIP and thanks for the electricity.
- **Carpenters' Hall** • 320 Chestnut St
215-925-0167
Has the Philly three: cute, old, and brick.
- **Chestnut Mall** • Chestnut St & Columbus Blvd
Exploring the well-lived life of William Penn.
- **Christ Church Grounds** • N 5th St & Arch St
Where BF is buried—amongst other notables.
- **Christ Church Park** • Market St & S 2nd St
Dogs, squirrels, and OC workers on lunch breaks.
- **Dream Garden Mosaic** • 601 Walnut St
Maxfield Parrish's creation dominates the lobby.
- **Elfreth's Alley** • Arch St & Race St
The oldest residential street in the US, baby.
- **Empty Lot** • South St & Lombard St
It could be the biggest real-estate waste in the city.
- **Franklin Court** • Market St & S 3rd St
Museum and "ghost" sculpture of Franklin's digs.
- **Franklin Square** • N 6th St & Race St
We wonder who this park is named after?
- **The Gazela** • Columbus Blvd & Market St
Many-masted boat is more than a century old.
- **Independence Hall** • 550 Chestnut St
877-444-6777
Home of the first gay rights protests in 1965! Also signing of Constitution, et al.

- **Independence Visitor's Center** •
Market St & N 6th St
215-965-7676
Learn about Philly's rich cultural history—and use the free public pit stop if you are in need.
- **Liberty Bell** • Market St & S 5th St
215-965-2305
The only reason anyone ever visits us.
- **Lightning Bolt Sculpture** • 300 N 6th St
Electro-tastic.
- **Mikveh Israel** • 44 N 4th St
215-922-5446
Oldest Jewish congregation with an impressive set of scrolls.
- **Mother Bethel African Methodist Episcopal Church** • 419 S 6th St
215-925-0616
Enclosed section of truly creepy-looking grave markers.
- **National Constitution Center** • 525 Arch St
215-409-6600
A Presidential wonderland.
- **North 3rd Street Biking Hazard** •
N 3rd St & Vine St
Yo bikers. Beware this stretch of road. Bike up 5th instead.
- **Old St. Joseph's Church** • 321 Willings Alley
215-923-1733
Stunning stained glass a testament to old-world can-do.
- **Penn's Landing Marina** •
S Columbus Blvd & Penns Landing S
Gaze at the $30 million yachts and feel crappy about yourself.
- **Philadelphia Police Headquarters** •
750 Race St
Fighting crime in a '70s glass circular building.
- **Race Street Pier** • Race St & Columbus Blvd
215-629-3200
Beautiful revitalized public space provides sweeping views of, um, Jersey.
- **Real World House** • 249 Arch St
The very house those brats used to flop in when they weren't getting wasted.
- **Rose Garden** • Walnut St & S 4th St
A serene bit of civic space too rarely used.
- **Second Presbyterian Church** •
N 3rd St & Arch St
Sections of the burial grounds reserved for Africans.
- **St. Peter's Church** • 313 Pine St
215-925-5968
Est. 1761, so you know it's gotta be good.

- **Steel Kangaroos** • Lawrence Ct
  Mandatory public art.
- **The United States Mint** •
  151 N Independence Mall E
  215-408-0112
  It's surprisingly easy to stand outside and look suspicious.
- **Vietnam Veteran Memorial** •
  Spruce St & S Columbus Blvd
  Honoring those who served and gave their lives.
- **WYSP** • 101 S Independence Mall E
  215-625-9460
  Crappy rock station often gives out schwag here.

Coffee

- **Double Shots Espresso Bar** • 211 Chestnut St
  215-351-5171
  Lots of seating inside.
- **Menagerie Coffee** • 18 S 3rd St
  Top-notch artisanal espressos and hand-pours.
- **Old City Coffee** • 221 Church St
  215-629-9292
  Awesome, awesome locally roasted coffee.
- **Philadelphia Java Co.** • 518 S 4th St
  215-928-1811
  Yes, this is the coffee shop in Always Sunny.

Home to perhaps more whipped-up-to-frothing bars/clubs per capita than any other area of the city, as long as you like your scenes loud and your booze pricey, you've got it all here. That said, **The Khyber** is a great spot for not only music but also comedy, **The Victoria Freehouse** is a fun British-style pub, and you'll silently assent to **Sugar Mom's** nifty subterranean setting.

Nightlife

- **Bleu Martini** • 24 S 2nd St
  215-940-7900
  Yet another trendy OC watering hole. Wear complicated shoes.
- **Buffalo Billiards** • 118 Chestnut St
  215-574-7665
  Poolhall has much to recommend it, including strong drinks.
- **The Continental** • 138 Market St
  215-923-6069
  Lavish drinks and mostly shallow conversation.
- **Cooperage Wine and Whiskey Bar** • 601 Walnut St
  215-226-2667
  Happy hour in the Curtis Center.
- **Cuba Libre** • 10 S 2nd St
  215-627-0666
  Known for its pretty rollicking mojitos.
- **Downey's** • 526 S Front St
  215-625-9500
  Weekend karaoke great, all else meh.
- **Drinker's Tavern** • 124 Market St
  215-351-0141
  Amazing replica of frat house basement.
- **Eulogy Belgian Tavern** • 136 Chestnut St
  215-413-1918
  Trappist ales have a way of kicking your ass, so be careful.
- **The Irish Pol** • 45 S 3rd St
  215-238-9353
  Free beer AND air conditioning!
- **Khyber Pass Pub** • 56 S 2nd St
  215-238-5888
  Rock institution a rite-of-passage for indie kids.
- **Morgan's Pier** • 221 N Columbus Blvd
  215 279-7134
  It gets crowded, but stays fun.
- **National Mechanics Bar and Restaurant** • 22 S 3rd St
  215-701-4883
  Beetlejuice-like. Excellent.

- **Paddy Whacks Pub** • 150 South St
  215-464-7544
  Share in the joy (but mostly pain) of being a Philly sports fan.
- **The Plough & the Stars** • 123 Chestnut St
  215-733-0300
  Fight through the Jersey crowd to the bar, then expect to wait.
- **Race Street Café** • 208 Race St
  215-627-6181
  Lots of polished wood makes your buzz more noteworthy.
- **Red Sky** • 224 Market St
  215-925-8080
  Let me get this straight: an ultra-trendy bar? In OC? Really?
- **Revolution House** • 200 Market St
  215-625-4566
  Service is hit or miss, but the roofdeck does not disappoint.
- **Rotten Ralph's** • 201 Chestnut St
  215-925-2440
  Upstairs: chow. Downstairs: rollicking bar with decent prices for the area.
- **Society Hill Hotel Bar** • 301 Chestnut St
  215-925-1919
  An elegant throwback.
- **Stratus Lounge** • 433 Chestnut St
  215-925-2889
  Very limited view for a rooftop bar.
- **Sugar Mom's** • 225 Church St
  215-925-8219
  Underground grotto bar has pool, video games (including Erotic Photohunt!) and a rocking juke.
- **Triumph Brewing Company** • 117 Chestnut St
  215-625-0855
  Hoppy fun time.
- **The Victoria Freehouse** • 10 S Front St
  215-543-6089
  Freeshen ya drink, guvnah?
- **Woolly Mammoth** • 430 South St
  215-923-8780
  Take-out beer. Loud and grimy.

🍴Restaurants

- **Amada** • 217 Chestnut St
215-625-2450 • $$$
Authentic tapas is superb, and homemade sangria makes it even better.
- **Bistro 7** • 7 N 3rd St
215-931-1560 • $$$
Spendy, contemporary BYOB French stuff.
- **Bistro Romano** • 120 Lombard St
215-925-8880 • $$$
Eat heavy Italian under dim candlelight.
- **Blackbird Pizzeria** • 507 S 6th St
215-625-6660 • $
Surprisngly tasty vegan pizza. (Hey, vegans need junk food, too.)
- **Buddakan** • 325 Chestnut St
215-574-9440 • $$$
Pricey Starr Restaurants Asian fusion - everybody has a birthday there.
- **Campo's Deli** • 214 Market St
215-923-1000 •
Over-stuffed sandwiches served by underfed sandwich makers.
- **Chloe** • 232 Arch St
215-629-2337 • $$$
Excellent food in an intimate setting.
- **The Continental** • 138 Market St
215-923-6069 • $$
Starr's biggest success, the drinks and food are hip, and consumed voraciously by Jersey.
- **Cooperage Wine and Whiskey Bar** •
601 Walnut St
215-226-2667 • $$
Happy hour in the Curtis Center.
- **Cuba Libre** • 10 S 2nd St
215-627-0666 • $$$$
Fine mojitos, great atmosphere. Food? Um, we guess.
- **DiNardo's Famous Seafood** • 312 Race St
215-925-5115 • $$
Gulf-coast soft shells are the major draw.
- **Eulogy Belgian Tavern** • 136 Chestnut St
215-413-1918 • $$
Great beer selection highlights a so-so menu.
- **Farmicia** • 15 S 3rd St
215-627-6274 • $$
Farm to table nom noms. Great brunch.
- **Farmicia** • 15 S 3rd St
215-627-6274 • $$
Adjoining Metro Cafe makes bagels like whoa.

- **Fork** • 306 Market St
215-625-9425 • $$
Upscale without being obnoxious.
- **The Franklin Fountain** • 116 Market St
215-627-1899 • $
1920's ice cream parlor, a true Old City gem.
- **Gianfranco Pizza Rustica** • 6 N 3rd St
215-592-0048 • $
Some think it's the best. It's not, but it ain't bad.
- **Han Dynasty** • 123 Chestnut St
215-922-1888 • $$
Very spicy, very good.
- **Karma** • 114 Chestnut St
215-925-1444 • $$
High-end Indian fare but still veggie-friendly.
- **Kisso Sushi Bar** • 205 N 4th St
215-922-1770 • $$
Service with a never ending smile.
- **La Famiglia** • 8 S Front St
215-922-2803 • $$$
Impeccable high-end Italian fare.
- **La Locanda Del Ghiottone** • 130 N 3rd St
215-829-1465 • $$
Gluttonously huge portions. Not that there's anything wrong with that.
- **Margherita Pizzeria** • 60 S 2nd St
215-922-7053 • $
Flamboyant toppings, by the slice.
- **Marmont Steakhouse & Bar** • 222 Market St
215-923-1100 • $$$
Quantity over quality.
- **Marrakesh** • 517 S Leithgow St
215-925-5929 • $$
Sit on circular sofas and stuff your face with phyllo.
- **Mexican Post** • 104 Chestnut St
215-923-5233 • $
Average chow but solid margaritas.
- **Mizu Sushi Bar** • 220 Market St
215-238-0966 • $$
Creative little BYOB.
- **Moshulu** • 401 S Columbus Blvd
215-923-2500 • $$$$
Elegant food in a century-old sailing vessel. Avast ye matey.
- **Mrs. K's Koffee Shop** • 325 Chestnut St
215-627-7991 • $
Breakfast all day, bottomless coffee.
- **National Mechanics Bar and Restaurant** •
22 S 3rd St
215-701-4883 •
"It's gourmet food, and it's drunk food."

Map 4

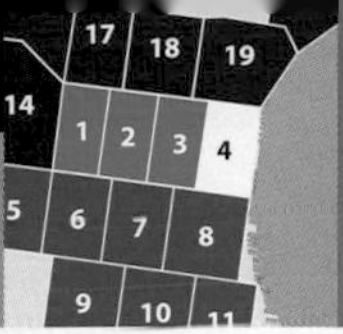

Chloe continues to be a perennial favorite amongst foodies and those trying to dodge Old City while in Old City. Nibble great (and pricey) tapas at **Amada**. Hit the make-your-own Bloody-Mary bar during brunch at **National Mechanics**. And devour a sundae from **Franklin Fountain**.

- **Old City Coffee** • 221 Church St
  215-629-9292 •
  Good-vibes lunch spot with serious coffee.
- **Pagoda Noodle Café** • 125 Sansom St
  215-928-2320 • $$
  Grab a bite on your way to the Ritz East.
- **Philadelphia Java Co.** • 518 S 4th St
  215-928-1811 • $
  Like hanging out in the Berenstein Bears house, but with your laptop.
- **Pizzicato** • 248 Market St
  215-629-5527 • $$
  Stunning—and that's just the waitstaff.
- **The Plough & the Stars** • 123 Chestnut St
  215-733-0300 • $$$
  If you can fight off the NJ scenesters, the food is fine.
- **Positano Coast** • 212 Walnut St
  215-238-0499 • $$$
  Excellent al fresco Italian.
- **Race Street Café** • 208 Race St
  215-627-6181 • $$
  Decent burgers, great brew selection.
- **Ristorante Panorama** • 14 N Front St
  215-922-7800 • $$$
  Along with Spasso and Famiglia, the murderer's row of high end Italian fare.
- **Serrano** • 20 S 2nd St
  215-928-0770 • $$$
  Worth braving Old City on the weekend for their pumpkin gnocchi.
- **Sonny's Famous Steaks** • 228 Market St
  215-629-5760 •
  Cheesesteaks like no other cheesesteak, considering you'll be drunk when you eat these ones.
- **Spasso** • 34 S Front St
  215-592-7661 • $$
  Affordable Italian and their clams have earned them a rep.
- **The Victoria Freehouse** • 10 S Front St
  215-543-6089 • $$
  Bloody authentic British pub, complete with Scotch eggs and mushy peas.
- **Xochitl** • 408 S 2nd St
  215-238-7280 • $$$
  Like *anyone* can pronounce the name after a few margaritas.
- **Zahav** • 237 St James Pl
  215-625-8800 • $$$
  Culinary greatness from the Middle East.

🛍 Shopping

- **a.k.a. music** • 27 N 2nd St
  215-922-3855
  A music buff's dream: hard-to-find CDs and LPs.
- **Brave New Worlds Comics** • 55 N 2nd St
  215-925-6525
  Secret den of comictude.
- **Charlie's Jeans** • 233 Market St
  215-627-3390
  If you have to ask the price, set your face on stun.
- **Gourmet of Olde City** • 26 N 3rd St
  215-627-8890
  Bricks 'o chocolate.
- **Mode Moderne** • 159 N 3rd St
  215-627-0299
  Drag your living room kicking and screaming into the 21st century.
- **Olde City Tattoo** • 44 S 2nd St
  215-627-6271
  Displays all of your life's major accomplishments.
- **The Papery** • 1219 Locust St
  215-922-1500
  Super cute.
- **Pierre's Costumes** • 211 N 3rd St
  215-925-7121
  Well over 100,000 costumes.
- **Shane Confectionery** • 110 Market St
  215-922-1048
  Excellent sweets from the oldest continuously-run confectionery in the US.
- **Sugarcube** • 124 N 3rd St
  215-238-0825
  Vintage and contemporary fashions.
- **Tartes** • 212 Arch St
  215-625-2510
  Tartes cupcakes bring all the old, fur-swathed society ladies to the yard
- **Vagabond** • 37 N 3rd St
  267-671-0737
  Seasonal fashions and original designs.
- **Wawa Food Market** • 518 S 2nd St
  215-629-1050
  A godsend for 3 am munchies.

Map 5 • Gray's Ferry

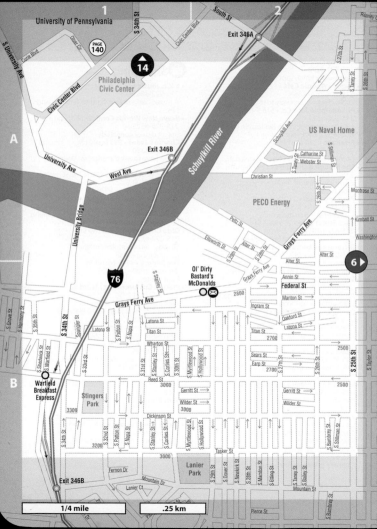

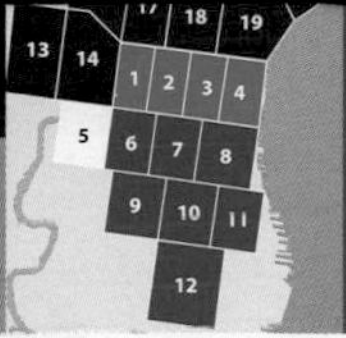

Map 5

Close to Center City and while not an outward beauty, Gray's Ferry has its own kind of tree-starved, industrially ravaged gorgeousity. Get your cheap mob thrills at the **Warfield Breakfast Express**, where La Costa Nostra member Joe Ciancaglini was almost rubbed out back in '93.

O Landmarks

• **Ol' Dirty Bastard's McDonalds** •
S 29th St & Grays Ferry Ave
The site of ODB's last arrest (in 2002) before
his death (in 2004).
• **Warfield Breakfast Express** •
Reed St & S Warfield St
Failed mob hit on Joey Ciancaglini caught
on tape.

Restaurants

• **La Rosa's Café** • 1300 S Warfield St
215-339-1740 • $
If you ever need a breakfast pizza, this is the
joint to hit up.
• **Moe's Hot Dog House** • 2601 Washington Ave
215-465-6637 • $
Dog toppings galore, plus veggie & turkey
options.

Map 6 • **Graduate Hospital / Gray's Ferry**

Time was, this area was known more for urban decay than anything else. Since then, things have definitely turned around. West South Street has gotten much-needed new blood and new bars, and while being in a subway dead-zone doesn't really help, the area is well worth the walk.

☕ Coffee

- **La.Va Café** • 2100 South St
  215-545-1508
  Could be better or worse. Serves Israeli food.
- **Ultimo Coffee** • 2149 Catharine St
  215-545-3565
  Philly's best coffee, thanks to an unusual brewing process.

🍸 Nightlife

- **American Sardine Bar** • 1800 Federal St
  215-334-2337
  Superb drafts and nibblies. Check out the beer garden.
- **Grace Tavern** • 2229 Grays Ferry Ave
  215-893-9580
  Dark, but not dingy bar for a casual night out.
- **Resurrection Ale House** •
  2425 Grays Ferry Ave
  215-735-2202
  Awesome drafts with mediocre food.
- **Robert's Twilight Lounge** • 700 S 20th St
  Honest to goodness neighborhood dive bar with one hell of a house band.
- **Ten Stone** • 2063 South St
  215-735-9939
  English pub has darts, billiards, and a stone fireplace.

🍴 Restaurants

- **Divan Turkish Kitchen & Bar** • 918 S 22nd St
  215-545-5790 • $$$
  Turkish delights.
- **Grace Tavern** • 2229 Grays Ferry Ave
  215-893-9580 • $
  The best green beans you'll ever eat.
- **Honey's Sit 'n Eat** • 2101 South St
  215-732-5130 • $
  Newest location of the popular Jewish Southern hybrid.
- **Miles Table** • 1620 South St
  267-318-7337 • $$
  Fresh and tasty. Excellent homemade bagels.
- **My Thai** • 2200 South St
  215-985-1878 • $
  Cozy and casual, with just the right amount of sass to its cooking.
- **Phoebe's Bar-B-Q** • 2214 South St
  215-546-4811 • $
  Take-out only, but worth the mess.
- **Sidecar Bar & Grille** • 2201 Christian St
  215-732-3429 • $$
  Subtle gentrification amidst the unsubtle sound of the gun.
- **SoWe Bar Kitchen** • 918 S 22nd St
  215-545-5790 • $$
  Local pub with decent grub.
- **Ten Stone** • 2063 South St
  215-735-9939 • $$
  Traditional British pub with American food. Go figure.

🛍 Shopping

- **Bicycle Therapy** • 2211 South St
  215-735-7849
  The best bike-repair joint in the city.
- **Fireside Camp Supply** • 2207 South St
  267-928-2757
  Escape from the concrete jungle!
- **The Igloo** • 2223 Grays Ferry Ave
  267-858-4290
  FroYo…in the Year 2000.
- **Loop** • 1914 South St
  215-893-9939
  Gorgeous, high-end yarns when AC Moore just won't do.
- **Rita's** • 2124 South St
  267-428-3533
  Great spot for tasty custard and wooder ice.

Map 6

Map 7 · **Southwark West**

Map 7

Looking for proof that South Philly changes radically from block-to-block? You've got it right here, buddy. From new condos to crumbling lots, from some of the best food in the city to dubious holes-in-the-wall (okay, sometimes they're the same thing); this is one of the most varied areas of the city.

O Landmarks

- **Cous' Little Italy** • 901 S 11th St
  Angelo Bruno, ancient Don, eats his last meal here before getting whacked.
- **Godmobile** • E Passyunk Ave & Tasker St
  Repent or perish.
- **Holiday Lights** • Tasker St & S 13th St
  Year round orgy of holiday lights.
- **Lady Day Placard** • S Broad St & South St
  Billie was born in Philly, remember.
- **Philadelphia's Magic Gardens** •
  1022 South St
  215-733-0390
  Isaiah Zagar's masterpiece in progress.
- **Stenciled Face** • 1248 S 13th St
  Is it the King or Mary Poppins? You decide.
- **Vulpine Athletic Club** • Federal St & S 12th St
  Where James "Jimmy Brooms" Diadorrio met his ugly demise.

Coffee

- **B2** • 1500 E Passyunk Ave
  215-271-5520
  Nancy Trachtenberg's second Benna's location.
- **Black n Brew** • 1523 E Passyunk Ave
  267-639-6070
  Cute shop with solid food menu.

Farmers Markets

- **Broad & South** • South St & S Broad St
  Wednesdays, 2 pm-7 pm, in season.

Nightlife

- **Bob & Barbara's Lounge** • 1509 South St
  215-545-4511
  Perhaps the city's best boozy entertainment center. PBR, ping pong, and drag queens.
- **Boot & Saddle** • 1311 S Broad St
  267-639-4528
  Solid bar with live shows in a smallish space.
- **The Cambridge** • 1508 South St
  267-455-0647
  Underrated pub with a respectable draft list.
- **Devil's Den** • 1148 S 11th St
  215-339-0855
  A spacious South Philly beer snob paradise.
- **Dolphin Tavern** • 1539 S Broad St
  215-278-7950
  Cheap beer and strippers. NFT pick.
- **Hawthornes** • 738 S 11th St
  215-627-3012
  Bottles, drafts, and sammies with seats by the fire.
- **Jet Wine Bar** • 1525 South St
  215-735-1116
  Wine version of a local pub. Worth a visit.
- **Pub on Passyunk East (P.O.P.E.)** • 1501 E Passyunk Ave
  215-755-5125
  Hipsters unite.

Map 7

Southwark West

🍴 Restaurants

- **August** • 1247 S 13th St
  215-468-5926 • $$
  Downtown style across from Passyunk Square.
- **Bitar's** • 947 Federal St
  215-755-1121 • $
  Baked—not fried—falafel, plus lots of gyros.
- **Carmen's Country Kitchen** • 1301 S 11th St
  215-339-9613 • $
  Tiny and quirky, but avant garde food is
  sublime.
- **Chiarella's Ristorante** • 1600 S 11th St
  215-334-6404 • $$
  Italian food…just like grandma used to make.
- **Chickie's Italian Deli** • 1014 Federal St
  215-462-8040 • $
  Standout hoagies and hot sammies. Try the
  Chicken Italiano.
- **Circles** • 1514 Tasker St
  267-687-1778 • $$
  Don't knock the cheesesteak eggrolls til you
  try 'em.
- **Da Vinci Ristorante** • 1533 S 11th St
  215-336-3636 • $$
  Unique Italian with great desserts.
- **Dante & Luigi's** • 762 S 10th St
  215-922-9501 • $$
  Heaping out the gravies since 1899.
- **Devil's Den** • 1148 S 11th St
  215-339-0855 • $$
  Mediocre food, but the beers are delish.
- **Entree Bistro** • 1608 South St
  215-790-0330 • $$
  Superb New American bistro with a hint of
  Italiano.

- **Fond** • 1537 S 11th St
  215-551-5000 • $$$
  Elegant little bistro with an emphasis on
  seafood.
- **Francoluigi's** • 1549 S 13th St
  215-755-8900 • $
  Huge-portioned BYOB packs in the locals. Lots
  of singing.
- **Govinda's** • 1408 South St
  215-985-9303 • $$
  Excellent whole-food eats from vegan
  hypnotherapists.
- **Green Eggs Cafe** • 1306 Dickinson St
  215-226-3447 • $$
  Light and sweet, it's time to eat.
- **Hawthornes** • 738 S 11th St
  215-627-3012 • $$
  Bottles, drafts, and sammies with seats by
  the fire.
- **Isgro Pastries** • 1009 Christian St
  215-923-3092 • $
  Fattening you up since 1904. Just order cakes
  in advance.
- **Izumi Sushi** • 1601 E Passyunk Ave
  215-271-1222 • $$
  Freshest fish this side of Washington Ave.
- **Jamaican Jerk Hut** • 1436 South St
  215-545-8644 • $
  Check out their Caribbean-inspired outdoor
  space.
- **JNA Institute of Culinary Arts** •
  1212 S Broad St
  215-468-8800 • $$$
  Four course, $25 prix-fixe dinners? Yes please!
- **Lazaro's** • 1743 South St
  215-545-2775 • $
  You like slices the size of Bangladesh? This is
  the joint for you.

Map 7

If you can't find food or fun here then you're just being willful and obstinate. So anyway, speaking of vittles: goodness gracious, that food! Head to **P.O.P.E.** for a frosty one, a delectable pastry at **Isgro**, and a delicious BYOB dinner at **August**. And did we mention that the best dive bar on Earth is here? Long live **Bob & Barbara's**.

- **Magpie** • 1622 South St
  267-519-2904 • $
  Artisan pies, sweet and savory. Try the pie milkshake.
- **Ms. Tootsie's** • 1314 South St
  215-731-9045 • $$
  Catfish, collards, mac & cheese.
- **Nam Phuong** • 1100 Washington Ave
  215-468-0410 • $
  Tasty pho and avocado shakes.
- **Pure Fare** • 1609 South St
  267-687-2292 • $
  Great lunch option when you feel guilty about skipping the gym.
- **The Quick Fixx** • 1511 South St
  267-273-1066 • $
  Casual BYO for the carb lover.
- **Rex 1516** • 1516 South St
  267-319-1366 • $$
  Southern vittles at their finest.
- **Ricci's Hoagies** • 1165 S 11th St
  215-334-6910 • $
  Old-school deli stuffs the hoagies with charm.
- **Sam's Morning Glory Diner** • 735 S 10th St
  215-413-3999 • $$
  Huge lines, but pancakes will make you weep.
- **Sawatdee** • 534 S 15th St
  215-790-1299 • $$
  Average Thai.
- **So Crepe** • 1506 South St
  267-761-9310 • $$
  So French. (Seriously.)
- **Supper** • 926 South St
  215-592-8180 • $$$
  Farm-to-table; seriously, it's up in Newtown Square.

🛍 Shopping

- **Anvil Iron Works** • 1022 Washington Ave
  215-468-8300
  Gates, grates and everything in between!
- **Bare Feet Shoes** • 427 South St
  215-922-0488
  Fun 'n cheap threads 'n kicks.
- **Belle Cakery** • 1437 E Passyunk Ave
  215-271-2299
  Splurge on the olive bread. You won't regret it.
- **Harry's Occult Shop** • 1238 South St
  215-735-8262
  Sorry black arts enthusiasts—White Magic only at Harry's.
- **Sweet Freedom Bakery** • 1424 South St
  215-545-1899
  Gluten-free, dairy-free indulgence for even non-vegans.

Map 8 • Bella Vista / Queen Village

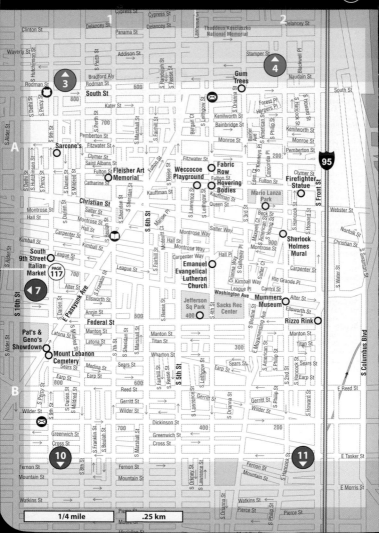

Map 8

Anyone who bought in early is a lucky duck, and anyone who rents just got here too late. Home to everything from the delicious **Italian Market** to the testosterone-engorged horror that is South Street, it's hard to believe that if you head south of Washington, the housing is actually affordable. Really, it's true.

○ Landmarks

- **Emanuel Evangelical Lutheran Church** •
  1001 S 4th St
  Saving Philly souls since 1868.
- **Fabric Row** • S 4th St & Bainbridge St
  From prom dresses to curtain rods.
- **Firefighter Statue** • S Front St & Queen St
  Don't miss the weird-looking Dalmatian at his feet.
- **Fleisher Art Memorial** • 719 Catharine St
  215-922-3456
  Art classes, exhibits, galleries on the DL.
- **Hovering Bodies** • S 4th St & Catharine St
  School kids' body molds now disintegrated into horror movie.
- **Jefferson Square Park/Sacks Rec Center** •
  Washington Ave & S 4th St
  Hoops, soccer and a pool to take a plunge afterward.
- **Mario Lanza Park** • S 2nd St & Queen St
  Great doggie run and film series.
- **Mount Lebanon Cemetery** •
  S 9th St & Passyunk Ave
  Early African burial ground, but the bodies have been moved.
- **Mummers Museum** • 1100 S 2nd St
  215-336-3050
  Philly's answer to Mardi Gras krewes.
- **Pat's & Geno's Showdown** •
  S 9th St & E Passyunk Ave
  Stand in the crosswalk and watch humanity degrade itself by the second.
- **Rizzo Rink** • 1001 S Front St
  215-685-1593
  Proud home of the Rink Rats.
- **Sarcone's** • 734 S 9th St
  215-922-1717
  Get your bread on and don't pass up the pizza.
- **Sherlock Holmes Mural** •
  S 2nd St & Christian St
  Hidden maze of characters and images abound.
- **South 9th Street Italian Market** •
  S 9th St b/w Wharton St & Fitzwater St
  215-278-2903
  You kiddin' me? Cheese, meat, bread, pasta.
- **Street Magician** • South St & S Orianna St
  David Blaine he ain't.
- **Weccacoe Playground** •
  Catherine St & S 5th St
  215-339-0975
  Best public tennis court in CC.

☕ Coffee

- **Alhambra Cafe** • 609 S 3rd St
  215-922-2202
  Chai from scratch, plus hookah.
- **Anthony's Italian Coffee** • 903 S 9th St
  215-627-2586
  In the Italian Market.
- **The Bean Café** • 615 South St
  215-629-2250
  South Street standby.
- **Benna's Café** • 1236 S 8th St
  215-334-1502
  For a pre- or post-Pat's brew.
- **Cafe Fulya** • 727 S 2nd St
  267-909-9937
  Turkish pastries and coffee.
- **Chapterhouse Café & Gallery** • 620 S 9th St
  215-238-2626
  Fantastic little place.
- **Gleaner's Cafe** • 917 S 9th St
  215-923-3205
  Coffee amongst carnivores.
- **Red Hook Coffee and Tea** • 765 S 4th St
  215-923-0178
  Occasionally off, generally good.

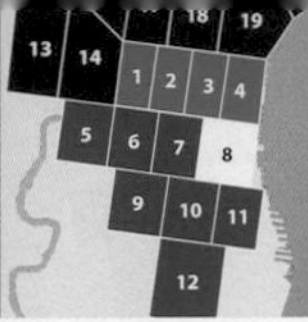

Map 8

Bella Vista / Queen Village

Nightlife

- **12 Steps Down** • 831 Christian St
215-238-0379
South Philly's esoteric basement booze hall.
- **Bainbridge Street Barrel House** •
625 S 6th St
267-324-3553
Yet another amazing draft list—not that we're complaining.
- **Bridget Foy's** • 200 South St
215-922-1813
South Street people-watching from an upscale environment.
- **Cheers to You** • 430 South St
215-923-8780
Unpretentious sports bar has decent beer, many TVs.
- **Connie's Ric-Rac** • 1132 S 9th St
215-279-7587
Grungy, black and fit for a show.
- **Copabanana** • 344 South St
215-923-6180
Classiest place on South Street.
- **The Dive Bar** • 947 E Passyunk Ave
215-465-5505
Former old man bar repopulated with hipsters.
- **For Pete's Sake** • 900 S Front St
215-462-2230
Typified eatery, bar has good taps.
- **Friendly Lounge** • 1039 S 8th St
215-627-9798
Corner tavern with old tables and Highlife. Who needs more?
- **Garage** • 1231 E Passyunk Ave
Canned beers and arcade games in a former auto-body shop.
- **Growlers** • 736 S 8th St
267-519-3242
Decent draft list and pub grub, but the fireplace seals the deal.

- **The Industry** • 1401 E Moyamensing Ave
215-271-9500
Show your favorite bartender a good time. You owe him.
- **Jon's Bar and Grille** • 300 South St
215-592-1390
Good outdoor seating area allows you to see South in full regalia.
- **L'Etage** • 624 S 6th St
215-592-0656
Classy French-themed lounge, with wine and cheese platters to match.
- **New Wave Café** • 784 S 3rd St
215-922-8484
Rock solid food and a swinging booze crowd. Plus, Quizzo.
- **O'Neal's** • 611 S 3rd St
215-574-9495
A sports bar with a DJ? It works, but makes for some strange crossovers.
- **Ray's "Happy Birthday" Bar** •
1200 E Passyunk Ave
215-365-1169
The quintessential dark corner bar.
- **Reef Restaurant and Lounge** • 605 S 3rd St
215-629-0102
A real life Margaritaville.
- **Royal Tavern** • 937 E Passyunk Ave
215-389-6694
Standard Tap South: great menu and beer choice.
- **Saloon** • 750 S 7th St
215-627-1811
Reportedly where Tony Bennett eats when he's in town.
- **Tattooed Mom** • 530 South St
215-238-9880
Regulars pack into the one major bar on South that isn't for tourists.
- **Theatre of Living Arts** • 334 South St
215-922-2599
Indie-band paradise, right down to the crappy bathrooms.

At night, feast and quaff at one of the more in-the-know Philly treasures, the **Royal Tavern**. There is good beer at **Bainbridge Barrel House**, and **Garage** has skee-ball. **Tattooed Mom** is another great spot, even if the pool table is taken (and it probably will be). See also the eponymously named **The Dive Bar** or **Ray's Happy Birthday Bar**, where dirty hipsters and old neighborhood men break bread.

Restaurants

- **Beau Monde** • 624 S 6th St
  215-592-0656 • $$$
  Elegant French creperie. Comment charmant!
- **Bibou** • 1009 S 8th St
  215-965-8290 • $$$
  A must for the Francophile.
- **Bridget Foy's** • 200 South St
  215-922-1813 • $$$
  Strong drinks and a nice spot to survey the crowd
- **Café Huong Lan** • 1037 S 8th St
  215-629-9966 • $
  Vietnamese hoagies done with flair.
- **Café Nhu Y** • 802 Christian St
  215-925-6544 • $
  A Vietnamese veggie hoagie that will slap your ass and call you sonny.
- **Caffe Valentino** • 1245 S 3rd St
  215-336-3033 • $$
  For a nice meal before a shitty UA Theatre film.
- **Cucina Forte** • 768 S 8th St
  215-238-0778 • $$
  A creepy little place with nothing going for it.
- **Dmitri's** • 795 S 3rd St
  215-625-0556 • $
  Popular neighborhood BYOB; be prepared to wait.
- **Famous 4th Street Deli** • 700 S 4th St
  215-922-3274 • $
  Great cookies, and the largest order of eggs you have ever seen.
- **Famous 4th Street Delicatessen** •
  700 S 4th St
  215-922-3274 • $$
  Legit pastrami and massive sammiches fit for your bubbe.
- **Federal Donuts** • 1219 S 2nd St
  267-687-8258 • $
  Legendary handmade donuts and Korean twice-fried chicken.
- **Fitzwater Café** • 728 S 7th St
  215-629-0428 • $
  Blissful eggs and great pancakes.
- **For Pete's Sake** • 900 S Front St
  215-462-2230 • $$
- **Geno's Steaks** • 1219 S 9th St
  215-389-0659 •
  Neon-drenched, with opinions to match.
- **Gnocchi** • 613 E Passyunk Ave
  215-592-8300 • $$
  Their eponymous dish does them justice.
- **Golden Empress Garden** • 610 S 5th St
  215-627-7666 • $$
  Ho-hum Chinese with many veggie options.
- **Hikaru** • 607 S 2nd St
  215-627-7110 • $$
  Delicate specialty rolls in keeping with the low-key atmosphere.
- **Hosteria Da Elio** • 615 S 3rd St
  215-925-0930 • $$$
  There really is an Elio, and he's a magician with a whisk.
- **The Industry** • 1401 E Moyamensing Ave
  215-271-9500 • $$
  Show your favorite waitress a good time. You owe her.
- **Ishkabibble's** • 337 South St
  215-923-4337 •
  Fast, late night chow at its finest.
- **Jim's Steaks** • 400 South St
  215-928-1911 •
  For those who love smelling of onions while standing in line.
- **Johnny Rockets** • 443 South St
  215-829-9222 • $
  If you like your burgers served with '50s-style doo-wop, be our guest.
- **La Fourno** • 636 South St
  215-627-9000 • $
  Good pastas, solid wood-fired 'za.
- **Latest Dish** • 613 S 4th St
  215-629-0565 • $$$$
  DJ spins tunes as you throw down irresistible chow.
- **Lil' Pop Shop** • 534 S 4th St
  215-923-3509 • $
  All manner of fancy (and addictive) popsicles.
- **Lorenzo & Sons Pizza** • 305 South St
  215-800-1942 • $
  Philly's most famous (not necessarily best) pie.
- **Lorenzo's Pizza** • 900 Christian St
  215-922-2540 • $
  Very parm-heavy but it definitely sticks to your ribs.
- **Lovash** • 236 South St
  215-925-3881 • $$
  Decent Indian with a bit of fire in its loins.
- **Maoz** • 248 South St
  215-625-3500 • $
  Dutch falafel chain with all-u-can eat toppings.

Map 8

Bella Vista / Queen Village

- **Monsu** • 901 Christian St
215-440-0495 • $$$
Spectacular Sicilian. Affordable and BYOB under one roof!
- **Mustard Greens** • 622 S 2nd St
215-627-0833 • $$
You must try the garlic noodles. Trust us.
- **Napoli Pizzeria** • 944 E Passyunk Ave
215-336-3833 • $
Panzerotti: a pizza, deep fried. This is so good, it's worth the heart attack.
- **New Wave Café** • 784 S 3rd St
215-922-8484 • $$
Locals pub with elegant chow.
- **Nomad Pizza** • 611 S 7th St
215-238-0900 • $
Have we died and gone to Brooklyn?
- **Paesano's** • 1017 S 9th St
215-440-0371 • $
Dense meat or vegetable-filled sandwiches.
- **Pat's King of Steaks** • 1237 E Passyunk Ave
215-468-1546 •
When you've gotta have a cheesesteak at 5 am.
- **Phileo Yogurt** • 416 South St
215-873-8361 • $
Pretty good pay-by-the-ounce Pinkberry knock-off.
- **Ralph's** • 760 S 9th St
215-627-6011 • $$
Serving up pasta for more than a century.
- **Royal Tavern** • 937 E Passyunk Ave
215-389-6694 •
Mellowed hipsters drink like kings.
- **Sabrina's Cafe** • 910 Christian St
215-574-1599 • $$
Brunch specials and great décor, plus polenta fries.
- **Saloon** • 750 S 7th St
215-627-1811 • $$$$$
Reportedly where Tony Bennett eats when he's in town.
- **Snockey's** • 1020 S 2nd St
215-339-9578 • $$
Down and dirty oyster house.
- **South Street Diner** • 140 South St
215-627-5258 • $$
24 hours of cheap, reliable, grub.
- **South Street Philly Bagels** • 613 S 3rd St
215-627-6277 • $
Best bagel in the city.

- **Taco Loco** • Jefferson Square Park
215-883-9191 • $
Brutally good taco truck parked on Washington Ave.
- **Tamarind** • 117 South St
215-925-2764 • $$
Dutiful Thai in casual atmosphere.
- **Taqueria La Veracruzana** •
908 Washington Ave
215-465-1440 • $
Not much to look at, but authentic and delicious.
- **Termini Brothers** • 1523 S 8th St
215-334-1816 • $
The cannoli is legend. Spoken of in whispers.
- **The Ugly American** • 1100 S Front St
215-336-1100 • $$
Only place we know of for a "classy" garbage plate.
- **Ulivo** • 521 Catharine
215-351-1550 • $$
Cozy, above average Italian BYO.
- **Villa di Roma** • 936 S 9th St
215-592-1295 • $
If loving their ricotta/mozzarella pasta is wrong, then we don't want to be right.

🛍 Shopping

- **Adidas** • 436 South St
267-514-1952
For meatheads and fashionistas alike.
- **Anastacia's Antiques** • 617 Bainbridge St
215-928-9111
Yeah, we bought an antique speculum here; wanna fight about it?
- **Atomic City Comics** • 638 South St
215-625-9613
Comics, Japanese animation, cult films and beyond.
- **Bella Boutique** • 527 S 4th St
215-923-8174
Pre-worn designer wear ain't cheap, apparently.
- **Bella Vista Beer Distributor** • 755 S 11th St
215-627-6465
Best option in the city when a six-pack just won't do.
- **Center City Soft Pretzel Co.** •
816 Washington Ave
215-463-5664
Opens at midnight. Gourmet and cheap.

Get your Schwinn on at **Via Bicycle**. **Sabrina's** poofs up pancakes with fruity oomph, and they've got killer omelets, too. **Villa di Roma** embraces the red sauce while **Federal Donuts** "elevates" doughnuts and Korean fried chicken—there's plenty of room for all of it, waistbands notwithstanding. And then there's the vortex of cheap meat and whiz at **Jim's**, **Ishkabibble's**, **Pat's**, and **Geno's**.

- **Cohen & Co Hardware** • 615 E Passyunk Ave
  215-922-3493
  Friendly, slightly odd staff make it worthwhile.
- **Crash Bang Boom** • 528 S 4th St
  215-928-1123
  Where all today's punks score combat boots
  and eye shadow. Formerly Zipperhead.
- **Di Bruno Brothers** • 930 S 9th St
  215-922-2876
  Say cheese.
- **EB Games** • 505 South St
  215-625-0795
  Everything from Scrabble to GTA.
- **Essene Market & Cafe** • 719 S 4th St
  215-922-1146
  Organic, vegan market and cafeteria. Plus lots
  of vitamins.
- **Fante's Kitchen Shop** • 1006 S 9th St
  215-922-5557
  Exhaustive inventory of all kitchen goodies.
- **Garland of Letters** • 527 South St
  215-923-5946
  New-age books, trinkets, and many, many
  types of candles.
- **Goldstein's** • 809 S 6th St
  215-468-0564
  Italian imports since 1902. Loads of
  suspenders, too.
- **Hats in the Belfry** • 633 South St
  215-922-6770
  Grab a cool Gandalf hat and be the envy of
  your D&D club.
- **Head House Books** • 619 S 2nd St
  215-923-9525
  An independent running on integrity fuel, not
  to mention huge, glossy gift books.
- **House of Tea** • 720 S 4th St
  215-923-8327
  Some varieties more expensive than good
  hashish.
- **John's Water Ice** • 701 Christian St
  215-925-6955
  A South Philly institution.
- **Masquerade** • 1100 S Columbus Blvd
  215-952-0980
  Basically a Wal-Mart of costuming.
- **Maxie's Daughter** • 724 S 4th St
  215-829-2226
  The heart of fabric row.

- **Moon and Arrow** • 754 S 4th St
  215-469-1448
  Great finds, from vintage threads to furniture.
- **Mostly Books** • 529 Bainbridge St
  215-592-8380
  Books, furniture, and "20th Century Artifacts."
- **Nocturnal Skateshop** • 610 S 3rd St
  215-922-3177
  X-Games street champ Kerry Getz is the
  owner.
- **Philadelphia Bar & Restaurant Supply** •
  629 E Passyunk Ave
  215-925-7649
  From non-stick ladles to sweet wine keys.
- **Philadelphia Eddie's Tattoo** • 621 S 4th St
  215-922-7384
  Ask for Troy.
- **Philly AIDS Thrift** • 710 S 5th St
  215-922-3186
  Prepare to be overstimulated with amazing
  finds.
- **Repo Records** • 538 South St
  215-627-3775
  Joke: How many indie kids does it take to
  screw in a lightbulb? Answer: You don't know?
- **Retrospect** • 508 South St
  267-671-0116
  Clothes, knick-knacks and furniture—though
  hardly cheap.
- **Rita's** • 239 South St
  215-629-3910
  Great spot for tasty custard.
- **Sarcone's Deli** • 734 S 9th St
  215-922-1717
  Hoagie fixins live up to the bread.
- **Triple Play Sports** • 827 S 9th St
  215-627-4898
  Customized fan-ware and lots of USA pride.
- **Urban Jungle** • 1526 E Passyunk Ave
  215-952-0811
  Turn your city patio into a green getaway.
- **Urban Princess** • 750 S 4th St
  215-278-7675
  Clothes, jewelry, homemade soaps, and more.
  Treat yo self!
- **Via Bicycle** • 606 S 9th St
  215-627-3370
  Unpretentious and nothing fancy—but
  cheap.

Map 9 • **Point Breeze / West Passyunk**

Map 9

Hey, want to see where Beanie Sigel claims he got shot? That's here: head to 22nd and his namesake street. Things around this neighborhood are sort of friendly and the rents are super-cheap (with good reason), but parking at night is nigh impossible. Yeah, that's right: *nigh*.

O Landmarks

- **Melrose Diner** • 1501 Snyder Ave
  215-467-6644
  Parking lot was the site of brutal mob hit of Frank Baldino.

Coffee

- **Ultimo Coffee** • 1900 S 15th St
  215-339-3177
  Well-regarded coffee shop with regular Friday tastings.

Nightlife

- **DiNic's** • 1528 Snyder Ave
  215-923-6175
  Flyers-centric bar has decades of history and dust.
- **JR's Bar** • 2327 S Croskey St
  215-336-4020
  Punk music. Cheap beer. Sign us up.
- **South Philadelphia Tap Room** •
  1509 Mifflin St
  215-271-7787
  Stylish gastropub with impressive draft list.

Restaurants

- **Barrel's** • 1725 Wolf St
  215-389-6010 • $$
  No-frills Italian joint, popular for lunch.
- **Gennaro's Tomato Pie** • 1429 Jackson St
  215-463-5070 • $$
  Exactly what it sounds like but better. Crisp and simple.
- **Hardena Resto Waroeng Surabaya** •
  1754 S Hicks St
  215-271-9442 • $$
  Delicious, tiny, unpretentious Indonesian hole in the wall.
- **L'Angolo** • 1415 W Porter St
  215-389-4252 • $$
  Homemade Italian. Ravioli. To. Die. For.
- **La Stanza** • 2001 Oregon Ave
  215-271-0801 • $$$
  Standard Italian, but the joint's on stilts.
- **Melrose Diner** • 1501 Snyder Ave
  215-467-6644
  A breakfast institution 24 hours a day.
- **South Philadelphia Tap Room** •
  1509 Mifflin St
  215-271-7787 • $$
  Stylish gastropub with impressive draft list.
- **Valanni** • 1229 Spruce St
  215-790-9494 • $$$
  In the heart of the gayborhood, it's eclecticism with zero pretentiousness.

Shopping

- **South Philly Comics** • 1621 Passyunk Ave
  267-318-7855
  Comic geeks love that it's open late.

Map 10

A busy (and somewhat congested) section of South Philly that features lots of residential living space stacked not-so-neatly on top of itself. South Broad takes on the appearance of a blocked artery during peak rush hours, and the curious parking custom of leaving your car in the middle of the goddamn street hardly helps matters.

O Landmarks

- **King of Jeans** • 1843 E Passyunk Ave
  Learn to believe again; admire the King of Jeans sign.
- **Sneakers on a Wire** • 1226 Morris St
  Hanging VANS.

Farmers Markets

- **Fountain Farmers' Market** •
  S 11th St & Tasker St
  Wednesday afternoons, in season.

Nightlife

- **Cantina Los Cabalitos** • 1651 E Passyunk Ave
  215-755-3550
  Toss down tequila and nibble on nachos.
- **Le Virtu** • 1927 E Passyunk Ave
  215-271-5626
  Restaurant industry folks get 20% off at the bar. Word.
- **Lucky 13** • 1820 S 13th St
  215-336-8467
  Bottled beer and meatball subs.
- **Stateside** • 1536 E Passyunk Ave
  215-551-2500
  Bourdain loves this place. Make what you will of that.
- **Stogie Joe's** • 1801 E Passyunk Ave
  215-463-3030
  Cozy local with a killer upside down pizza.
- **Watkins Drinkery** • 1712 S 10th St
  215-339-0175
  Chill neighborhood pub with excellent draft list.

Restaurants

- **Bomb Bomb BBQ Grill** • 1026 Wolf St
  215-463-1311 • $$
  BBQ is expected here, but the quality Italian food is something only locals know about.
- **Criniti Restaurant** • 2611 S Broad St
  215-465-7750 • $
  Unpretentious, inexpensive spaghetti house.
- **El Zarape** • 1648 E Passyunk Ave
  215-336-1293 • $$
  Authentic Mexican cusine great for take-out.
- **Khmer Kitchen** • 1700 S 6th St
  215-755-2222 • $
  Best Cambodian in the Tri-state area.
- **La Rosa Pizzeria** • 2106 Broad St
  215-271-5246 • $
  Sicilian style 'za. Go for the potato.
- **Le Virtu** • 1927 E Passyunk Ave
  215-271-5626 • $$$
  Dine in a garden? In South Philly? For real!
- **Mamma Maria** • 1637 E Passyunk Ave
  215-463-6884 • $$$$
  Seven-course prix fixe varies from evening to evening.
- **Marra's** • 1734 E Passyunk Ave
  215-463-9249 • $
  Zounds! The thin crust pie is heavenly.

- **Mazza Healthy Mediteranean** •
  1100 Jackson St
  215-952-2600 • $$
  Amazing hummus, falafel, etc.
- **Mr. Martino's Trattoria** • 1646 E Passyunk Ave
  215-755-0663 • $$
  Elegant, understated, and the food is bliss.
- **Paradiso** • 1627 E Passyunk Ave
  215-271-2066 • $$$
  Fine contemporary dining with waiters who compare the gnocci to "angel pillows."
- **Pop's Water Ice** • 1337 W Oregon Ave
  215-551-7677 • $
  Water Ice from a non-chain, taste the difference.
- **Scannicchio's** • 2500 S Broad St
  215-468-3900 • $$
  NJ legend finally opens branch in Philly.
- **Stateside** • 1536 E Passyunk Ave
  215-551-2500 • $$
  Bourdain loves this place. Make what you will of that.
- **Tre Scalini** • 1915 E Passyunk Ave
  215-551-3870 • $$$
  The food is extraordinary; the décor, horrendous.
- **Will** • 1911 E Passyunk Ave
  215-271-7683 • $$$
  Artful, French inspired cuisine.

Map 10

Revamped Passyunk Avenue has something for everyone. **Paradiso** serves Italian in a sophisticated setting while down the street, **Cantina** buzzes with hipsters buzzed on margaritas. For a low-key evening, try a specialty pizza at **Marra's** or head to **Lucky 13** for beer and meatball shots.

Shopping

- **Beautiful World Syndicate** •
  1619 E Passyunk Ave
  215-467-0401
  Hit or miss record shop—give yourself plenty of time to rifle.
- **Fabric Horse** • 1737 E Passyunk Ave
  215-995-1026
  Beautifully constructed, hipster-as-all-hell bags etc.
- **Fabulous Finds Boutique** • 1535 S Broad St
  215-336-5226
  From evening gowns to baby booties.
- **Home** • 1815 E Passyunk Ave
  215-551-1180
  The mom and pop furniture store of tomorrow.

- **Interior Concepts Furniture** •
  1701 E Passyunk Ave
  215-468-6226
  Leather furniture, beds, and salesmen.
- **Mia** • 1748 E Passyunk Ave
  215-465-2913
  Rodeo-drive-style upscale boutique in South Philly.
- **Occasionette** • 1825 E Passyunk Ave
  215-465-1704
  Shabby chic party supplies, gifts, and housewares.
- **Shoe Barrel** • 1812 E Passyunk Ave
  215-755-0942
  Affordable shoes for every occasion...not that you need an excuse.

Map 11 · **South Philly East**

For all intents and purposes, the area is connected to the stadiums, if for no other reason than its proximity to both 95 and Columbus—the two main routes to the sports complex. It is also the land of the Mummers, with "Two Street" being their main thoroughfare.

○ Landmarks

- **Asylum Arena** • 7 W Ritner St
  Mixed-use arena occasionally hosts crazy awesome wrestling.

Farmers Markets

- **Dickinson Square Farmers' Market** •
  Morris St & Moyamensing Ave
  Sundays, 10 am-2 pm, in season.

Nightlife

- **Penn's Port Pub** • 1920 S Columbus Blvd
  215-336-7033
  Strip club where "auditions are always welcome."

Restaurants

- **Chick-Fil-A** • 2204 S Columbus Blvd
  215-271-2313 • $
  The crème-de-la-crème of fast food branches out beyond the mall.
- **Chuck E. Cheese's** • 9 Snyder Ave
  215-551-4080 • $
  Some would find the visage of a giant rat hovering over your food disconcerting.
- **Gooey Looie's** • 231 McClellan St
  215-334-7688 • $
  Giant, cheap, and amazing cheesesteaks without the tourists.
- **Tony Luke's** • 39 E Oregon Ave
  215-551-5725 •
  No higher honor amongst the various sandwich gods.

Shopping

- **Bare Feet Shoes** •
  1944 S Christopher Columbus Blvd
  215-389-0107
  Fun 'n cheap threads 'n kicks.
- **Ikea** • 2206 S Columbus Blvd
  215-551-4532
  Have a handy friend or hammer ready.
- **Lowe's** • 2106 S Christopher Columbus Blvd
  215-982-5391
  Hardware for your inner construction worker.
- **Schafer's Muffler & Brakes Center** •
  1924 S Columbus Blvd
  215-755-1270
  Friendly service for sad cars.

53

Map 12 · **Stadiums**

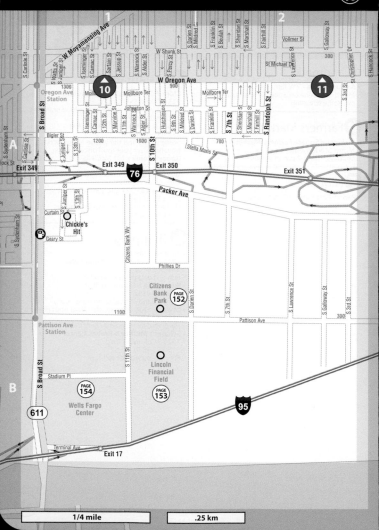

Oh to live in the shadow of the goalposts and foul poles! Of course, for this extreme proximity to Philly's fabled stadia, you must pay a heavy price in daily aggravation, from extreme noise pollution (lots of booing, which carries surprisingly far), to always-jammed streets and drunken louts peeing on your zinnias.

O Landmarks

- **Chickie's Hit** • Curtain St & Juniper St
  Frank Narducci shot 10 times after a court date.
- **Citizens Bank Park** • 1 Citizens Bank Way
  215-563-6000
  World phucking champions!"
- **Lincoln Financial Field** • 1020 Pattison Ave
  215-463-2500
  Where the Iggles call home.

Nightlife

- **McFadden's** • 1 Citizens Bank Way
  215-952-0300
  Beer and beer tub girls.
- **XFINITY Live!** • 1100 Pattison Ave
  855-406-4119
  A veritable mall of bars.

Restaurants

- **McFadden's** • 1 Citizens Bank Way
  215-952-0300 • $$
  Sports bar in the Phillies Citizen's Bank Park.
- **Medora's Mecca** • 3101 S 13th St
  215-336-1655 • $$
  Quiet place, amazing tiramisu.
- **Pastificio Deli** • 1528 Packer Ave
  215-467-1111 • $
  Hidden gem with one of Philly's best hoagies.
- **Talk of the Town** • 3020 S Broad St
  215-551-7277 • $$
  Stop by for a breakfast 'wich on your way to the game.

Map 12

Map 13 · **West Philly**

Map 13

West Philly's giant, gorgeous Victorian houses give this neighborhood a distinct feeling, and the tenants of the houses vary widely from squatting anarchists to African immigrants to college kids and more. Don't miss Clark Park—it's a hub of community activity.

○ Landmarks

- **A-Space** • 4722 Baltimore Ave
  215 727 8170
  A = Anarchy = nothing for sale
- **Clark Park** • Baltimore Ave & S 43rd St
  Established in 1895 in the heart of University City.
- **Pinwheel House** • Wallace St & N 42nd St
  A folk-art explosion of pinwheels and whirligigs.
- **Slought Foundation** • 4017 Walnut St
  215-701-4627
  Not-for-profit cultural organization with public programs in contemporary art.

Coffee

- **Green Line Cafe** • 4239 Baltimore Ave
  215-222-3431
  Popular West Philly spot.
- **Green Line Cafe** • 4426 Locust St
  215-222-0799
  Popular West Philly spot.
- **Kaffa Crossing** • 4423 Chestnut St
  215-386-0504
  Fair Trade coffee and Ethiopian grub at this café with a mission.
- **Satellite Cafe** • 701 S 50th St
  215-729-1211
  Coffee with vegan/vegetarian options.

Farmers Markets

- **Clark Park** • Baltimore Ave & S 43rd St
  215-568-0380
  One of the best, with a variety of vendors.
- **Walnut Hill Farm Stand** • 4610 Market St
  Thursdays, 4 pm-7 pm, in season.

Nightlife

- **Cavanaugh's** • 119 S 39th St
  215-386-4889
  College party scene offering more than kegs of Busch Lite.
- **Dock Street Brewing Co.** • 701 S 50th St
  215-726-2337
  Great pizza & a slew of beers brewed on site.
- **Fiume** • 229 S 45th St
  Tiny little hipster bar.
- **Gojjo** • 4540 Baltimore Ave
  215-386-1444
  Friendly place appeals to students, grads and locals.
- **Lalibela Cafe** • 4441 Chestnut St
  215-450-3480
  Hookah convenient to Penn. BYOB and WiFi.
- **Local 44** • 4333 Spruce St
  215-222-2337
  Bitchin' draft beer selections, meh on the food.
- **Luxor Cafe** • 132 S 45th St
  215-909-9762
  West Philly hookah. Open late. No booze.
- **Smokey Joe's** • 210 S 40th St
  215-222-0770
  Penn's unofficial watering hole has seen many a fine academian fall to ruin.
- **University Pinball** • 4006 Spruce St
  215-387-2561
  No drinks, but lots of 18+ arcade fun after curfew.

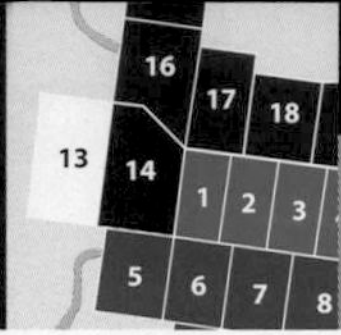

Map 13

Map 13

West Philly

16 17 18
13 14
1 2 3
5 6 7 8

🍴 Restaurants

- **Aksum** • 4630 Baltimore Ave
267-275-8195 • $$$
Mediterranean BYOB (with hookah option).
- **Allegro Pizza** • 3942 Spruce St
215-382-8158 • $
Good pizza! Beer! Good pizza and beer!
- **Colonial Pizza** • 400 S 43rd St
215-387-7702 • $
Some people swear by it, others don't. Serves beer.
- **Desi Chaat House** • 501 S 42nd St
215-386-1999 • $$
"Mild to wild."
- **Desi Village Restaurant** • 4527 Baltimore Ave
215-382-6000 • $
Indian on Baltimore Ave.
- **Distrito** • 3945 Chestnut St
215-222-1657 • $$$
Big, expensive, campy, fun.
- **Ethio Cafe & Carry Out** • 4400 Chestnut St
215-222-2104 • $
Tasty, inexpensive Ethiopian eats.
- **Evan's Pizza** • 4311 Locust St
215-386-8881 • $
Get your 40's here, but not your pizza.
- **Gold Standard Cafe** • 4800 Baltimore Ave
215-727-8247 • $$
Brunch option on Baltimore Ave.
- **Greek Lady** • 222 S 40th St
215-382-2600 • $
Began as a lunch truck, now popular enough for a building.
- **Kabobeesh** • 4201 Chestnut St
215-386-8081 • $
Tasty kabobs of many varieties.
- **Kaffa Crossing** • 4423 Chestnut St
215-386-0504 •
Fair Trade coffee and Ethiopian grub at this café with a mission.
- **Kilimandjaro** • 4317 Chestnut St
215-387-1970 • $$
Large-portioned, African goodness.

- **Koch's Deli** • 4309 Locust St
215-222-8662 • $$
Seriously good sandwiches, and sometimes they feed you pickles.
- **Le Bercail** • 4519 Baltimore Ave
267-292-5805 • $$
West Philly Senegalese.
- **Lee's Deli** • 4700 Baltimore Ave
215-724-1954 • $
Good breakfasts and a chicken cheesesteak folks go nuts for.
- **Lil' Pop Shop** • 265 S 44th St
215-222-5829 • $
All manner of fancy (and addictive) popsicles.
- **Marigold Kitchen** • 501 S 45th St
215-222-3699 • $$$
Extremely fine dining frequented by the university crowd.
- **Mood Cafe** • 4618 Baltimore Ave
215-222-1037 •
Indian lassis, chaats and milkshakes.
- **Pasqually's Pizza and Pasta** • 200 S 43rd St
215-387-6100 • $$
Food? Meh. Beer? Oh yes.
- **Pattaya** • 4006 Chestnut St
215-387-8533 • $$
Not your father's Thai restaurant: exotic and challenging.
- **Pho & Cafe Saigon** • 4248 Spruce St
215-222-6800 • $
Lychee milkshake? Yes please! Tasty, tasty place.
- **Queen of Sheba** • 4511 Baltimore Ave
215-382-2099 • $
Ethiopian, open 'til 2 am with full bar.
- **Saad's Halal** • 4500 Walnut St
215-222-7223 • $
Friendly, funny, delicious, and cheap as hell.
- **Tandoor India** • 106 S 40th St
215-222-7122 • $$
Good, but go for the buffet, not the menu.
- **Vientiane Cafe** • 4728 Baltimore Ave
215-726-1095 • $$
Beautifully good Thai food.
- **Vietnam Cafe** • 816 S 47th St
215-729-0260 • $$
Fish sauce and lime on the cheap in West Philly.

The West Philly melting pot is perhaps best demonstrated by the incredible variety in restaurants, from Ethiopian (**Kaffa Crossing**, **Ethio**) to Pakistani (**Kabobeesh**) to Thai (**Vientiane Cafe**) to fancy Mexican (**Distrito**). Dock **Street Brewing Co.** features a slew of beers brewed on site, and **Fiume** and **Local 44** both do the trick.

🛍 Shopping

- **Bindlestiff Books** • 4530 Baltimore Ave
  215-222-2432
  Tiny, cute, mostly new remainders.
- **Donut Plus** • 4325 Chestnut St
  215-222-0811
  "Donut" miss it! See? See what we did there?
- **Eak Chuong Grocery** • 4421 Chestnut St
  215-386-1254
  For all your rice flour and black bean sauce needs.
- **Firehouse Bicycles** • 701 S 50th St
  215-727-9692
  Community-minded full-service bike store.
- **The Fresh Grocer** • 4001 Walnut St
  215-222-9200
  Fresh? Yes. Overpriced? Also yes.
- **Fu-Wah Mini Mart** • 810 S 47th St
  215-729-2993
  Famous tofu and Vietnamese hoagies!
- **Garden Court Eatery** • 4725 Pine St
  215-748-0748
  Six packs of beer—and food, too.
- **International Foods and Spices** •
  4203 Walnut St
  215-222-4480
  Inidan-Pakistani grocery.
- **Little Baby's Ice Cream** • 4903 Catharine St
  215-921-2100
  Unusual and delicious scoops.
- **Makkah Market** • 4249 Walnut St
  215-382-0909
  Hot foods (falafel!!) and awesome groceries.
- **Mariposa Food Co-op** • 4824 Baltimore Ave
  215-729-2121
  Food co-op focusing on local and sustainably grown food.
- **The Marvelous!** • 4916 Baltimore Ave
  215-726-8742
  CDs and comics: living together as god meant them to.
- **Metropolitan Bakery** • 4013 Walnut St
  215-222-1492
  The people who make bread for half the city.
- **Milk & Honey Market** • 4435 Baltimore Ave
  215-387-6455
  Local, organic market with to-go food.
- **The Natural Shoe Store** • 220 S 40th St
  215-382-9899
  Expansive array of shoes at disparate prices.
- **The Second Mile Center** • 214 S 45th St
  215-662-1663
  HUGE thrift store. Watch for occasional Saturday half-off sales.
- **State Liquor Store** • 4906 Baltimore Ave
  215-726-4046
  God help the PLCB.
- **Toviah Thrift Shop** • 4211 Chestnut St
  215-382-7251
  Come for the needles in the haystack of crap. Stay to talk to proprietor Larry.
- **Wawa Food Market** • 3744 Spruce St
  215-387-0029
  A godsend for 3 am munchies.

Map 14 · **University City**

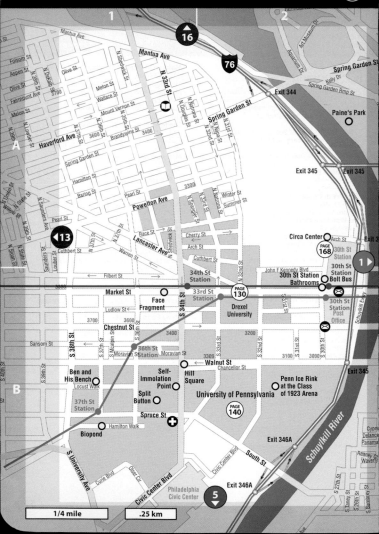

Map 14

If "University City" seems a bit forced to you, you're not crazy—the neighborhood didn't even exist until the mid-1950s when it was created as a marketing ploy. From time to time things have been tense between students and neighbors thanks to "Penntrification," but mostly the area remains a small safe haven for collegians.

⭘ Landmarks

- **30th St Station Bathrooms** •
  Market St & S 30th St
  Recreate *Witness* and pretend you're a little Amish child.
- **Ben and His Bench** • Locust Walk & S 37th St
  Cuddle up with Ben F. and read the newspaper.
- **Biopond** • 3740 Hamilton Walk
  A quiet lunch spot replete with benches and fishpond.
- **Bull Bus** • N 30th St and Market St
  30th Street Bolt Bus Station. The best and cheapest way to travel!
- **Cira Centre** • N 30th St & Arch St
  Look kids, a gigantic Lite-Brite!
- **Drexel Dragon Statue** • Market St & S 34th St
  What does Drexel University have in common with the Renaissance Fair?
- **Face Fragment** • S 35th St & Market St
  Half a face with Roman nose, no eyes.
- **Hill Square** • Walnut St & S 34th St
  Great view of the city, and a series of benches upon which to recline.
- **Paine's Park** •
  MLK Jr. Dr and Benjamin Franklin Pkwy
  Check out the great views before falling on your face.
- **Penn Ice Rink at the Class of 1923 Arena** •
  3130 Walnut St
  215-898-1923
  Skate year round. Thanks '23ers!
- **Self-Immolation Point** • S 34th St & Locust St
  Where artist/activist Kathy Chang burned herself to death.
- **Split Button** • Spruce St & S 36th St
  Claes Oldenburg gives Penn students something to think about.
- **UPenn's Edible Forest** • Sansom St & S 36th St
  Hazardous shrubbery maintained by college students. You can eat it if you want.

🍎 Farmers Markets

- **University Square Farmers' Market** •
  Walnut St & S 36th St
  Wednesdays, 10 am-3 pm, in season.

🍸 Nightlife

- **Bridgewater's Pub** • 2951 Market St
  215-387-4787
  For getting drunk before getting on the R5. Good beer.
- **Mad Mex** • 3401 Walnut St
  215-382-2221
  Big college hang-out has decent grub and plenty of booze.
- **Mikey's American Grill & Sports Bar** •
  3180 Chestnut St
  215-222-3226
  A sports bar on a college campus. Meh.
- **New Deck Tavern** • 3408 Sansom St
  215-386-4600
  Sports and students congregate in high volume.

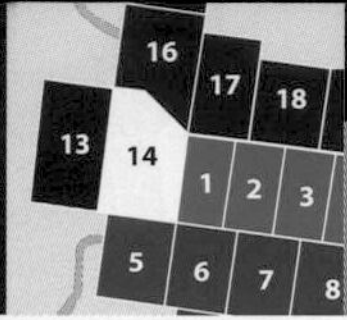

Map 14

University City

🍴 Restaurants

- **Abner's Cheesesteaks** • 3813 Chestnut St
  215-662-0100 •
  Or you can just have them FedEx you a
  sandwich.
- **Baby Blues BBQ** • 3402 Sansom St
  215-222-4444 • $$
  Penn kids get all the good stuff, right down to
  the barbecue.
- **Bobby's Burger Palace** • 3925 Walnut St
  215-387-0378 • $$
  Decent burgers and shakes, minus the lines at
  Shake Shack.
- **Doc Magrogan's Oyster House** •
  3432 Samsom St
  215-382-3474 • $$$
  Oysters: now available in shot form.
- **Ed's Buffalo Wings & Pizza** •
  3513 Lancaster Ave
  215-222-4000 • $$
  Great for those in the mood for both hummus
  and wings.
- **Han Dynasty** • 3711 Market St
  215-222-3711 • $$
  Very spicy, very good.
- **Harvest Seasonal Grill & Wine Bar** •
  200 S 40th St
  215-662-1100 • $$
  Upscale casual farm to table eats.
- **Lemon Grass Thai** • 3630 Lancaster Ave
  215-222-8042 • $$
  Charming Thai cuisine. Order extra corn
  fritters.
- **Mad Mex** • 3401 Walnut St
  215-382-2221 • $$
  Student-friendly joint has edible burritos,
  good beer.

- **New Deck Tavern** • 3408 Sansom St
  215-386-4600 • $$
  Bar food of a standard order, but whiskey
  selection is a plus.
- **Pari Cafe Creperie** • 3417 Spruce St
  215-222-6500 • $
  Real men eat crepes.
- **Penne** • 3600 Sansom St
  215-823-6222 • $$$
  The Hilton's pasta emporium has abundance
  of wine.
- **Picnic** • 3131 Walnut St
  215-222-1608 • $$
  Gourmet deli has the goods to go.
- **Pod** • 3636 Sansom St
  215-387-1803 • $$$
  If Kubrick had opened a sushi bar…
- **Powelton Pizza** • 3635 Lancaster Ave
  215-387-1213 • $
  Decent pizza in University City. Try the pesto.
- **Shake Shack** • 3200 Chestnut St
  267-338-3464 • $
  UPenn's version of the popular milkshake and
  burger joint.
- **Sitar India** • 60 S 38th St
  215-662-0818 • $$
  Don't miss their great buffet.
- **Slainte** • 3000 Market St
  215-222-7400 • $
  Less scary than the pub that was there before.
- **Sweetgreen** • 3925 Walnut St
  215-386-1365 • $$
  Salads and wraps with a local flair.
- **White Dog Café** • 3420 Sansom St
  215-386-9224 • $$$
  Progressive liberal idealists served locally-
  sourced organica and tasty cocktails.

The University City District's main goal is to take everything Center City does and make a bastardized version of it. While this leaves a sour taste in our mouths, one can't forget that the area is full of excellent restaurants, bars, food carts, and theatres. Oh, and frat parties: Lite beer in the house!

🔒 Shopping

- **American Apparel** • 3661 Walnut St
  215-222-2091
  Get the "crazy waif in a leotard-thong" look.
- **Avril 50** • 3406 Sansom St
  215-222-6108
  Pre-Internet spot for all your international newspaper needs.
- **Eastern Mountain Sports** • 3401 Chestnut St
  215-302-0030
  Decent selection of camping gear, wait for the sales.

- **Insomnia Cookies** • 3417 Spruce St
  877-632-6654
  Delivers cookies until 3 am. We're not kidding
- **Philadelphia Runner** • 3621 Walnut St
  215-662-5100
  Everything you need to try and make running actually enjoyable.
- **Trophy Bikes** • 712 N 2nd St
  215 222 2020
  Best place in town for a folding bike.
- **Urban Outfitters** • 110 S 36th St
  215-387-6990
  Meeting ground of hipsters and UPenn students.
- **Wawa Food Market** • 3604 Chestnut St
  215-222-6422
  A godsend for 3 am munchies.

Map 15 · **Strawberry Mansion**

Map 15

This gritty North Philly nabe hugs less-frequented portions of Fairmount Park from East Park Reservoir to spooky Mount Vernon Cemetery. Cecil B. Moore Avenue—named for the famed Philadelphia Civil Rights activist—serves as main artery on the south. Save for a few exceptions, dining is limited to take out and casual fare.

O Landmarks

• **The Thinker** •
N 22nd St & Benjamin Franklin Pkwy
215-568-6020
We know, we know. A cliché. But it's still cool.

Nightlife

• **The Bishop's Collar** • 2349 Fairmount Ave
215-765-1616
Neighborhood fave. Come for the beer. Stay for the beer.
• **St. Stephen's Green** • 1701 Green St
215-769-5000
A great addition to the 'hood.

Restaurants

• **The Bishop's Collar** • 2349 Fairmount Ave
215-765-1616 • $$
Sandwiches and good barfood highlight this AM staple.
• **Bridgid's** • 726 N 24th St
215-232-3232 • $$
Popular neighborhood joint has good chow and great beer.
• **Fiqs** • 2501 Meredith St
215-978-8440 • $$
Mediterranean BYOB hot spot has class to spare.
• **Jack's Firehouse** • 2130 Fairmount Ave
215-232-9000 • $$
Former fire station still brings the BBQ heat.
• **London Grill** • 2301 Fairmount Ave
215-978-4545 • $$$
Weirdly enough, expect Asian, Latin, AND Mediterranean chow.
• **Rembrandt's** • 741 N 23rd St
215-763-2228 • $$
Perhaps the best plate of calamari in the city.

Map 16 • Brewerytown

Map 16

Named for the large number of breweries that once populated the area, the people in this neighborhood range from cold-cash professionals to college students to families trying to make ends meet. Its proximity to both I-76 and the infamous loop down Kelly Drive makes it hugely desirable for just about everyone—but be warned that when real-estate marketers refer to part of it as "up-and-coming," a lot of the area hasn't quite, er, come "up" yet.

O Landmarks

- **Ann Newman Giant Wooden Slide** •
  W Oxford St & N 33rd St
  Smith Playground's single greatest attraction.
- **Art Museum Steps** •
  N 22nd St & Benjamin Franklin Pkwy
  Recreate Rocky's infamous romp like all the other jackasses.
- **Kelly Natatorium** • Waterworks Dr
  The Waterworks' now defunct swimming pool and aquarium.
- **Lloyd Hall** • 1 Boathouse Row
  215-685-3936
  Scullers and skaters share the space.
- **Philadelphia Museum of Art** •
  2600 Benjamin Franklin Pkwy
  215-763-8100
  Sorry, Rocky: it's much more interesting on the inside.

Nightlife

- **North Star Bar** • 2639 Poplar St
  215-787-0488
  Cool live music most nights, damn fine drinks every night.

Restaurants

- **Butter's Soul Food** • 2821 W Girard Ave
  215-235-4724 • $
  Take-out soul food—fried chicken, ribs, greens, etc.
- **Era** • 2743 Poplar St
  215-769-7008 • $$
  Cheap Ethiopian food & drinks.
- **Trio** • 2624 Brown St
  215-232-8746 • $$$
  Thai BYOB.

Map 17

Lots of families, students, and young couples are here, living in sin and duplexes. The area is close to both Fairmount Avenue and 676, which makes it convenient to many places (except public transit). On the positive side, **Eastern State Penitentiary** is one of the best attractions in Philly and has a rocking Halloween haunted house.

O Landmarks

- **Barnes Foundation** •
  2025 Benjamin Franklin Pkwy
  215-278-7000
  The collection's controversial move to the city is to your benefit. Go!
- **Eastern State Penitentiary** •
  2027 Fairmount Ave
  215-236-3300
  Take a tour, buy a t-shirt. Get the daylights scared out of you.
- **Rodin Museum** •
  2151 Benjamin Franklin Pkwy
  215-568-6026
  More than just the Thinker.

Coffee

- **Mugshots** • 2100 Fairmount Ave
  267-514-7145
  Coffee with a view of Eastern State Pen.

Farmers Markets

- **Fairmount Farmers' Market** •
  22nd St & Fairmount Ave
  Thursdays, 3 pm-7 pm, in season.

Nightlife

- **Urban Saloon** • 2120 Fairmount Ave
  215-232-5359
  Pretty sharp place to watch the Phillies.

Restaurants

- **Angelino's** • 849 N 25th St
  215-787-9945 • $
  It"s pizza! Nothing that wild about it.
- **The Belgian Café** • 2047 Green St
  215-235-3500 • $$$
  New addition to the Monk's family.
- **BlueCat** • 1921 Fairmount Ave
  267-519-2911 • $$
  Latin may be dead, but the food ain't.
- **Dominics Fish Market** •
  2842 Cecil B. Moore Ave
  215-232-7120 • $
  All the fresh seafood you might expect—only cheaper.
- **Little Pete's** • 2401 Pennsylvania Ave
  215-232-5001 • $
  A greasy spoon with no apologies.
- **Pizzeria Vetri** • 1939 Callowhill St
  215-600-2629 • $$
  Marc Vetri, is there anything you can't do?
- **Rose Tattoo Café** • 1847 Callowhill St
  215-569-8939 • $$$
  Like being on the set of a Tennessee Williams opus.
- **Rybread** • 2319 Fairmount Ave
  215-769-0603 • $$
  Killer sandwiches and a nice outdoor patio.
- **Sabrina's Cafe** • 1804 Callowhill St
  215-636-9061 • $$$
  New location. Same great food and long wait.
- **Umai Umai** • 533 N 22nd St
  215-988-0707 • $$$
  Sushi with BYO Sake.
- **Yuri Deli** • 1618 N 29th St
  215-763-7395 • $
  Small spot filled with bunly goodness.

Shopping

- **Beehive** • 1719 Fairmount Ave
  215-235-4483
  Sweet little hair salon.
- **JK Market** • 2001 Green St
  215-236-2788
  Nice little corner store.
- **Philly Flavors** • 2004 Fairmount Ave
  215-232-7748
  Small means huge.
- **Wawa Food Market** • 2040 Hamilton St
  215-988-0648
  A godsend for 3 am munchies.

Map 18 · **Spring Garden / Francisville**

Map 18

By day this area is dominated by students of all kinds, but it gets pretty quiet after dark. Housing is still affordable, excluding the loft/studio condo spaces that dot the landscape. It's less friendly at night thanks to the abandoned Reading railroad tracks, so put away the map, yeah?

○ Landmarks

- **Divine Lorraine Hotel** • 699 N Broad St
  Onetime divine guesthouse, ravaged by time.
- **Metropolitan Opera House** •
  N Broad St & Fairmount Ave
  Former opera house used in fine *12 Monkeys* film.

Nightlife

- **The Institute** • 549 N 12th St
  267-318-7772
  Their catchphrase? "Beer is fun." We agree.
- **Prohibition Taproom** • 501 N 13th St
  215-238-1818
  Often changing beer list, plus early and late happy hours.
- **The Trestle Inn** • 339 N 11th St
  267-239-0290
  Grime and go-go girls. Awesome.
- **Union Transfer** • 1026 Spring Garden St
  215-232-2100
  The Electric Factory's classier cousin.

Restaurants

- **Alla Spina** • 1410 Mt Vernon St
  215-600-0017 • $$$
  Italian gastropub.
- **Bufad** • 1240 Spring Garden St
  215-238-9311 • $$
  Amazing wood fired pizza.
- **Café Lift** • 428 N 13th St
  215-922-3031 • $$
  Potentially too hip and delish for the past-prime yuppies who tend to always be there.
- **City View Pizza** • 1547 Spring Garden St
  215-564-1910 • $
  Standard-issue pizza joint, big with CCP students.
- **Jose's Tacos** • 469 N 10th St
  215-765-2369 • $
  Ignore the gourmet Mexican explosion: Jose's has the goods.
- **Osteria** • 640 N Broad St
  215-763-0920 • $$
  More tasty (and a little cheaper) Italian grub by Mr Vetri.
- **Route 6** • 600 N Broad
  215-391-4600 • $$$
  Stephen Starr's seafood shanty.
- **Sazon** • 941 Spring Garden St
  215-763-2500 • $$
  Venezuelan for the show-off man-on-a-budget.
- **Wazobia** • 616 N 11th St
  215-769-3800 • $
  Authentic Nigerian cuisine.
- **West Tavern** • 1440 Callowhill St
  215-563-6134 • $
  Old-man joint that reeks of smoke, grease, and greatness.

Shopping

- **The Diving Bell Scuba Shop** • 681 N Broad St
  215-763-6868
  Just don't watch *Open Water* first.

Map 19 · **Northern Liberties**

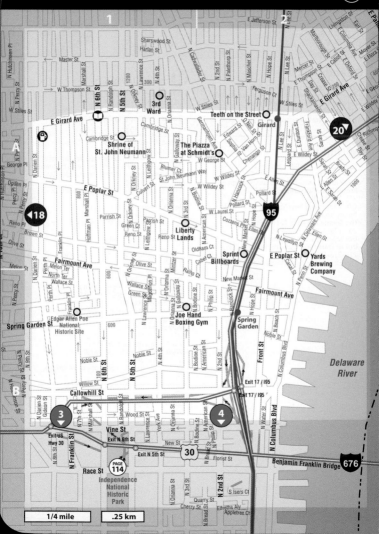

Map 19

Northern Liberties might be getting too hip for its own good—and it doesn't help when people call it "NoLibs." The post-hip yuppie types are moving in and rents are going up up up. Don't let that scare you, though—it's still a great 'hood.

O Landmarks

- **3rd Ward** • 1227 N 4th St
  267-608-1016
  Another Brooklyn import: co-working space and classes.
- **Edgar Allen Poe National Historic Site** •
  532 N 7th St
  215-597-8780
  Is it creepy to think he penned "The Black Cat" when you see the real chimney in his real basement? Yes it is.
- **Joe Hand Boxing Gym** •
  543–547 N 3rd St
  215-271-4263
  Kids train beside future Golden Glove/Olympic champs.
- **Liberty Lands** • N 3rd St & Poplar St
  Recently reclaimed from junkies and winos.
- **The Piazza at Schmidt's** •
  Germantown Ave & N 2nd St
  Shops, restaurants, and a giant TV: oh my!
- **Shrine of St. John Neumann** • 1019 N 5th St
  215-627-3080
  Shrine of canonized Philly Bishop. Yes, that's him right there in the altar.
- **Sprint Billboards** • Poplar St & N Hancock St
  Can't miss 'em along I-95.
- **Teeth on the Street** •
  W Girard Ave & N Hope St
  Teeth. On the street. With a rubber glove.
- **Yards Brewing Company** •
  901 N Delaware Ave
  215-634-2600
  Free weekend tours and a tasting room?
  Sign us up!

Coffee

- **Higher Grounds** • 631 N 3rd St
  215-922-3745
  A coffee shop with a punny name? No way!
- **One Shot Cafe** • 217 W George St
  215-627-1620
  A rare NoLibs coffee joint that doesn't wreak of hipster.
- **One Shot Coffee** • 1040 N 2nd St
  215-627-1620
  Little spot on Liberties Walk.
- **The Random Tea Room and Curiosity Shop** • 713 N 4th St
  267-639-2442
  For those who love the leaf more than the bean.

Nightlife

- **The 700** • 700 N 2nd St
  215-413-3181
  Crowded, smoky lower bar; extremely crowded, smoky dance floor upstairs.
- **The Abbaye** • 637 N 3rd St
  215-627-6711
  Belgian bistro uses good beer liberally throughout menu.
- **Bar Ferdinand** • 1030 N 2nd St
  215-923-1313
  Delicious libations that will make you forget you're in Philly.
- **The Barbary** • 951 Frankford Ave
  215-634-7400
  Hipster dance parties, plus occasional all-ages shows.
- **Barcade** • 1114 Frankford Ave
  215-634-4400
  Exactly what it sounds like, but somehow cooler.
- **Bottle Bar East** • 1308 Frankford Ave
  267-909-8867
  Bottles and cans, just clap your hands.
- **Club Ozz** • 1155 N Front St
  215-203-7201
  Stripping under the El for the utterly wasted.
- **Electric Factory** • 421 N 7th St
  215-627-1332
  Large venue for bigger rock shows: stick to the balcony.
- **Finnigan's Wake** • 537 N 3rd St
  215-574-9317
  Slam a Miller Lite while listening to a cover band jam Puddle of Mudd tunes.
- **The Fire** • 412 W Girard Ave
  267-671-9298
  Good rock shows, minimal amounts of hipsters.
- **Johnny Brenda's** • 1201 Frankford Ave
  215-739-9684
  Fishtown hipster hang.
- **Liberties** • 705 N 2nd St
  215-238-0660
  Food plus beer equals foooodbeeeer.
- **The M-Room** • 15 W Girard Ave
  215-739-5577
  Puppet Karaoke. Need we say more.

- **McFadden's** • 461 N 3rd St
  215-928-0630
  Great spot to drink shooters with 21-year olds.
- **North 3rd** • 801 N 3rd St
  215-413-3666
  A blood-orange margarita, under the right
  circumstances, can be life-altering.
- **North Bowl** • 909 N 2nd St
  215-238-2695
  Swankiest bowling ever. All ages until 9 pm.
- **Ortlieb's** • 847 N 3rd St
  267-324-3348
  Old school venue has smokey drinks and
  smokier jazz.
- **Saint Lazarus** • 102 W Girard Ave
  267-978-4510
  Relaxed, atmospheric vibe with music-drink
  focus.
- **Silk City Diner** • 435 Spring Garden St
  215-592-8838
  Energetic crowd.
- **Standard Tap** • 901 N 2nd St
  215-238-0630
  The legend grows about this trend-setting
  No-Libs marvel.

Restaurants

- **The Abbaye** • 637 N 3rd St
  215-627-6711 • $$
  Belgian bistro uses good beer liberally
  throughout menu.
- **Bar Ferdinand** • 1030 N 2nd St
  215-923-1313 • $$
  Yummy tapas brunches and dinners. Ole!
- **Bubba's Texas BBQ** • 19 W Girard Ave
  267-324-3530 • $$
  Bangin' brisket.
- **Cafe Estelle** • 444 N 4th St
  215-925-5080 • $$
  Worth getting up for brunch and homemade
  pastries.
- **Circles** • 812 N 2nd St
  267-687-1309 • $$
  Don't knock the cheesesteak eggrolls til you
  try 'em.
- **Darling's Diner** • 1033 N 2nd St
  267-239-5775 • $
  Famous cheesecake at a mediocre, neo-retro
  diner.

- **East Girard Gastropub** • 200 E Girard Ave
  267-761-9343 • $$
  Oyster special in Fishtown? Sounds about
  right.
- **El Camino Real** • 1040 N 2nd St
  215-925-1110 • $$
  Three words: Fried pickle chips.
- **The Foodery** • 837 N 2nd St
  215-238-6077 • $
  Sandwiches and legendary make-your-own
  six pack.
- **Green Eggs Cafe** • 719 N 2nd St
  215-922-3447 • $$
  Light and sweet, it's time to eat.
- **Hikari** • 1040 N American St
  215-923-2654 • $$$
  Good sushi. BYO sake.
- **Honey's Sit 'n Eat** • 800 N 4th St
  215-925-1150 • $
  The wait for brunch just goes on and on.
- **Il Cantuccio** • 701 N 3rd St
  215-627-6573 • $$
  Small, trend-setting trattoria, simple but
  effective.
- **Johnny Brenda's** • 1201 Frankford Ave
  215-739-9684 • $
  Hipster hang has the best food in Fishtown!
- **Las Cazuelas** • 426 W Girard Ave
  215-351-9144 • $$
  Mexican seafood that will knock your
  calcetines off.
- **Liberties** • 705 N 2nd St
  215-238-0660 • $$$
  Food plus beer equals foooodbeeeer.
- **Modo Mio** • 161 W Girard Ave
  215-203-8707 • $$$
  Pros: delicious. Cons: full of themselves, not of
  large portions.
- **North 3rd** • 801 N 3rd St
  215-413-3666 • $$
  Yummy chalkboard specials abound in this
  busy bar/bistro.
- **One Shot Cafe** • 217 W George St
  215-627-1620 • $$
  Bitchin' breakfasts.
- **Paesano's** • 152 W Girard Ave
  267-866-9566 • $
  Dense meat or vegetable-filled sandwiches.
- **Pizzeria Beddia** • 115 E Girard Ave
  $$
  Delicious, simple whole pies.

Northern Liberties

Map 19

Give New Jersey Delaware Avenue—when it comes to beer, we'll take Northern Liberties. The **Standard Tap** is still the OG for local beer on, well, tap. Visit **Yards Brewing Company** because the beer is worth it. Elsewhere, **Bar Ferdinand** is a great date-night spot and venerable **Silk City** never disappoints.

- **Popolino** • 501 Fairmount
  215-928-0106 • $$$
  Roman style trattoria. Amazeballs.
- **Pura Vida** • 527 Fairmount Ave
  215-922-6433 • $
  Guatemalan, cheap, and so good.
- **PYT** • 1050 N Hancock St
  215-964-9009 • $$
  Burgers and boozy milkshakes from the Paperstreet guy.
- **Radicchio** • 402 Wood St
  215-627-6850 • $$
  Old City's version of a simple little BYOB with updated Italian cuisine.
- **Rustica** • 903 N 2nd St
  215-627-1393 • $
  Gianfranco's No-Libs extension: good and salty.
- **Soy Café** • 630 N 2nd St
  215-922-1003 • $
  Homemade fake cheese will make you scream, "I-can't-believe-it's-VEGAN!"
- **Standard Tap** • 901 N 2nd St
  215-238-0630 • $$$
  Flagship joint with sumptuous dinners and brunches.
- **Taco Riendo Restaurant** • 1301 N 5th St
  215-235-2294 • $
  Solid, no frills Mexican. Try the horchata!
- **Tiffin** • 710 W Girard Ave
  215-922-1297 • $$
  Indian delivery.

🛍 Shopping

- **Art Star** • 623 N 2nd St
  215-238-1557
  Gallery and crafty boutique. Get your handmade here.
- **Borderline Records & Tapes** •
  525 W Girard Ave
  From one man's private collection, yours for a song.
- **Brown Betty Dessert Boutique** •
  722 N 2nd St
  215-629-0999
  Desserts aren't just baked; they're nurtured.

- **City Planter** • 814 N 4th St
  215-627-6169
  Garden pots (planters), but no plants. But what a collection it is!
- **Creep Records** • 1050 N Hancock St
  267-239-2037
  Headshop-record store hybrid with occasional live music.
- **Delicious Boutique & Corseterie** •
  212 E Girard Ave
  215-413-0375
  Because it's always time for a $500 corset.
- **Euphoria** • 1001 N 2nd St
  215-238-9209
  Smoothies.
- **The Foodery** • 837 N 2nd St
  215-238-6077
  Mix and match your brewskis.
- **Jerusalem** • 115 W Girard Ave
  215-634-1991
  Middle Eastern culinary delights.
- **Northern Liberties Mailbox Store** •
  630 N 3rd St
  215-627-6215
  Cute mail supplies and all sorts of shipping.
- **Otolith** • 2133 Huntingdon St
  215-426-4266
  Great shop. Save the fish by eating them.
- **Palm Tree Market** • 717 N 2nd St
  215-925-4707
  Upscale corner store for when you're out of fresh mozzarella.
- **The Random Tea Room and Curiosity Shop** • 713 N 4th St
  267-639-2442
  Delicious wifi and tea.
- **Spring Garden Market** •
  400 Spring Garden St
  215-928-1288
  New market with fruits, fish and all things fresh.
- **Trax Foods** • 1204 N Front St
  215-423-5801
  Deli and small grocery in area that needed it.
- **Very Bad Horse** • 1050 N Hancock St
  267-455-0449
  Where Steven Tyler would shop if he were 22 and cool.

Map 20 · **Fishtown / Port Richmond**

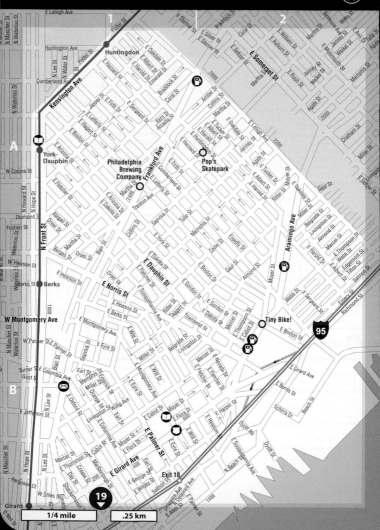

A longtime working-class, European immigrant area, Fishtown and Port Richmond are brimming with neighborhood bars and pride. This area has recently received a shot in the arm from downtown refugees seeking affordable first buys. Even though housing prices are shooting up in response, it remains a relatively affordable area.

○ Landmarks

- **Philadelphia Brewing Company** •
  2440 Frankford Ave
  215-427-2739
  Building dates back to the Weisbrod & Hess
  Oriental Brewing Company in 1885.
- **Pop's Skatepark** • Trenton Ave & E Hazzard St
  Abandoned playground transformed to
  neighborhood skate park.
- **Tiny Bike!** • E York St & Aramingo Ave
  Notice! Regular-sized boy rides unnaturally
  tiny bike. Ooh and ahh at will.

💻 Coffee

- **Coffee House Too** • 2514 E York St
  267-324-5888
  Featuring Dallis Brothers Coffee.
- **Leotah's Place** • 2033 E York St
  267-519-9031
  Community-minded fairtradeorganic coffee
  house.
- **Lola Bean** • 1325 Frankford Ave
  215-634-5652
  Happy hipsters lovin' their joe.
- **Milkcrate Cafe** • 400 E Girard Ave
  267-909-8348
  Caffeine and vinyl.
- **Reanimator Coffee** •
  1523 E Susquehanna Ave
  215-425-5805
  Perfection in mug form.
- **Rocket Cat Cafe** • 2001 Frankford Ave
  215-739-4526
  Fishtown hipster hangout.
- **Steap and Grind** • 1619 Frankford Ave
  267-858-4427
  Leaves or beans, you can't lose.

☕ Farmers Markets

- **Greensgrow Farmstand** •
  2501 E Cumberland St
  215-380-4355
  Fresh goods from the urban farm.

🍸 Nightlife

- **Atlantis, The Lost Bar** • 2442 Frankford Ave
  215-739-4929
  Perfect neighborhood pub.
- **Cedar Point Bar & Kitchen** • 2370 E Norris St
  215-423-5400
  Southern fried beer bar.
- **El Bar** • 1356 N Front St
  215-634-6430
  Under-the-elevated-train-type bar. Shake,
  rattle and drink.
- **Fette Sau** • 1208 Frankford Ave
  215-391-4000
  Meat, beer, and whiskey. Philly is the new
  Brooklyn.
- **Fishtown Tavern** • 1301 Frankford Ave
  215-687-8406
  It's dark and red and awesome inside.
- **Frankford Hall** • 1210 Frankford Ave
  215-634-3338
  Massive German beer garden surprisingly
  low on brahs.
- **Green Rock Tavern** • 2546 E Lehigh Ave
  215-203-0840
  Cans, PBC, and more pierogies than you can
  shake a stick at.
- **Interstate Drafthouse** • 1235 E Palmer St
  267-455-0045
  Hidden gem for the beer snob.
- **Kraftwork** • 541 E Girard Ave
  215-739-1700
  Hipsters and beer snobs living in harmony.
  Now that's brotherly love.
- **Kung Fu Necktie** • 1248 N Front St
  215-291-4919
  A dive with a candelabra.
- **Les & Doreen's Happy Tap** •
  1301 E Susquehanna Ave
  215-634-1123
  Maybe someday the hip kids will like it here.
  The karaoke night'll likely get 'em.
- **Lloyd Whiskey Bar** • 529 E Girard Ave
  215-425-4600
  Somehow underrated whiskey bar.
- **Loco Pez** • 2401 E Norris St
  267-886-8061
  Sipo tequila y cerveza.

Map 20

Fishtown / Port Richmond

- **Memphis Taproom** • 2331 E Cumberland St
  215-425-4460
  Affordable amazing beers? I can get behind that.
- **Murph's Bar** • 202 E Girard Ave
  215-425-1847
  Comfortable place to be? The jury is still out.
- **Yards Brewing Company** •
  901 N Delaware Ave
  215-634-2600
  Philly's best home brew.

🍴 Restaurants

- **Best Deli II** • 2616 E Lehigh Ave
  215-291-9310 • $
  Fine, but perhaps a bit of an inflated self-image.
- **Cedar Point Bar & Kitchen** • 2370 E Norris St
  215-423-5400 • $$
  Southern fried beer bar.
- **Ekta** • 250 E Girard Ave
  215-426-2277 • $
  Hot, tiny, well-priced Indian/Pakistani.
- **Fette Sau** • 1208 Frankford Ave
  215-391-4888 • $$
  Meat, beer, and whiskey. Philly is the new Brooklyn.
- **Ida Mae's Bruncherie** • 2302 E Norris St
  215-426-4209 • $
  Traditional Irish breakfast or tofu scramble. You decide.
- **Jovan's Place** • 2327 E York St
  215-634-3330 • $$
  Portions fit for a Hapsburg.

- **Les & Doreen's Happy Tap** •
  1301 E Susquehanna Ave
  215-634-1123 • $
  Two fryers, a cash register, and a lady.
- **Loco Pez** • 2401 E Norris St
  267-886-8061 • $$
  Popular (read: crowded) Mexicalian.
- **Mugshots Diner** • 2424 E York St
  215-426-2424 • $$
  Only if Applebee's is closed.
- **The Pickled Heron** • 2218 Frankford Ave
  215-634-5666 • $$$
  French. No actual pickles or herons, though.
- **Pizza Brain** • 2313 Frankford Ave
  215-291-2965 • $$
  Enjoy artisan pies in the world's first pizza museum.
- **Sketch** • 413 E Girard Ave
  215-634-3466 • $$
  Very tasty, if you leave the hype at home.
- **Soup Kitchen Cafe** • 2146 E Susquehanna Ave
  215-427-1680 • $$
  Damn fine soups 'n sammies.
- **Steak 'N Shake** • 2573 Frankford Ave
  877-938-9033 • $
  A bovine feast.
- **Stock's Bakery** • 2614 E Lehigh Ave
  215-634-7344 • $
  Stock up on all your baked goods needs. Forgive us.
- **Sulimay's Restaurant** • 632 E Girard Ave
  215-423-1773 • $
  High-class eggs and wondrous pancakes.
- **Tacconelli's Pizza** • 2604 E Somerset St
  215-425-4983 • $
  So good you need to call ahead to reserve your dough. No joke.

Ida Mae's is a must for any self-respecting pancake lover. Tacconelli's serves up perfect pizza. Memphis Taproom has an incredible list of brews (and vegan eats). Green Rock works well as your local but keep Frankford Hall in your back pocket for destination beer. Caffeine up at Rocket Cat, Reanimator or Milkcrate.

🔒 Shopping

- **Bicycle Stable** • 1420 Frankford Ave
  215-634-0633
  For your wheels!
- **Circle Thrift** • 2233 Frankford Ave
  215-423-1222
  Thrift store with weird church space upstairs.
- **DiPinto** • 407 E Girard Ave
  215-427-7805
  Guitars for real
- **Dollar Plus Party Fair** • 2415 E Lehigh Ave
  215-634-2760
  Screw Dollar Tree.
- **Jay's Pedal Power** • 512 E Girard Ave
  215-425-5111
  Strange bikes and regular bikes from a well-established shop.
- **Little Baby's Ice Cream** • 2311 Frankford Ave
  267-687-8567
  Unusual and delicious scoops (tucked inside Pizza Brain).

- **Little Shop of Treasures** • 419 E Girard Ave
  267-446-5574
  Hooray for junk shops.
- **Milkcrate Cafe** • 400 E Girard Ave
  267-909-8348
  Caffeine and vinyl.
- **Philadelphia Record Exchange** •
  1524 Frankford Ave
  215-925-7892
  Excellent jazz and rock stuff, plus tons of vinyl.
- **Scoops** • 812 E Thompson St
  215-634-7629
  Ice cream window with the works; namely,
  pizza nuggets and happy patrons.
- **Stock's Bakery** • 2614 E Lehigh Ave
  215-634-7344
  Port Richmond's pride rocks the best
  poundcake around.
- **Whipped Bakeshop** • 636 Belgrade St
  215-598-5449
  Cupcakes 'n cakecups. Say whaaa?

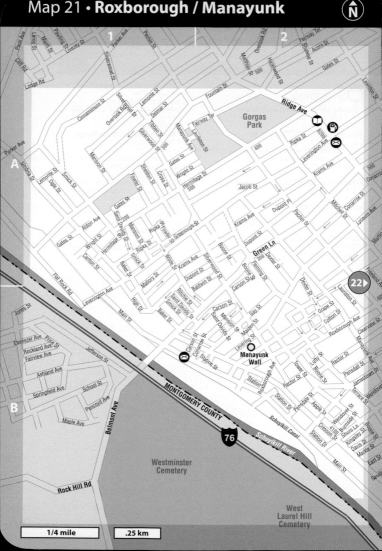

Map 21 · **Roxborough / Manayunk**

Map 21

Referred to mostly—particularly by landlords—as just "Manayunk," this area is synonymous with Main Street—where young, post-collegiate pals and gals can be seen biking down the Tow Path, boozing in the evening hours, and spicing up their prep with a splotch of chintz. The nation's largest agricultural high school—W.B. Saul—is nearby on Henry Avenue.

○ Landmarks

- **Manayunk Wall** • Levering St & Main St
  Philadelphia International Championship
  bicycle races race here. How 'bout that.

Coffee

- **Crossroads Coffee House** • 6156 Ridge Ave
  215-487-1923
  Featuring beans from Counter Culture Coffee
  Roasters.

Farmers Markets

- **Gorgas Park Farmers' Market** •
  Ridge Ave & Acorn St
  Fridays, 2 pm-6 pm, Jun-Oct.
- **Pretzel Park** • 4300 Silverwood St
  267-237-1489
  Saturdays, 10 am-2 pm, in season.

Nightlife

- **The Bayou Bar and Grill** • 4245 Main St
  215-482-2560
  All you can eat crab nights and frat party feel.
- **Bourbon Blue** • 2 Rector St
  215-508-3360
  An upscale rock n' roll joint in the mighty
  'Yunk.
- **Castle Roxx** • 105 Shurs Ln
  267 566 5459
  Relaxed out-of-the-way joint.
- **Flat Rock Saloon** • 4301 Main St
  215-483-3722
  One of the biggest Belgian beer selections in
  all of Philly.
- **Kildare's** • 4417 Main St
  215-482-7242
  The new hot spot in the 'Yunk.
  Recommended: the Dirty Hoe.
- **Manayunk Brewery & Restaurant** •
  4120 Main St
  215-482-8220
  A multitude of home-brews highlights this
  popular hangout.

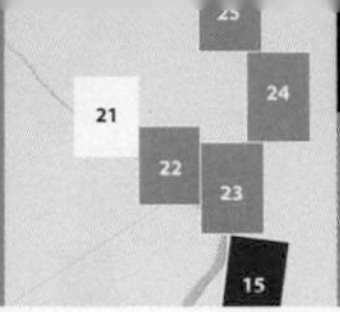

Map 21

Roxborough / Manayunk

🍴 Restaurants

- **Adobe Cafe** • 4550 Mitchell St
  215-483-3947 • $$
  Southwestern-style steakhouse offers seitan options.
- **Chabaa Thai Bistro** • 4371 Main St
  215-483-1979 • $$
  Pad thai to tha max.
- **The Couch Tomato Café** • 102 Rector St
  215-483-2233 • $
  Worth a slice if you're in the neighborhood.
- **Il Tartufo** • 4341 Main St
  215-482-1999 • $$
  Get some mozzarella, baby.
- **Jake's and Cooper's Wine Bar** • 4365 Main St
  215-483-0444 • $$$$
  Pricey Manayunk flagship that got the ball rolling.

- **Kildare's** • 4417 Main St
  215-482-7242 • $$$
  Fine Irish Food. Recommend the Boxys.
- **Le Bus** • 4266 Main St
  215-487-2663 • $
  Continental style with top-shelf baguettes.
- **Manayunk Brewery & Restaurant** •
  4120 Main St
  215-482-8220 • $$
  Lots of outdoor space and solid sushi.
- **Marchiano's Bakery** • 4653 Umbria St
  215-483-8585 • $
  Do you really know life until you know cheesesteak bread?
- **Taqueria Feliz** • 4410 Main St
  267-331-5874 • $$
  High end Mexican in a casual setting.
- **Zesty's** • 4382 Main St
  215-438-6226 • $$
  Nice Greek spot.

Roxborough / Manayunk

You'll either love everything or detest most of it. But either way, for the love of burritos, please visit **Adobe**, one of the city's best Mexican spots. Not into Mexican? Join the post-frat party downtown, or visit the array of toned-down furniture stores and maternity shops, which give big clues to who really lives here—nesting grown ups.

🛍 Shopping

- **Main Street Music** • 4444 Main St
  215-487-7732
  Indy music store.
- **Meadowsweet Mercantile** • 4390 Main St
  215-756-4802
  Awesome handmade furniture from
  reclaimed materials.

- **Pompanoosuc Mills** • 4120 Main St
  215-508-3263
  Great high-end furniture.
- **Vamp Boutique** • 4231 Main St
  215-487-2340
  Boutique fashion for ladies that you can
  actually afford.
- **Worn Yesterday** • 4235 Main St
  215-482-3316
  Your youngsters will be natty with the help of
  this Manayunk staple.

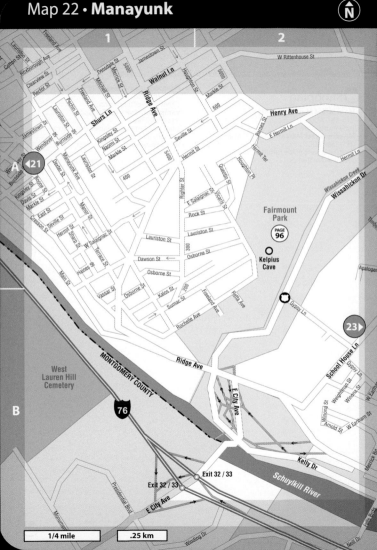

Map 22 · **Manayunk**

N

1 2

W Rittenhouse St

Cotton St

Freeland Ave

Roxborough Ave

Clearview St

Rector St

Jamestown Ave

Parnside Ave

Merrick St

Michael St

Jamestown St

Walnut Ln

Houghton St

Markle St

5600

5500

Henry Ave

Barnes St

E Hermit Ln

Hermit Ter

Freeland Ave

Pechin St

Shurs Ln

Kingsley St

Ridge Ave

Seville St

Hermit St

Hermit Ln

Wendover St

Burnside St

Naomi St

Markle St

5400

Hermit St

Quentin St

Houghton Pl

Hermit Ln

A 421

Jamestown St

Baker St

Boone St

Manayunk Ave

Lauriston St

Minor St

400

Righter St

E Salaignac St

Vicars St

Wissahickon Creek

Wissahickon Dr

Kingsley St

Davis St

Markle St

Seville St

East St

Crasson St

Hermit St

W Salaignac St

W Terrace St

Haines St

Rock St

Fairmount
Park

PAGE
96

Apaloger

Dexter St

Lauriston St

Lauriston St

300

Kelpius
Cave

Main St

Vassar St

Dawson St

Osborne St

Osborne St

Osborne St

Kalos St

200

Sumac St

Freeland Ave

Pella Ave

Gypsy Ln

23▶

Rochelle Ave

Ridge Ave

School House Ln

Gypsy Ln

West
Lauren Hill
Cemetery

MONTGOMERY COUNTY

E City Ave

Weightman St

Winona St

Winona St

W Earlham St

B

76

Winona St

Arnold St

W Earlham St

Kelly Dr

Timber

Merrick Rd

Neill Dr

Presidential Blvd

Exit 32 / 33

Exit 32 / 33

E City Ave

Schuylkill River

Winding Dr

Monum

1/4 mile

.25 km

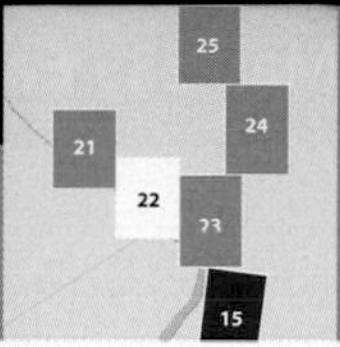

Map 22

An ever-popular area to live for its simultaneous access to downtown and to nature, it seems every third person here is wearing spandex and is on their way to the Wissahickon Trail. More residential than upper Main Street, there's more room to breathe and less rent to pay.

O Landmarks

• **Kelpius Cave** • Sumac St & Wissahickon Park
Historic monk retreat now used for secret bong shelter.

Nightlife

• **Dawson Street Pub** • 100 Dawson St
215-482-5677
A small escape from the normal Manayunk crowd.

Restaurants

• **Han Dynasty** • 4356 Main St
215-508-2066 • $$
Very spicy, very good.

Map 23 · **East Falls**

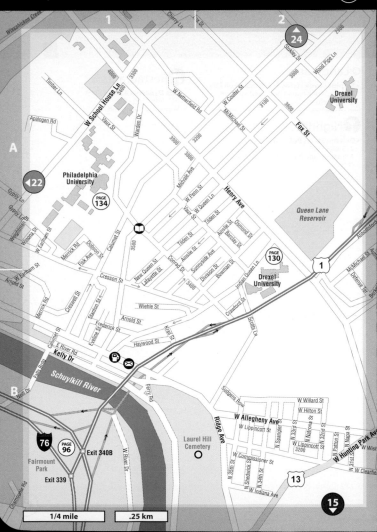

Map 23

Convenient to Center City while preserving a country feeling, East Falls has been home to many famous Philadelphians. Grace Kelly lived here before that whole princess gig came up, for one. A short drive away from the main goings-on, the perks are proximity to River Drive for a run and owning your own delightful, ivy-covered chunk of yesteryear.

O Landmarks

- **Laurel Hill Cemetery** • 3822 Ridge Ave
  215-228-8200
  Ancient, Victorian-style, and oddly beautiful.

Farmers Markets

- **East Falls Farmers' Market** •
  Ridge Ave & Kelly Dr
  Saturdays, 10 am–2 pm, in season.

Restaurants

- **Falls Taproom** • 3749 Midvale Ave
  215-849-1222 • $$
  Plenty on draft with good food to go with it.
- **Johnny Manana's** • 4201 Ridge Ave
  215-843-0499 • $$
  Unusual Mexican, but forget that and check the tequila shelf.

Map 24 · **Germantown South**

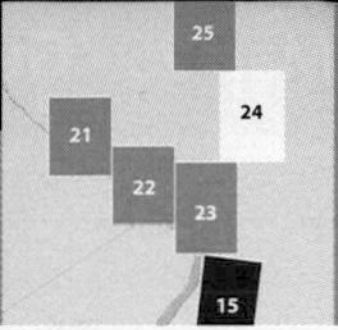

Map 24

The area was drained in the early nineties by white flight, and ever since has been regrouping into what most of us would call a block-by-block neighborhood. But what gorgeous blocks they can be—full of history (check out Rittenhouse Town), bursting greenery, and some very cool people.

O Landmarks

- **Germantown Town Hall** •
  5928 Germantown Ave
  Gorgeous Beaux Arts/Classical Revival
  building for sale for just $400,000.
- **Sun Ra Arkestra House** • 5626 Morton St
  Where the Arkestra for this jazz genius lived
  and played, Marshall Allen continues in the
  same vein.

Farmers Markets

- **Germantown Farmers' Market** •
  6026 Germantown Ave
  Fridays, 2 pm-6 pm, in season.

Restaurants

- **House of Jin** • 234 W Chelten Ave
  215-848-7700 • $$
  Fusing Chinese, Japanese, and American jazz?
  Whatever.
- **K&J Caribbean and American Diner** •
  5603 Greene St
  215-849-0242 • $
  Have some red beans with your french toast.
- **Nile Cafe** • 6008 Germantown Ave
  215-843-6453 • $$
  Southern-style vegan.

Map 25 · **Germantown North**

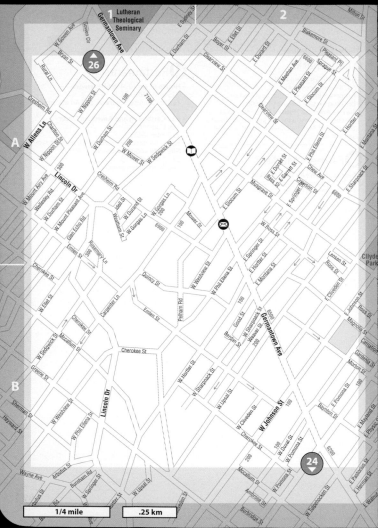

Lutheran Theological Seminary

1/4 mile

.25 km

Map 25

Tree-lined streets, ivy-covered mansions—and it's only minutes away from downtown. Progressive-minded families build roots here and enjoy the locally sourced organic options along Germantown Avenue.

☕ Coffee

- **High Point Cafe** • 7210 Cresheim Rd
215-248-1900
In Allens Lane train station.
- **High Point Cafe** • 602 Carpenter Ln
215-849-5153
A wholesome chill spot.
- **Point of Destination** • 6460 Greene St
215-849-7771
Right by the train station

🍅 Farmers Markets

- **Weaver's Way Farmers' Market** •
Greene St & Carpenter Ln
More than just fresh goods at this popular co-op.

🍴 Restaurants

- **Bacio** • 311 Mt Pleasant
215-248-2740 • $$$
Germantown date spot.
- **Earth Bread + Brewery** •
7136 Germantown Ave
215-242-6666 • $$
By "Earth Bread" they mean "Pizza."
- **Geechee Girl Cafe** • 6825 Germantown Ave
215-843-8113 • $$
Try a Southern specialty from the Low Country of South Carolina & Georgia.
- **Golden Crust Pizza** • 7155 Germantown Ave
215-248-2929 • $
Pedestrian, uninspired. Kids love it.
- **Lincoln Pizzeria** • 277 W Mt Pleasant Ave
215-248-2233 • $$
Much-loved pizza.

- **McMenamin's Tavern** •
7170 Germantown Ave
215-753-9911 • $
Mount Airy locals unite!
- **Mi Puebla Restaurant** •
7157 Germantown Ave
215-247-1779 • $$
Decent! Mexican! Food!
- **Rib Crib** • 6333 Germantown Ave
215-438-6793 • $
Meaty joint has cult following.
- **Tiffin** • 7105 Emlen St
215-242-3656 • $$
The famous Indian delivery expands to the northern regions.
- **Toto's Pizzeria** • 6555 Greene St
215-848-4550 • $$
Good time for Pizza? Have a good pizza this time.
- **Umbria** • 7131 Germantown Ave
215-242-6470 • $$
Cozy little BYOB that remains a hit with locals.

🛍 Shopping

- **Big Blue Marble Bookstore** •
551 Carpenter Ln
215-844-1870
An independent with lots of events for progressive parents and their wannabe kids.
- **Joa Mart** • 361 W Hortter St
215-438-2820
Awesome small grocery.
- **Weaver's Way Co-op** • 559 Carpenter Ln
215-843-2350
Become a member and save money on high quality food.

Map 26 • **Mt Airy**

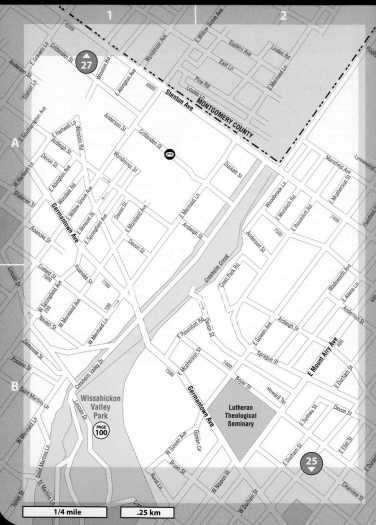

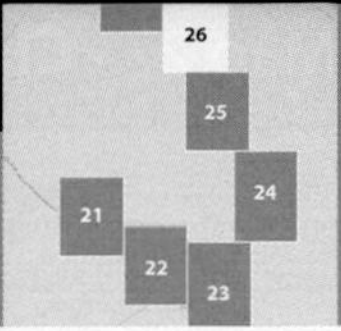

Map 26

Families and the coupled are attracted to Mt. Airy's lush greenery and choice shopping on Germantown Avenue. Not surprisingly, it's becoming more difficult to buy here, since nobody wants to sell.

Farmers Markets

• **Chestnut Hill Growers' Market** •
Germantown Ave & Winston Rd
Saturdays, 9:30 am-1:30 pm, year-round.

Restaurants

• **Bredenbeck's Bakery & Ice Cream Parlor** •
8126 Germantown Ave
215-247-7374 • $
Fight through the line to score sweet ice cream treats.
• **CinCin** • 7838 Germantown Ave
215-242-8800 • $$
Highly-rated Chinese in a largely non-Asian community.
• **Roller's at Flying Fish** •
8142 Germantown Ave
215-242-0707 • $$
Gourmet international cuisine, prepared by masters.
• **Trolley Car Diner** • 7619 Germantown Ave
215-753-1500 • $
Classic food, classic look. Ice cream served on an old trolley.

Map 27 · Chestnut Hill

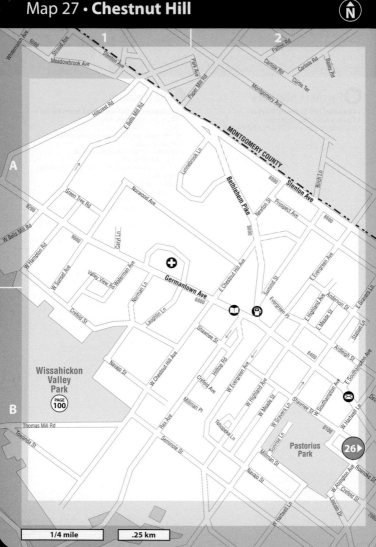

Map 27

The Hill is a cobblestone mix of New England-esque shopping (white, cute, and useless) with breaks along the way for some exceptional eats. The beautiful old houses with gardens that tumble onto the sidewalk will inspire you to get your stroll on.

Coffee

• Chestnut Hill Coffee Co. •
8620 Germantown Ave
215-242-8600
Gorgeous coffee, roasted right there.

Farmers Markets

• Chestnut Hill Farmers' Market •
8229 Germantown Ave
215 242 5905
Indoor; Thursdays & Fridays, 9 am-6 pm;
Saturdays, 8 am-5 pm.

Restaurants

• Campbell's Place • 8337 Germantown Ave
215-242-1818 • $$
Pub fare in a busy neighborhood joint.

• Chestnut Grill & Sidewalk Cafe •
8229 Germantown Ave
215-247-7570 • $$
Cajun-flavored fare with Asian accents.

• Chestnut Hill Coffee Co. •
8620 Germantown Ave
215-242-8600 •
Prim desserts match thoroughly-crafted espresso drinks.

• Heirloom • 8705 Germantown Ave
215-242-2700 • $$$$
Seasonal menus, local ingredients; BYOB.

• McNally's Tavern • 8634 Germantown Ave
215-247-9736 • $
Established in 1921 and home of the world-famous Schmitter.

• Metropolitan Bakery •
8607 Germantown Ave
215-753-9001 • $
Great breads, rolls, soups—and brownies to die for.

• Mica Restaurant • 8609 Germantown Ave
267-335-3912 • $$$$$
Multi-star seasonal tasting menus from Chip Roman.

• Osaka • 8605 Germantown Ave
215-242-5900 • $$$
Solid sushi; fun specialty rolls.

• Thai Kuu • 35 Bethlehem Pike
267-297-5715 • $$$
Above-average Thai in beautiful setting with prices to match.

Shopping

• Cake • 8501 Germantown Ave
215-247-6887
Sweets in a former greenhouse.

• The Chestnut Hill Cheese Shop •
8509 Germantown Ave
888-343-3327
Family-owned cheese bazaar.

• Hideaway Music • 8612 Germantown Ave
215-248-4434
Nice collection of high quality vinyl and posters.

• Kitchen Kapers • 8530 Germantown Ave
215-242-2866
Cove of all things culinary.

• Mango • 8622 Germantown Ave
215-248-9299
Hempy clothing, endless incense, and crafty gifts.

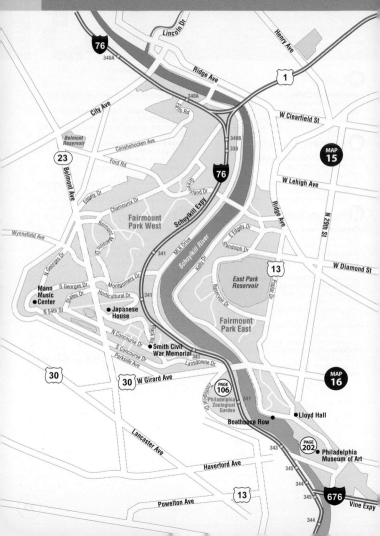

General Information

NFT Maps: 15 & 16
Address: 4231 N Concourse Dr
Philadelphia, PA 19131
Phone: 215-683-0200
Website: www.phila.gov/parksandrecreation/
Pages/default.aspx

Overview

Although all three major Philly parks (Fairmount Park, Wissahickon Valley Park, and Pennypack Creek Park) are part of the Fairmount Parks System, when we refer to "Fairmount Park" here, we mean only this particular section, not the entire sprawling Parks System. Okay? Okay.

Fairmount Park is where the sports fields are located. People usually go there to be active, whether it's playing in a softball league, jogging along Kelly Drive, or rowing on the Schuylkill. There's also a very popular free "disc golf" course near Strawberry Mansion. This park is not the place to go when you want to commune with nature, smoke an apple bong, or gulp home-stilled Kahlua. That said, the locals on the west side do throw some kickin' barbecues in summertime over at the Belmont Plateau.

Fairmount Park is also home to the Mann Center, the Philadelphia Museum of Art, the Japanese House, and the Smith Civil War Memorial (the place where the Statue of Liberty was supposed to end up).

The Drives

Kelly and MLK Drives make up what locals call "the Loop." (Until recently, MLK was known as West River Drive, and Kelly, somewhat less recently, as East River Drive. Locals sometimes go by the old names, so don't be confused by them.) The paved path that runs along these roads on the east and west banks of the Schuylkill River is 8.4 miles if you cross the river at the Falls Bridge and loop back to the beginning. The trail (happily separated from the curvy road, where idiots tend to drive way too fast) is Philly's somewhat misbegotten answer to South Beach: there are lots of expertly fit, hot-assed singles giving each other the long once-over as they pass (and sometimes barely avoiding smashing into each other) on bike, blades, or foot. On Saturdays and Sunday from April to October, most of MLK Drive is closed to cars between 8 am and 5 pm, giving walkers, cyclists, runners, skaters, and anyone else without an engine at their disposal open use of the road.

The Loop is also home to numerous runs, bike races, and regattas. If a few miles of open road are required for a race, you can bet at least some of it will occur here. It's also the host of charity walks like the annual AIDS Walk, the Walk for the Whisper (ovarian cancer), and Philadelphia Cares Day.

Boathouse Row

www.boathouserow.org

Just around the corner from the Art Museum, ten charming and colorful 19th-century Victorian structures comprise Boathouse Row, including the oldest rowing club in the country, Bachelor Barge Club, founded in 1853. It's definitely worth seeing the Row at night when the houses are lit like Whoville at Christmas. One of the best views, believe it or not, is from the Schuylkill Expressway—at least when you're stuck in traffic you'll have something nice to look at.

Lloyd Hall

1 Boathouse Row, Kelly Dr, 215-685-3936;
Hours vary by season
Open to the public, Lloyd Hall has a multi-purpose gym, lockers, and restrooms, making it a popular meeting place for those heading out on the Loop.

How to Get There—Driving

We can't tell you how to get to every spot in the park. It's over 1,000 acres with countless destinations. In general, if you want to get to the western section, take the MLK Drive. If you want to go to the eastern part, take Kelly Drive.

From I-95 to Fairmount Park East, take 676 W to the Ben Franklin Parkway exit. Make a left onto the parkway, then keep the Art Museum on your left, and you will end up on Kelly Drive. From I-95 to Fairmount Park West, do the same except once you're on the parkway, keep the Art Museum on your right (you have to go around Eakins Oval in front of the museum), and you'll end up on MLK Drive (unless you goof and end up on the Spring Garden Bridge or back on the Parkway heading towards the city).

From the west, take the Schuylkill (I-76) Eastbound For Fairmount Park East and get off at the exit for Lincoln Drive/Kelly Drive #340A. Stay in the left-hand lane to exit on Kelly Drive. For Fairmount Park West, take the Montgomery Avenue Exit #341. Go left at the bottom of the ramp, and you'll run into MLK Drive.

Parking

Parking depends entirely on where and when you visit the park. There are free parking lots scattered throughout, but on warm and sunny weekends, you'd better arrive early.

How to Get There—Mass Transit

Again, this really depends on where you want to go. Your best bet is to go to www.septa.com and click on the link for the "Plan My Trip" page. Addresses for most points in the Park can be found through the park's website.

General Information

Environmental Center Address: 8600A Verree Rd
Philadelphia, PA 19115
Environmental Center Phone: 215-685-0470
Fairmount Park System Phone: 215-683-0200

Overview

Once used as hunting and fishing grounds by the Lenni-Lenape Indians, Pennypack Creek Park was established in 1905. Today, the 1,600 acres of woodlands, meadows, wetlands, and fields still provide a great habitat for wildlife: More than two hundred species of birds and a variety of native mammals, reptiles, and amphibians call Pennypack home (including the occasional rogue alligator). Located right in the middle of Philly's Northeast section, the park runs roughly from Huntingdon Pike all the way over to I-95 N. Hiking trails and biking trails (both off-road and paved) are filled with people walking their dogs and children.

A 65-acre stretch called Pennypack on the Delaware was added to the southern end of the park in 1998. New additions include a large recreational complex with soccer and softball fields, a paved path, fishing piers, picnic venues, and extraordinary views of the Delaware River.

Pennypack Environmental Center

8600 Verree Rd, 215-685-0470;
Surrounded by a bird sanctuary, the Pennypack Environmental Center on Verree Road is a massive historical and environmental information bank. In addition to the earthy animal displays, the center also has an Early America exhibit and a new 300-gallon aquarium. The resource library is open to the general public, but materials are not available for loan. The center is open weekdays from 9 am until 4 pm, and some weekends for special events.

Fox Chase Farm

8500 Pine Rd, 215-728-7900; www.foxchasefarm.org
Fox Chase Farm on Pine Road is the only remaining working farm in Philadelphia, and it doubles as a school campus. The farm is open to the general public only for special events and festivals, including the once-a-month Saturday Morning Open House. For a complete schedule of events, check the website or visit the Pennypack Environmental Center. Activities in the past have included tours of the farm and workshops in various crafts, wood working, ice cream churning, and flower pressing. Most of the activities cost $3-$5 per person.

Friends of Pennypack Park

215-934-PARK; www.friendsofpennypackpark.org
While the budget for Pennypack Park has remained the same for the past two decades, many of the improvements to the park have been carried out by hundreds of local volunteers. The park is almost always crowded with the neighbors who have fallen in love with the park, and it's clear how much they care by the many trash cans, lack of garbage, and friendly passersby. The FOPP website has information about everything from the best place for wedding photos to why the dams have not been repaired to which musicians are playing during Pennypack Park's summer concert series.

How to Get There—Driving

The park is huge, and depending on where you want to go and what you want to see in the park, there are many entrances. From Center City Philadelphia, take I-95 N about five miles to the Bridge Street exit (Exit 27). Continue on Aramingo Avenue 0.3 miles to Harbison Avenue. Take Harbison for about two miles and turn right on East Roosevelt Avenue. Take East Roosevelt 1.7 miles to the park entrance. You can also take the Cottman and Rhawn Street exit off I-95, make a right on State Road, then a left on Rhawn Street take that for about 2 miles until the area turns green, then look for parking on side streets, or find the entrance on the left.

Parking

There is loads of free parking within the park, and on side streets around the park. Never fear because the PPA's evil clutch does not reach here, but police will ticket for normal violations.

How to Get There—Mass Transit

Many buses will take you close or into Pennypack Park, depending on which part of the park you're headed to. For the southeast side of the park, ride bus 10, 20, 14, or 77. To get to the northwest section and the Environmental Center, hop on the 67. For the northernmost tip of the park, take the 88.

By Regional Rail, take the Trenton Line and get off at Holmesburg Junction at the southern end of the park. You can also take the West Trenton Line to Bethayres and walk a few minutes south to reach the northern end.

General Information

Environmental Center Address:
　　　300 Northwestern Ave
　　　Philadelphia, PA 19118
Environmental Center Phone:
　　　215-685-9285
Websites:　www.fow.org
　　　www.phila.gov/parksandrecreation/
　　　Pages/default.aspx

Overview

While Pennypack Park is deep trails and rolling hills, Wissahickon is huge cliffs and gorges where you can actually climb and feel challenged. Part of the massive Fairmount Parks System, the Wissahickon Valley consists of 1,800 acres of urban forest. While Fairmount Park East/West is known for its ball fields and recreational areas, just like Pennypack, the Wissahickon Valley offers Philadelphians the opportunity to really get back to nature.

The Park is also loaded with Wissahickon schist (that's a type of rock, for you non-geologists) and many varieties of trees, such as Lofty Hemlock, American White Elm, and Native Beech.

The valley is an ideal location for hiking, canoeing and kayaking, rock climbing, mountain biking, picnicking, ice skating, fishing, and horseback riding. (Permits are required to bicycle or ride horseback on all trails except Forbidden [Wissahickon] Drive.) The mountain bike trail is a 30-mile loop that swoops and drags over the terrain—many sections are fine for amateurs, but there are enough technical climbs and downhills to keep even experienced riders entertained.

Trail Highlights

The remnants of Philly's first water fountain can also be found along the trail (it eventually had to be sealed when its spring became too polluted--how appropriate). Devil's Pool, once a spiritual area for the Lenape tribes, can be reached on foot from Valley Green by taking the footpath on the eastern bank and walking downstream to the mouth of Cresheim Creek. For a truly stunning view, take a walk to Lover's Leap. Enter the main footpath at the Ridge Avenue entrance and follow the west bank over to Hermit's Lane Bridge. You'll find yourself peering over a giant precipice to the gorge below. Legend has it

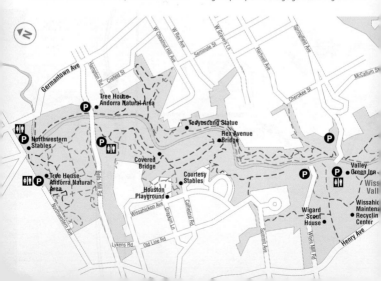

the daughter of a mighty Indian chief and her lover plunged to their deaths in a desperate attempt to escape the woman's wily marital arrangement to an old chieftain.

Maps of the Wissahickon trails (and other parts of the Fairmount Park system) can be printed for free on the Fairmount Park website, or you can purchase maps at the Wissahickon Park Environmental Center.

How to Get There—Driving

Park, big. Roads, many. In other words, it all depends on where you want to go. If you've never been to the Wissahickon Valley before, consider cruising up Lincoln Drive, which takes you right along part of the Wissahickon Creek. To get to Lincoln Drive from the Schuylkill/76, get off at Exit 340A Lincoln Drive/Kelly Drive. From the exit ramp, get in the middle lane and follow the signs for Lincoln Drive.

Henry Avenue is a good way to get to many points as well. From the Schuylkill/76, still get off at Exit 340A, but instead follow the signs for Ridge Avenue E (stay left, left, then left again). At the dead end, go right onto Ridge Avenue South Drive through three lights,

then turn left on Midvale Avenue. Go through three lights again, and turn left on Henry Avenue. The Park runs along the right hand side of Henry Avenue.

Parking

It's not hard to find parking in the Wissahickon Valley Park. There are numerous locations throughout the park where parking is free.

How to Get There—Mass Transit

For the southern part of the park, take the Manayunk/Norristown Line to Wissahickon Station or any of the buses that go through the Wissahickon Transit Center (1, 9, 27, 35, 38, 61, 65, 124, 125, R). The Chestnut Hill West Line makes regular stops to the east of the park including Chelten Ave, Tulpehoken, Upsal, Carpenter Lane, Allen Lane, St Martins, Highland, and Chestnut Hill West. Using septa.com's "Plan My Trip" feature will help you find your way by public transportation.

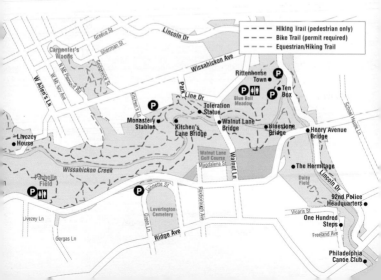

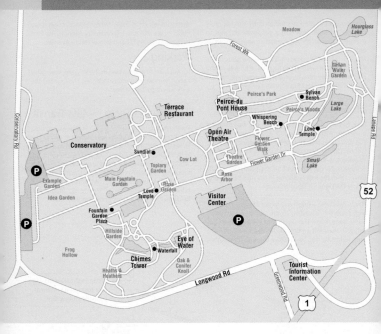

Conservatory

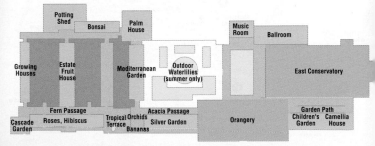

General Information

Address:	1001 Longwood Rd
	Kennett Square, PA 19348
Phone:	610-388-1000
Website:	www.longwoodgardens.org
Hours:	Open daily from 9 am
	(closing time depends on season)
Admission:	Adults $18, Seniors (62+) $15,
	Students (5-22) $8, Children (under 4) free.
	Prices for performances vary

Overview

If you're not into horticulture, you're probably not reading this. If you are, you'll be happy to learn that over 11,000 different types of plants grow at Longwood. We strongly urge you to look at their website, which includes dozens of pages dedicated to the gardens.

Although Longwood is sprawled out over 1,050 acres, most visitors limit themselves to the impressive collection of forty outdoor gardens, indoor gardens, and heated greenhouses located within a 4-acre radius. Because of the wealth of wondrous plants, it's difficult to give all of them individual shout-outs, but we feel compelled to point out the breathtaking orchid display in the Conservatory. And the Bonsai exhibit. And the various banana trees. And the super-cool insect-catching plants display. And that's just the indoor plants. The fountains are also a huge draw year-round, with various water shows playing daily and special holiday presentations come Christmastime.

When you've had enough greenery, head inside the stately Du Pont House and check out the exhibits on the life of chemical magnate Pierre du Pont and those of his most prominent descendents. You can even listen to an audio clip of the "Du Pont Song," a rousing ditty that declares, in words a hundred years ahead of their time, "Du Pont is the man!" Indeed.

Eating

If you look in your wallet and exclaim, "There's just way too much money in here!" we recommend the Terrace Restaurant located next to the Conservatory. The cafeteria (in the same building) is a more reasonably priced dining option. If you enjoy a limited budget, you can always pack some food and eat it in the picnic area located outside of the gardens.

Pets

Service dogs are the only animals permitted at Longwood. There are no kennels or other pet-housing facilities, so no chance for Queenie to weigh anchor on the Italian Water Garden.

Annual Events

Every year Longwood features a variety of pretty spectacular events. We recommend checking the website for their current schedule, but here are some past celebrations that you can expect to see permutations of again:

Mid-January - Mid-March - Welcome Spring
Witness the early blooming stages of bulbs. Expect to see the classic daffodils and tulips as well as their more exotic relatives, like the blue poppy.

Mid-March - Early April - Easter Display
The conservatory is filled with over 1,000 lilies. Outside, bulbs tentatively press upward through the still thawing soil.

April & May - Acres of Spring
Outdoor color-fest with purple phlox, white foam flowers, and azaleas to die for.

June - September - Festival of Fountains
Visit the fountain gardens for concerts and water spectaculars, all while sitting surrounded by roses and water lilies. If you go to one event at Longwood all year, make it one of the "Fireworks & Fountains" evenings that are part of this festival. You haven't seen fireworks until you've seen rich people fireworks.

Mid-September - Early October – GardenFest
The garden railway takes visitors on a ride through the heritage trail, while experts point out autumn gourds and squash. The Gardens also host talks and demonstrations on the art of gardening.

October - Autumn's Colors
Indoor and outdoor gardens alike explode in shades of yellow, red, and gold. Local bands perform during the weekends.

November - Chrysanthemum Festival
See chrysanthemums in quantities and shapes that you've never seen before.

Late November - December – Christmas
400,000 tasteful decorative lights transform the gardens into a winter wonderland. Water and light shows set to music are staged in the Open-Air Theater.

How to Get There—Driving

From Philly and vicinity, take I-95 to Route 322 W (Exit 3A), to Route 1 S. Longwood is located just off Route 1 once you cross Route 52. Alternatively, take I-76 to I-476 S, to Route 1 S.

Parking

Free parking is available in the parking lot. On busy days, expect a short trek from your car to the visitor center. Accessible parking is located next to the visitor center but it fills up quickly; passenger drop-off at the visitor center is permitted.

How to Get There—Mass Transit

Become buddies with a car owner or join a Car Share program (Enterprise CarShare or Zipcar). If your social skills suck or you don't have a license, take the Wilmington/Newark Line to Wilmington on SEPTA Regional Rail. From Center City to Wilmington, Delaware, you'll pay $6.50 one-way if you buy your ticket ahead of time, or $8 if you purchase it on the train. From there, you'll have to take a taxi or rent a car, since there is no regularly scheduled public transit to Longwood. Taxis run about $30 one-way. So, to recap: SEPTA = $13.00 round trip. Taxi = $60 round trip. Total = $71 + tip for cab driver. You make the call.

Squares, Circles, and Small Parks

General Information

Websites:
www.phila.gov/parksandrecreation/
Pages/default.aspx
www.ushistory.org/lovepark
www.friendsofclarkpark.org

Overview

When William Penn initially imagined the city of Philadelphia back in 1682, he pictured "a green country town" filled with lush trees and garden escapes. Penn envisaged multiple city squares that would provide a welcome retreat from the swirl of city activity—certainly an advanced method of city planning.

Each of the five city squares originally bore the names of their locations: Northeast, Northwest, Center, Southwest, and Southeast. Many decades later, in the nineteenth century, the parks were renamed after important historical figures. Aside from the five central squares, there are several other quaint neighborhood parks to wile away the time.

1. Logan Square

Logan Square, originally Northwest Square, was once the site of burial plots, pasturage, and public executions. In 1919, a French architect remodeled the square to include a large traffic circle with an area for gardens, monuments, and a memorial fountain. The fountain still serves as a memorial, but is most often used by hot children in the summertime as an impromptu public swimming area. Plenty of adult supervision is almost always at hand. If you happen to come by on the last day of school, you'll see a parade of girls from nearby Hallahan High School taking a traditional plunge, school uniforms and all.

2. Franklin Square

Just outside Old City's main drag, Franklin Square's once seedy green space was recently redone in honor of Ben Franklin's tercentency. Now home to a carousel, miniature golf, playgrounds, and a restored fountain, it's the sort of place that's fun when it's not overrun with screaming children.

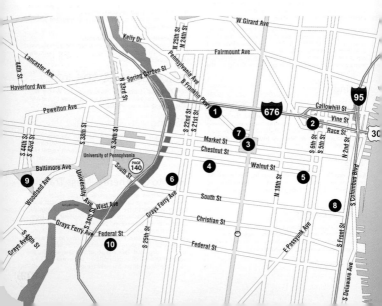

3. Penn Square

Center Square is the largest of the original five city parks. It was renamed Penn Square in tribute to William Penn, whose initial desire to see this land used for public buildings was overruled; instead, early Philadelphians used the space for residential properties. It wasn't until the late-19th century that the square became a location for new public buildings and the mammoth City Hall was built. The square has some of the most intriguing architecture in the city, including the imposing Penn statue, standing high over City Hall.

4. Rittenhouse Square

Southwest of Rittenhouse Square remains the most fashionable residential district in Philly, home to the equivalent of an affluent Victorian aristocracy. You can still see some of the mansions from that period, though most of the homes were turned into apartment buildings after 1913. Of all the squares, Rittenhouse Square is the most neighborly of the parks. Some of the city's best-loved sculptures reside here among the plants, annual flower markets, and outdoor art exhibits. Fancy bars and restaurants circle the area, keeping it chic and elite.

5. Washington Square

Washington Square, the Southeast Square, is known as the final resting place of more Revolutionary soldiers than anywhere else in the United States. It wasn't until 1825 that the city renamed the square and its uppity reputation began to grow. In the first half of the 20th century, this became the heart of Philly's publishing industry, and such popular publications as *The Saturday Evening Post* and *Ladies' Home Journal* were conceived here. Be sure to check out the Bicentennial Moon Tree. This sycamore was planted from a seed carried to the moon by the Apollo Space Mission. There is also a large public fountain in the center that serves as a great place for people and their pooches to chill out during summer months.

6. Fitler Square

Just a few blocks southwest of Rittenhouse Square and five blocks east of the Schuylkill River, Fitler Square is surrounded by a slew of expensive single-family dwellings and an array of fine restaurants, quaint shops, and small businesses. Named for Edwin H. Fitler, a well-regarded 19th-century mayor of Philadelphia, the square lays just a stone's throw from Philly's most commercial Center City shopping district. It plays host to a series of annual events like the Spring Fair, Easter Egg Hunt, and Christmas tree lighting. Woe betide you if you walk on the grass or let your dog do same; they are very pricklish about the lawn.

7. Love Park

This little enclave across from City Hall opened in the free-loving '60s. The park is famous for Robert Indiana's 20-foot tall LOVE sculpture, the symbol for the "City of Brotherly Love." For years, Love Park was a mecca for skateboarders, who came in droves to test their mettle against the park's ramps, stairs, and fountains. But the mayor has imposed a strict no-skating policy, forcing the young-uns to sneak around like ninjas in order to snag a few blissful runs.

8. Headhouse Square

This charming, cobblestone lined street square in Old City is definitely worth strolling. Surrounded by cozy restaurants and picturesque parks, Headhouse Square also houses the nation's oldest firehouse. For fourteen consecutive weekends during the year, beginning at Memorial Day, check out the Creative Collective Craft and Fine Arts Fair. It's a great way to spend the weekend, meeting with local artists, browsing their wares, and sending the kids off to any one of the free art workshops for an afternoon of T-shirt painting or puppet-making. Most shows are on Saturdays and run from 10 am to 10 pm. There is also a popular Farmer's Market here that runs from 10 am to 2 pm on Saturdays and Sundays throughout the summer.

9. Clark Park

Initially established in 1895, Clark Park (43rd St & Chester Ave), adds to the West Philly scene by attracting artists and musicians who showcase their talents throughout the nine acres of greenery. The Clark Park Music and Arts Community play a huge role in facilitating an array of festivals in the park. The CPMAC and The Friends of Clark Park are two key organizations working to help maintain and promote the park. Check out the life-sized Charles Dickens statue, or take a look at the Friends of Clark Park website to check out upcoming events.

10. Penn Treaty Park

Penn Treaty Park is located at the site of where William Penn and the Lenape Indians signed a friendship agreement. Well, maybe. There are actually no hard historical documents confirming this fact—but don't tell that to the statue of Penn that presides over the park. Today Penn Treaty Park serves as a beautiful spot on the edge of the Delaware River to go fishing (but we don't recommend eating anything that you catch), fly kites, barbecue, and smoke weed (apparently).

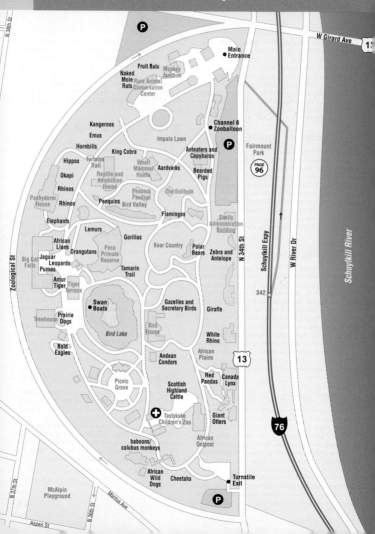

General Information

Address:	3400 West Girard Ave Philadelphia, PA 19104-1196
Phone:	215-243-1100
Website:	www.philadelphiazoo.org
Hours:	In-Season - Mar-Nov 9:30 am–5 pm daily Off-Season - Dec-Feb 9:30 am–4 pm daily
Admission:	In season (Mar-Oct): Adults, $20; Child(2-11), $16; Off season (Nov-Feb): Adults, $18; Child(2-11), $16; Children under 2 are free year-round.

Overview

Opened in 1874, the Philadelphia Zoo is the oldest in the country. Drawing 1.1 million visitors per year, it's laid out over 42 acres and has 1,300 animals from six continents, a remarkable display of historic architecture, an impressive botanical collection of over 500 plant species, and superior research and veterinary facilities.

But kids today have become more jaded than their predecessors. These days, maybe because of television shows like Animal Planet and the Discovery Channel, it seems to take more than a moping hippo hiding in the corner of his cage to excite the kiddies. So, like zoos in most cities, the Philadelphia Zoo has been evolving with the times and placing greater emphasis on its amusement park facilities than on its animals.

In order to fit in these new rides, the play areas, and—but of course—the ubiquitous market places, the zoo has scaled down its number of actual animals. Fewer than ten years ago, the zoo had 1,800 animals; today, the zoo's collection is down to 1,300 and dropping fast. Ironically enough, the Philly Zoo, known as the setting of the first chimpanzee birth in the country (1928), no longer houses chimps.

Rides and Activities

The Zooballoon (open April through October), takes visitors 400 feet above the ground to see the giraffes and zebras oddly juxtaposed against the Philadelphia skyline. The quaint Amoroso PZ Express Victorian-era train is another fun attraction for the kids (and adults) who prefer the comfort of feeling ground beneath their feet. The crowds around Bird Valley waiting to ride the Swan Boat (open April through October) are bigger than the ones trying to catch a glimpse of the rhino. And the Camel Safari does come complete with your own spitting, smelly camel ride. Make sure to bring along some extra cash if you're planning on partaking in the fun, as all of these rides cost $3–$15 on top of the entrance fee.

How to Get There—Driving

From I-76, take Exit 342 to Girard Avenue. Follow signs to the Zoo.

From I-95, take exit 676 W to I-76 W. Get off at Exit 342 to Girard Avenue. Follow signs to the Zoo.

Parking

As you drive toward the zoo, turn right on Girard Avenue or continue straight to the 34th Street parking lot. The cost of parking is $15 (unless you're a member—then it's free).

How to Get There—Mass Transit

Ride SEPTA bus 15 to 34th Street and Girard Avenue. Bus 32 stops at 33rd Street and Girard Avenue. Bus 38 stops close by at 34th Street and Mantua Avenue. A $2 shuttle departs half hourly from the Museum of Art in summer.

Zoo Tours

All tours are lead by volunteer docents and are $5. For more information about Zoo Tours, or to make reservations (which are required), call 215-243-5235.

Thematic Tours:
- Conservation/Endangered Species Tour
- Adaptations
- Reptiles and Amphibians
- Up Close and Personal (Adults only)
- Bible

About the Zoo Tours:
- Art and Architecture
- Horticulture

Children's Tours:
- The Five Senses Tour
- Adaptations

General Information

NFT Map: 4
Phone: 215-928-8801
Website: www.delawareriverwaterfront.com

Overview

Comprising 13 acres stretching from Spring Garden Street to Washington Avenue along the Delaware, Penn's Landing is gradually becoming more than just the port where all the Jersey kids get off the Camden ferry in order to snort glue and get their asses pierced on South Street. In spite of the improvements, it still houses the regrettable "Jersey Night Out" mix of huge, unbearably lame dance clubs and stripper bars, and many darkened sections of wharf and park where you can get into drunken throw-downs with like-minded barbarians.

Events

Despite all that, Penn's Landing does host many of Philly's biggest events and festivals each year. Many concerts take place at the Great Plaza (Columbus Blvd & Chestnut St), and others occur at the Festival Pier (Columbus Blvd & Spring Garden St), such as the Sippin' by the River Festival (www.sippinbytheriver. com) in September. Most recently, Philly's LGBT pride parade and festival culminated by the Marina, chock full of leather daddies, lesbian mothers, and everyone in between.

Blue Cross River Rink

Located on Columbus Boulevard and Market Street, the Blue Cross River Rink (www.delaware riverwaterfront.com/places/blue-cross-riverrink) hosts ice skating fun for everyone November through February (you can even skate with Santa a couple of times in December). Entry costs $8 for everyone ($9 on Friday and Saturday nights), and skate rental is an additional $3.. The rink is open 6 pm–9 pm weeknights (and until 1 am Friday nights), 12:30 pm–1 am on Saturdays, and 12:30 pm–9 pm on Sundays. Check the website or call 215-925-RINK before you go though, because sometimes the rink is closed for private rentals.

Other Attractions

There's the Seaport Museum, which chronicles the history of Penn's Landing, one of American's oldest ports. There are also some fine restaurants which reside near the Marina. And the aforementioned lame-ass clubs are towards the north, past the BF Bridge. Otherwise, you'll find interesting park

space and absolutely filthy-rich yachts if you walk south towards South Street. If you want to get out on the water—notice we said on, not in, pollution being what it is—and you don't own one of those expensive yachts, you'll find everything from 12-minute ferry rides to paddle wheel riverboat dining departing from the banks of the Delaware. Just don't ride one of those damn duck boats. If you live in Philly and ride a duck boat, you deserve to get punched in the face.

How to Get There—Driving

From I-95, take Exit 20 (Washington Ave/Columbus Blvd). Make a left onto Columbus Boulevard and proceed north.

From the Walt Whitman Bridge, take I-95 N to Exit 20. Follow directions above.

From I-76, travel east to I-676 E until you hit I-95. Take I-95 S to Exit 20, and follow the above directions.

Parking

There are loads of parking options around Penn's Landing. Most charge $12–$15 per day:

Festival Pier
   Spring Garden & Columbus Blvd - 300 spaces.
Pier 24
   Columbus Blvd & Cavanaugh's River Deck - 120 spaces.
Vine St & Columbus Blvd
   (across from Dave & Buster's) - 280 spaces.
Columbus Blvd & Market St - 400 spaces.
Columbus Blvd & Walnut St - 220 spaces.
Lombard Cir & Columbus Blvd - 220 spaces.
South Street Pedestrian Bridge &
   Columbus Blvd - 400 spaces.

Ticketed concert parking at Festival Pier costs $20. Monthly parking permits are also available the last five days through the first five days of every month. They offer 24-hour parking for permit holders, and can be purchased at the Penn's Landing Operations/ Visitor Center at 301 S Columbus Boulevard for first-time buyers. There is also ample street parking in the surrounding area if you 're willing to feed the meter every 2 hours.

How to Get There—Mass Transit

Take SEPTA bus 17 to Penn's Landing via 20th Street and Market Street, or bus 48 Tioga.

By subway, ride the Market-Frankford Line east, get off at 2nd Street, and walk south to Penn's Landing.

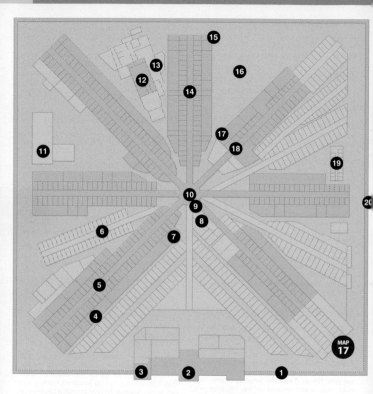

1. Facade
2. Front Tower
3. Administration Building Office
4. Synagogue
5. Cellblock 7
6. Cellblock 12
7. Al Capone's Cell
8. Chaplain's Office
9. Rotunda
10. Central Guard Tower
11. Chapel
12. Kitchen
13. Dining Hall
14. Cellblock 4
15. Exercise Yard
16. Baseball Diamond
17. Hospital
18. Outside the Operating Room
19. Death Row
20. Outside the Cellblocks

General Information

NFT Map: 17
Location: 22nd St & Fairmount Ave
Philadelphia, PA 19130
Phone: 215-236-3300
Website: www.easternstate.org
Hours: Open 7 days a week, year-round,
10 am–5 pm.
Admission: Adults $14, Seniors $12, Students
and Kids $10. Not recommended for
children under the age of 7.

Overview

There's no use denying it: Eastern State Penitentiary is a genuinely interesting, albeit touristy, destination.

Built in 1829 in what is now the Fairmount section of Philadelphia, ESP was once the largest and most expensive building in America. People flocked from around the globe to marvel at the prison's architecture and penal system. The prison was closed in 1971 and promptly fell into disrepair.

The non-profit preservationist group, Eastern State Penitentiary Historic Site, was formed in 1994, and today organizes tours and educational programs in an effort to restore the crumbling prison. Recently, several archaeologists were hired to excavate around the building's exterior, and came up with some actual buried, er… treasure. The findings included pieces of discarded silverware, glass bottles and bottle caps, and remnants of homemade tools possibly used for (what probably proved futile) escape plans.

ESP's once-oppressive environment is also used today as an art gallery. Art installations, motivated by the prison's history and created specifically for the space, are featured throughout the complex, and many change with the seasons. Recent installations have included "Ghost Cats" featuring 39 cat sculptures scattered around the grounds representing the colony of cats that ran wild in the penitentiary following its desertion in the 1970s. Another work, titled "The End of the Tunnel," featured a two-inch red steel pipe that snaked around the outside of the cell blocks and over the walls, symbolizing escape routes prisoners might have used.

During Halloween, the prison hosts a haunted house event called Terror Behind the Walls. Although it's ranked ninth in the country by HauntWorld Magazine, the truly creepy environment can be somewhat reduced by gaggles of teenagers talking on their cell phones behind you.

They also throw a big Bastille Day party every July. There's a playful reenactment of the Storming of the Bastille (influenced more by Monty Python than the French Revolution), followed by a French-themed street party. Tres Bien!

History

Eastern State Penitentiary was created by Quakers who believed that true penitence could come only from a life of solitude and reflection. To prohibit communication between inmates and guards, prisoners were required to wear masks anytime they left their cells. They received meals through small feed doors. Although the concept for Eastern State Penitentiary was based on ending ill treatment common in prisons of the day, the punishments exacted were far from pleasant. If inmates were caught trying to communicate with other prisoners, they would be denied meals or sentenced to solitary confinement for several days. If the infraction was more serious, an inmate might be chained to an outside wall in the winter months, stripped from the waist up, and doused with water until ice formed on his body. The "iron gag" was another form of punishment involving a five-inch piece of metal clamped onto a tongue. If captives exhibited resistance, the gag would be forced deeper into their mouth. At least one inmate died from the iron gag.

The prison is also famous for its inmates, some of whom have reached near-celebrity status. Over the years, ESP's quarters hosted the likes of gangster Al Capone and bank robber Willie Sutton.

How to Get There—Driving

From the north or west, take I-76 (Schuylkill Expressway) to Exit 344 (Old Exit 38)/I-676 (Vine Street Expressway). On I-676 take the first exit, Benjamin Franklin Parkway/23 Street, then take the first left onto 22nd Street. Pass the Philadelphia Museum of Art (on your left) and continue five blocks north, to Fairmount Avenue.

Coming from the south or east, take I-95 to Exit 22 (Old Exit 17) and follow I-676 W. Get off at the Art Museum/Benjamin Franklin Parkway exit. At the top of the ramp, turn right onto 22nd Street, pass the Philadelphia Museum of Art (on your left) and continue five blocks north to Fairmount Avenue.

Parking

While there is plenty of un-metered street parking in the area around the penitentiary, some streets have a two- or three-hour limit. If you're planning on taking your time touring the prison, there's a public lot next door which will cost between $3 and $10, depending on the length of your stay.

How to Get There—Mass Transit

Take the 7, 32, or 48 SEPTA bus to 22nd Street and Fairmount Avenue then walk east one block to the penitentiary. The 33 bus stops at 20th and Fairmount; walk west one block to the entrance. The 43 bus stops at 21st and Spring Garden Streets. Walk north to Fairmount Avenue, the next major street parallel to Spring Garden Street.

Big Bus (Stop #8) and Philadelphia Trolley Works (Stop #11) both stop right in front of the ESP, a sure sign that you're smack bang in the middle of the tourist route. Be sure to show your ticket stub from the tours and save $1 on admission to the prison. The Phlash trolley has an Eastern State Penitentiary stop at 22nd Street and Benjamin Franklin Parkway. Get off and walk four blocks north on 22nd Street to Fairmount Avenue.

Overview

To Philadelphians, Benjamin Franklin is more than just the picture on the $100 bill or the dude who flew a kite. Arriving here in 1723, he started, well, just about everything. He's responsible for our first fire company (Union Fire Company, 1736), our first insurance company (Philadelphia Contributionship, 1752), our first university (University of Pennsylvania, 1749), our first hospital (Pennsylvania Hospital, 1751), and our first library (Library Company, 1731). In addition, he was one of our first postmasters (appointed in 1737) and he ran one of our first newspapers, *The Pennsylvania Gazette*, in which he penned the very first political cartoon. Not to mention what he did for the country. (You remember that whole Declaration of Independence thing, right?)

He might have even gone a little overboard. But nobody's gone more overboard than us, especially since his 300th birthday in 2006 when we finally named what we all have a nasty, infectious, and idolatrous case of. We named our disease *Benergy*, and told everybody, drool-fanged, "We got it!"

Benergy, once named as such, provoked *Philadelphia Weekly* writer Steven Wells to lambaste our *Benefactor* for eight tight-fonted pages ("An avuncular saint, inventor and bootstrap capitalist—a PG-friendly, George-Bush-approved, sanitized, shrink-wrapped, deboned and prechewed establishment revolutionary for the whole family to enjoy.") all the while raising up quite rudely the revolutionary efforts of Thomas Paine, another Philadelphian, whose followers (i.e. traitors) claim had more to do with the Declaration of Independence than anybody, but who is largely back-f***ed by the rest of us because, well, he ain't Ben. Chill, Steven Wells. Don't get all *Bent* out of shape.

Panting and sighing, we've named just about everything we can after Ben—from our museums to our hoagie shops to our little babies. From almost any street corner in Philadelphia, you can spot something named after our man. Here are just a few choice examples—let's *Bengin*!

The Franklin Institute

222 N 20th St, 215-448-1200; www.2.fi.edu;
Daily 9:30 am–5 pm

It's virtually impossible to go to the Franklin Institute and not be overrun by children. That being said, it's still a good place for adults to go—if you're young at heart and you don't mind wading through school groups.

The Giant Heart, which opened in 1954, is a legend. If you're a kid, the legendary thing to do would be to get lost and cry inside of it, or at least get injured during rough play near a ventricle. If you're an adult, it's the number one spot in the city to have existential thoughts and wonder what the hell that smell is (hint: it's the reek of thousands of dirty children all walking through an enclosed space).

The Franklin National Memorial, located in the rotunda and free of charge, is the only national memorial held in private hands. Not one penny of federal funds helped to create it or support its upkeep. Oh, and there's a massive 20+ foot, 100+ ton statue of ol' BF there. After the rotunda, the Franklin Institute would like your money, please. Exhibits change regularly, so every few months you can go back and see something new. Prices vary depending on the exhibit, but expect to pay at least $20 for adults. The awesome 79-foot IMAX dome screen movies cost $9 for everybody.

Franklin at Franklin's University (a.k.a. the University of Pennsylvania)

Penn likes to call itself Franklin's University because Ben founded the joint in 1749. Two buildings are named after the big man: Franklin Field and the Franklin Building (we're not counting the meaningless Franklin Building Annex). The Franklin Building, located at 3451 Walnut Street and used for office space, is among the ugliest buildings on the historic campus. Penn's own website has only this to say about it: "Economical and utilitarian office tower that misses most of the important lines of development of the 1960s campus."

When you think of Ben Franklin, athleticism is probably not the first thing that springs to mind. Nevertheless, Franklin Field, located on 33rd Street between South and Walnut Streets, is old (built in 1922), attractive, and has some historical cache: The first televised football game was played there in 1940; it used to be the home of the Eagles and the yearly Army-Navy football game; it's the country's oldest two-tiered stadium; and it seats 52,000 to boot. Those who saw M. Night Shyamalan's *Unbreakable* (2000) will recognize Franklin Field as the nameless sports stadium that David Dunn (Bruce Willis) worked at as a security guard.

In addition to buildings named after him, it's hard to walk around campus without tripping over a statue of Benjamin Franklin:

- In front of **College Hall** sits a well-known plaster statue of a seated Ben that once resided in front of the old Post Office (9th and Chestnut Streets) as a tribute to Franklin, the United States' first Postmaster General.

- Outside **Weightman Hall** is a statue of a youthful Benjamin as he might have looked when he arrived in Philadelphia: seventeen years old, standing with a staff in one hand and a small bundle in the other. The adorning inscription reads: "I have been the more particular in this description of my journey that you may compare such unlikely beginnings with the figure I have since made there."

- At **37th Street and Locust Walk** is a life-sized bronze of Franklin reading one of his own publications: *The Pennsylvania Gazette*.

- On the second floor alcove of **Stiteler Hall** is a middle-aged, six-foot Ben Franklin holding a scroll in his left hand and a three-cornered hat in his right. Originally displaced from the Odd Fellows Cemetery Company and stored in a crate at Franklin Field for more than twenty years, the figure now resides on campus.

Franklin Statues Everywhere

Around the rest of the city, you'll see Ben popping up everywhere. Catch him wearing a firefighter's helmet at the Fire Hall at **4th and Arch Streets**, or at the **City Hall courtyard** looking out above the east entrance. On **Chestnut Street near 23rd**, Ben is featured seated in a huge mural. In addition, there's an abstract, very shiny bust of his head on **17th and Vine** (you'll see it while driving on I-676), and check out the lightning bolt sculpture at the base of the—you guessed it—Ben Franklin Bridge at **5th and Vine Streets**.

Benjamin Franklin Bridge

When they consider their bridges, most Philadelphians think two thoughts, neither of which is pleasant: New Jersey and traffic. However, the BFB is a beauty. A pedestrian footpath (oddly only open on one side at a time and then for set hours) allows you to run, walk, or bike the expanse. The light show it displays at night is mesmerizing when you're getting loaded at Penn's Landing.

The BFB was designed by Paul Cret, who was also involved in designing the Ben Franklin Parkway. Finished in 1926, the bridge connects Center City Philadelphia to Camden and was originally called the Delaware River Port Authority Bridge. In 1956, it was dedicated to Ben Franklin and renamed in his honor. Like all bridges, keep in mind that it's always free to get to New Jersey (jail doesn't charge rent either), but they make you pay to come back.

Benjamin Franklin Parkway

The view of Ben Franklin Parkway was made famous in the 1976 movie classic, *Rocky*. In it, Rocky Balboa (Sylvester Stallone) runs to the top of the Art Museum stairs, turns around and raises his arms in victory. Before him is the view of the parkway. This magic moment is recreated endlessly by tourists and visitors, who request their loved ones to make digital cell phone movies of themselves striding up the steps and holding their arms aloft.

Us locals prefer to climb on the museum's statues at two in the morning and watch all of the lights on the parkway turn green in unison—then red. And if you don't happen to have a pool in your apartment building complex, the Swann Memorial Fountain on 19th and Parkway is the perfect spot for requisite summer night dips.

Next time you're there, we've got a trick for all of you grown-ups with a juvenile sense of humor. From the top of the museum's steps, look south to the statue of William Penn atop City Hall. From this perspective, you'll see what we jokingly call the "the Penn Endowment." Heh.

The Parkway was constructed from 1917 to 1926 with the main objective of getting people from the business district to Fairmount Park. The aforementioned Philadelphia Museum of Art, the Rodin Museum, the Franklin Institute, and the Central Free Library are all along the Franklin Parkway, which has become a popular place for parades and other events by day, and for homeless somnambulists at night.

Franklin Square

Finally refurbished for Ben's 300th, this somewhat oddly placed park houses a carousel, a fountain, green space, a playground, and what we can only assume was one of Mr. Franklin's favorite pastimes, miniature golf.

Franklin Court

316 Market St, 215-965-2305; Daily 9 am–5 pm
This is the spot where Franklin's house stood before it was razed in 1812. That's right: razed. Whoops, our bad. In its place now stands a "ghost structure" (essentially the outline of the house done up in steel support beams) built for the 1976 bicentennial. When digging around in the rubble during its construction, some cool stuff turned up, including Franklin's privy pit.

B. Free Franklin Post Office & Museum

315 Market St, 215-592-1292; Mon–Sat, 9 am–5 pm, closed New Years Day and Christmas Day
Franklin first accepted the role of postmaster of Philadelphia in 1737, mainly to ensure that his newspaper, *The Pennsylvania Gazette*, was distributed properly. As a royal official, Franklin had "franking privileges," and signed his letters B. Free Franklin. Since he was allowed to send letters for free, some think that Franklin was alluding to the fact that his letters were being mailed at no charge. Others believe that "B. Free" was Franklin's statement to the colonies. Since he apologized for and profited from slavery, it's doubtful this was his cry to free the slaves he sold.

The B. Free Franklin Post Office and Museum is an actual working post office. Geeky philatelists will be especially happy to get a letter or postcard that has been cancelled with a hand-stamp bearing Franklin's "B. Free Franklin" signature. Also of note is the fact that this post office is the only one in the country *not* to fly the US flag outside. Why? Because there was no US flag in 1775 when the post office first opened.

Franklin's Grave

After Franklin's death on April 17, 1790, Carl Van Doren wrote, "No other town burying its great man, ever buried more of itself than Philadelphia with Franklin." His grave is located in the Christ Church Cemetery and can be seen through an iron gate at the southeast corner of 5th and Arch Streets. You can also pay a minimal fee to enter the cemetery during the day. Philadelphia tradition claims that throwing a penny onto Franklin's grave will bring good luck. The pennies are collected each night and promptly donated toward the creation of a *Benergy* clinic, where, hopefully, one day in the future, we can all get treated. And guess what we're going to name it.

Franklin Square
PAGE 122

Race St →

National Constitution Center

US Mint

Betsy Ross House

Independence Park Institute

Free Quaker Meeting House

● Benjamin Franklin's Grave

← Arch St

Christ Church Burial Ground

P

P

Christ Church

MAP 4

7th St

6th St

5th St

4th St

3rd St

2nd St

Independence Visitor Center (Security Screening Facility)

Market St

Declaration House

Liberty Bell Pavilion

Market Street Houses

Franklin Court

Independence Mall W

Independence Mall E

Independence Mall

Liberty Bell Center

Chestnut St

Old City Hall

Second Bank of the US

Pemberton House

Independence Hall

Philsophical Hall

New Hall Military Museum

First Bank of the US

Congress Hall

Library Hall

Carpenters' Hall

Sansom St

Independence Square (Security Screening Required)

18th Century Garden

Todd House

Bishop White House

Philadelphia Exchange

City Tavern

Dock St

Welcom Pa

Walnut St →

Thomas Paine Pl

Washington Square

Dock St

● Tomb of the Unknown Soldier of the American Revolution

PAGE 104

Rose Garden

St Joseph's Church

Willings Aly

Locust St

Magnolia Garden

General Information

NFT Map: 4
Websites: www.nps.gov/inde
              www.betsyrosshouse.org

Overview

Instead of the namby-pamby "Philadelphia: The Place That Loves You Back" slogan, perhaps the city should consider a new offering, "Philadelphia: Lots of Significant Stuff Happened Here 200 Years Ago." Tourists flock here because the city's history is so interconnected with the creation of the United States itself. Of course, jaded residents saunter right by these historic buildings where our forefathers determined the country's course with nary a glance. In fact, many of us avoid the Historical Park altogether until out of town guests force us to go downtown and see the Liberty Bell. Paris has the Eiffel Tower; we have the Liberty Bell. Hoo-rah.

INHP comprises "America's most historic square mile." Founded in 1956 on (of course) July 4th, INHP oversees eighteen landmark American institutions, but the most popular attraction by a landslide is the Liberty Bell.

We had to include the Betsy Ross House somewhere, and even though it is not part of INHP, it seems to fit in seamlessly (no sewing pun intended) with the INHP landmarks. And after all, the Betsy Ross House is Philadelphia's second-most visited tourist attraction after INHP.

We should mention, though, that we're pretty sure that's not actually her house. Yeah, her real house was demolished, and what we say is her house was the one next door. Whoops.

Admission

Inside the "security zone", access to all buildings is free and generally includes a tour guide and/or some sort of schpiel about the history of each building, including Independence Hall (plus its East and West Wings), Old City Hall, Congress Hall, and the Liberty Bell Pavilion. Outside of the security zone, the Declaration (Graff) House is also free, as is the Betsy Ross House (although their request for a "donation" feels suspiciously like a requirement). The one place you have to pay for a ticket is the National Constitution Center.

Between March 1st and December 31st

There's a lot of stuff to see, but it can all be covered in one pretty full day. Hit the Independence Visitor Center at 6th and Market Streets first, so you can score a free ticket for an Independence Hall tour. Your timed entry ticket could be anywhere from 45 minutes to three or four hours later, depending on how busy it is. Once you have your tour time secured, you can plan the rest of your day. In addition to all "the Man's" tours and sites, there's also a bunch of other tours, that show other aspects of historic Philadelphia. One thing to note: the Declaration (Graff) House is only open 9 am–11 am, whereas everything else is open throughout the afternoon.

Audio Tour

The 74-minute, self guided AudioWalk & Tour narration is available for rent at the Independence Visitor Center. The tour visits twenty important historical sites and the CD (player included) has 64 narrated segments. The cost is $16 for one person, $17 for two people, $18 for three people, and $20 for four people.

Independence Visitor Center

NW corner of Market St & 6th St, 215-965-7676; www.phlvisitorcenter.com; 8:30 am–6 pm (extended in summer till 7 pm)
This is the spot where you pick up the free tickets for your Independence Hall tour time. The food is at the back of the building on the right. It's also got overpriced food and an over priced gift shop; on the positive side, it does have a bathroom that might have a line.

Liberty Bell Center Museum

6th St b/w Market St & Chestnut St (security entrance on 5th St); www.nps.gov/inde/liberty-bell.html; 9 am–5 pm
This is it, the fulcrum of Philadelphia tourism. Used to be that you could touch it, but after some crazy took a hammer to it in 2001, they initiated the same "airport security" measure as everywhere else. A National Parks Department Ranger will give a little speech, allow a few brief moments for photography, and then shuffle you out towards Independence Hall.

Independence Hall

Chestnut St b/w 5th St & 6th St, 215-965-2305; www.nps.gov/inde/independence-hall-1.htm; 9 am–5 pm
The Independence Hall tour is where you line up and wait for your tour guide like a good school child. Tours run every fifteen minutes and last about half an hour. First stop is the East Wing of Independence Hall, where the ranger will tell you things about the hall and Philadelphia in general. The quality of your experience will depend entirely on the ranger you draw.

Independence Hall is split into two rooms: the Court Room and the Assembly Room. In the Court Room, you'll learn how a trial was held way back when. The good stuff is in the Assembly Room—that's where the Declaration of Independence and the U.S. Constitution were signed.

After you've covered Independence Hall proper, wander into the West Wing. The Declaration of Independence that was read out loud by Colonel John Nixon to the public for the first time on July 8, 1776 in the State House Yard (now Independence Square) resides here. You'll also find a second draft of the Articles of Confederation and Perpetual Union, a draft of the Constitution of the United States, and the inkstand that historians believe was used for the signing of the Declaration and the Constitution.

Congress Hall

6th & Chesnut Sts; www.nps.gov/inde/congress-hall.htm
A little bit further westward, you'll run into Congress Hall, which once housed the Senate and House of Representatives. Beyond that, it's special for another remarkable reason. During 1797, Philadelphia was the nation's capital (while Washington, DC, was being built), and on March 4th, George Washington transferred the power to run the country to John Adams, our second president. This was the first time in the modern age that power was transferred peaceably between two people who were not related.

Old City Hall

5th & Chestnut Sts; www.nps.gov/inde/old-city-hall.htm
To the east of Independence Hall is Old City Hall, which housed the city's government from 1791 to 1854 and was also the first Supreme Court of the United States. Upstairs was the Mayor's Office and Council Chambers and downstairs was the Mayor's Court, shared with the U.S. Supreme Court for nine years. You'll be struck by how small a space it is.

National Constitution Center

525 Arch St; www.constitutioncenter.org
Monday–Friday 9:30 am–5 pm, Saturday 9:30 am–6 pm, Sunday 12 pm–5 pm.
Tickets: $14.50 adults; $13 seniors (65+), youth (13-18), and students (with ID); $8 children (4–12); children under 4 and active military (with ID) are free.
All things Constitutional. You can see life-sized bronze statues of the signers, get your picture taken behind the presidential seal, and even complain to your congressional representative at the Participation Café. For $12, it's probably worth it. Currently there's massive landscaping in front of the Constitution center, and random storyteller areas in the surrounding region.

Betsy Ross House

239 Arch St, 215-686-1252; www.betsyrosshouse.org
Open 10 am–5 pm daily April–Oct; Closed Mondays Oct–Mar
Did Betsy Ross really make the first flag? We do know that her descendents claim that she made and helped design the first flag in 1776, although the flag we consider to be the Betsy Ross flag (with the 13 stars in a circle) did not appear until the 1790s. Whatever the case may be, this stop is a favorite of children, who don't know any better.

Declaration (Graff) House

7th St & Market St;
www.nps.gov/inde/declaration-house.htm
Open 9 am–11 am
This building, like many "historical" buildings in Philadelphia, was razed a long, long time ago. Then for the bicentennial, the city decided to rebuild it real quick in order to capitalize on some fat tourist dollars. Thomas Jefferson rented two rooms in this location from Jacob Graff, Jr. to escape the heat of the city.

City Tavern

138 S 2nd St at Walnut St; 215-413-1443;
www.citytavern.com; Opens at 11:30 am daily
Another building rebuilt for the bicentennial. The original burned down in 1834. While other reproductions (Betsy Ross House, Declaration [Graff] House, Franklin Court) are at best guesstimates, City Tavern is supposed to be a faithful reconstruction right down to the menus. Don't look for any low-carb meals here. Apparently 18th-century types required either bread or potatoes (usually both) with their giant slabs of meat. It isn't cheap, but you're dining in the same air space in which Washington, Jefferson, Adams, and Franklin once dined.

Parking

There's no lack of public parking near INHP—just be prepared to pay for it!

Central Parking Auto Park - 6th St b/w Market St & Arch St
Central Parking System – Market St b/w 8th St & 9th St
Parkway Parking - 8th St & Ranstead Street
Five Star Parking – 8th St & Chestnut St
Parking Plaza-Quaker City Auto – 8th St & Filbert St
HC Parking - 7th St & Cherry St
Bourse Parking – 4th St & Ranstead St

Whatever you do, do not try to park on the street unless you want to pick your vehicle up from one of the many impound lots. The PPA has this area on lockdown.

How to Get There—Mass Transit

The Market-Frankford line stops along Market Street at 8th, 5th, and 2nd Streets, with the 5th Street stop being the closest to the Independence Mall.

Many other trains stop at the 8th St/Market terminal, including the subway, trolley, and light rail. Take the Broad-Ridge Spur, Patco High Speed, or SEPTA bus routes 61 and 47 to the Market Street stop. Many, many other buses stop nearby; consult septa.com for all of the routes.

All SEPTA Regional Rail trains stop at the Market East Station, which is six blocks from INHP.

Then there's PHLASH. Nothing says, "Look at me, I'm a tourist!" like the big, purple PHLASH bus. But it is cheap and convenient, costing $2 per ride or $12 per day. The purple bus makes many stops along Market Street between Penn's Landing and City Hall, before cutting up Ben Franklin Parkway to the Philadelphia Museum of Art.

In addition to the food, there's also a large selection of random crap that the vendors will yell about. We don't know anywhere else where you can get a down winter jacket for $20.

Let us not forget Fante's at 1006 S 9th Street, one of the best kitchen stores in the country, not to mention, somewhat further south, the cheesesteak landmarks, Pat's and Geno's (Ninth St & Passyunk Ave). Beware where you pick to cheesesteak, purchasing from Geno's over Pat's carries with it an implied mentality. (Pick Pat's)

Then, if you're REALLY brave, there's the Italian Market Festival held in late May or early June; it features live music, activities, and mangoes on sticks. Check out italianmarketphilly.org/festival for the program schedule. The same organization also provides Christmas cheer through December.

How to Get There—Driving

From points north or south of Philly, take I-95 to the PA-611 N/Broad Street exit (Exit 14) towards Pattison Avenue. Merge onto S Broad Street. Turn right onto E Passyunk Avenue, then right onto Wharton Street.

From the west, take the US-422 E to I-76 E. Get off at the I-676 E/US-30 E exit (Exit 38) and turn left towards Central PA. Merge onto the Vine Street Expressway and exit at Broad Street/Central PA. Turn right onto N 15th Street. Make a left onto S Penn Square, another right on S Broad Street, and a left onto Washington Avenue. At S 10th Street, turn right, then make a left onto Wharton Street.

Parking

There are four lots that charge by the hour (reasonable rates) and three municipal parking lots in nearby streets. There is also free Saturday parking lot between S Darien Street and S Mildred Street, one block above Christian Street. However beware, the PPA does have this area on lockdown.

How to Get There—Mass Transit

Take bus 23 and get off at Christian Street. Turn right and walk one block to the market. By subway, take the Broad Street line and get off at Ellsworth-Federal. Walk east to 9th Street and turn left. Walk six blocks north and you'll arrive at the market.

General Information

NFT Map: 8
Address: 700-1100 S 9th St
                Philadelphia, PA 19147
Phone: 215-334-6008
Website: www.phillyitalianmarket.com
Hours: Tue–Sat: 9 am–5 pm, Sun: 9 am–2 pm

Overview

If going to a supermarket and seeing a freezer filled with frozen chickens isn't a personal enough experience for you, you might consider the Market. You can wander around living, breathing chickens, and many, many fresh carcasses (vegans can find all kinds of great stuff there, but they'll have to learn to avert their eyes). Freshness is what the Italian Market is all about, from meat to produce to bread to homemade cheese and spices.

Located in the heart of South Philly's vibrant Italian community, the Italian Market (sometimes referred to as "9th Street") is the country's oldest daily outdoor market—one hundred years and counting. Whereas the Italian Market used to be just that—Italian—there is a huge South East Asian and Latino presence in this section of South Philly.

Arch St

Dienner's Bar-B-Q Chicken

Lancaster County Dairy

Old City Coffee

Blue Mountain Vineyards & Cellars

Beiler's Bakery

Dutch Eating Place

Golden Fish Market

Metropolitan Bakery

$

PA General Store

Market Operations

The Rib Stand

Hatville Deli
Glick's Salads

Fisher's Soft Pretzels and Ice Cream

Seating Area

Foster's Gourmet Cookware

Foster's Gourmet Kitchen

Rick's Philly Steaks

Hatville Deli

12th Street Cantina

Amazulu
Kauffman's Lancaster County Produce

Don't Forget Your Pet

Bee Natural

Tootsie's Salad Express

Cold Storage

Carmen's Famous Hoagies

Olympic Gyro

Natural Connection

Dutch Country Meats

Andro's Fine Prepared Foods

Market Office Upstairs

Golden Bowl

Kamal's Middle Eastern Specialties

Martin's Quality Meats & Sausages

John Yi Fish Market

DiNic's

Spataro's

Spice Terminal

Seating Area

The Shoe Doctor

Bassett's Ice Cream

The Flower Basket
Four Seasons Juice Bar

Shanghai Gourmet

Mezze

Seating Area

Terralyn

Philbert

Seating Area

Flying Monkey Patisserie

Le Bus Bakery
Delilah's

Tea Leaf

Harry G Ochs & Son

Hershel's East Side Deli

The Original Turkey
Basic 4 Vegetarian

Tokyo Sushi Bar
Franks-A-Lot

Seating Area

Miscellanea Libri

Beer Garden

Profi's Creperie
Sang Kee Peking Duck

Nanee's Kitchen

OK Lee's Produce

Terralyn
De' Village

Godshall's Poultry

Coastal Cave

Seating Area

Pearl's Oyster Bar

Old City Coffee

Downtown Cheese
Cookbook Stall

Little Thai Market

Salumeria

Market Blooms and Garden

L Halterman Family Country Foods

Famous 4th St Cookie Co

Le Bus Bakery

Amy's Place
Chocolate by Mueller

Wan's Seafood

Giunta's Prime Shop

Iovine Brothers Produce

$

Market Information

Chocolate by Mueller

Termini Brothers Bakery
Down Home Diner

Down Home Diner

by george!

Iovine Brothers Produce

MAP 3

Filbert St

12th St

11th St

1 Livengood's Produce (Sat only)

	Groceries		Shops
	Bars/Beverages		Parkings
	Restaurants		Other

General Information

NFT Map:	3
Address:	12th St & Arch St
Phone:	215-922-2317
Website:	www.readingterminalmarket.org
Hours:	Mon–Sat: 8 am–6 pm, Sun 9 am–5 pm

Overview

A giant food market, with representative cuisine from all over the area (and then some), Reading offers everything from organic produce to Amish bakeries to fresh seafood.

From 1889 through 1985, the market lived in the train shed beneath the tracks of the station at 12th and Market streets. When the commuter-rail system was rerouted to bypass the station, the tracks were removed and the market remained. Today, many Philadelphians make Reading their lunch destination, while some venture into Amish breakfast territory, which is currently serving butter soup on a measly pancake (or, alternately, a pancake with the measles)... On our way home from work, we like to do our specialty grocery shopping here—selecting from locally grown fruit and vegetables and an excellent assortment of choice meat. Reading is, aside from the Italian Market, the best place to get cheese.

Reading is also the place for some choice people-watching. The contrast of function and dysfunction, tourists and locals, Midwestern conventioneers, cute babies, and the decrepit elderly is all so poetic. There's a sea-clogged piano near the 12th and Filbert Streets entrance, where seriously loony (and very sweet) old people stamp out arrhythmic Joplin, against the loud shouts just beyond them—"Shoeshine! Shoeshine!" Then there are the red plastic six-seater pull-trains full of adorable pre-schoolers, and the gawk-worthy DNA-similarity of all the Amish girls and boys. And now that Reading's been implanted with surprisingly never-faltering free wireless, there's really no reason not to sit here all day.

It's impossible to name all the varieties of chow involved, but here are some can't misses: **Downtown Cheese**, **Little Thai Market**, **Old City Coffee**, the farmer's market on Saturday, **Nanee's Kitchen** (Indian cuisine), **Kamal's Middle Eastern Specialties** where they'll give you a shot of wheatgrass, **LeBus** for all bread needs (that's right, **Metropolitan** is way more expensive and "artisanal," it turns out, is a euphemism for "too hard"), **Dutch Eating Place**, **DiNic's**, and lovine **Brothers Produce** for all the fruit you can carry. For some of the best donuts and baked goods on the planet, the friendly Amish folks at **Beiler's** will hook you up. Remember these two words: whoopie pie. Throw nutritional concerns aside and make a meal of a butter-dipped Amish soft pretzel and a scoop of ice cream from the legendary **Bassett's**. If you want to impress the snooty foodies who come to visit you (meaning, among others, anyone from NYC) take 'em here, load them up with a Vietnamese hoagie and a giant mint chocolate milkshake, then buy them a copper sauté pan. That'll learn 'em.

If you really want an insiders' view of the market you can take a Taste of Philly Tour with a local food expert. Learn about the vibrant history of the market, the story behind cheesesteaks, and lots more. Check out the events section on the website for more information.

How to Get There—Driving

From the Schuylkill/76, take Exit 344/676 E. From 676, take the second exit, Broad Street. From the exit ramp, continue straight on Vine Street and follow the signs that say "PA Convention Center." Turn right onto 12th Street and proceed two blocks to Arch Street. Reading Terminal Market is on the southeast corner of Arch and Market.
From I-95 S/N, take Exit 22/676 W. From 676 take the first exit, Broad Street. Turn right off of exit ramp onto 15th Street. Turn left onto Vine Street (second light) then right onto 12th St and proceed two blocks to Arch Street. Reading Terminal Market is on the southeast corner of Arch and Market.

Parking

$4 parking is available to market shoppers as long as you spend $10 at the market and get validation of purchase from any market merchant. The only catch is that you have to be done shopping in two hours. If you park for longer than 2 hours, the regular garage rates apply so check the current rates as you enter. To get this rate use the 12th and Filbert St Garage or the 11th and Arch St Garage. If you have patience and time to spare, there's a less complicated alternative—nearby metered parking.

How to Get There—Mass Transit

Take any of SEPTA's Regional Rail lines to the Market East Station and follow signs to the PA Convention Center and Reading Terminal Market.

From the Broad Street subway, get off at City Hall and walk east on Market Street. Turn left on 12th Street and walk one block until you hit RTM. From the Market/Frankford line, get off at 13th Street. Walk one block east to 12th Street and RTM is one block along 12th Street.

By trolley, get off at Juniper Station and walk two blocks east to 12th Street. Turn left onto 12th Street and walk one block to RTM.

There are loads of buses that pass close to the market. Routes 9, 17, 23, 33, 38, 44, 61 Express, and 121 all go by 12th and Market Streets.

119

Pennsylvania Convention Center

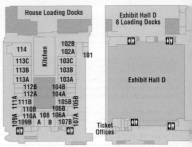

100 LEVEL (STREET LEVE

- House Loading Docks
- Exhibit Hall D — 8 Loading Docks
- 114
- 113C
- 113B
- 113A
- 112B
- 112A
- 111B
- 111A
- 110B
- 110A
- 109A
- 109B
- 108
- 106A
- 106B
- 107A
- 107B
- 105B
- 105A
- 104A
- 104B
- 103A
- 103B
- 103C
- 102A
- 102B
- 101
- Kitchen
- Exhibit Hall D
- Ticket Offices

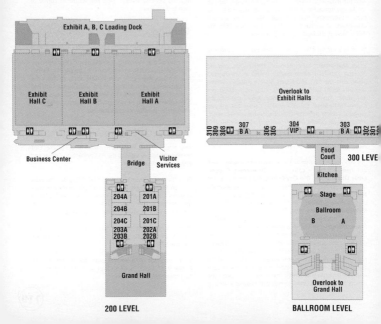

Exhibit A, B, C Loading Dock

Exhibit Hall C | Exhibit Hall B | Exhibit Hall A

Business Center | Bridge | Visitor Services

200 LEVEL

- 204A
- 204B
- 204C
- 203A
- 203B
- 201A
- 201B
- 201C
- 202A
- 202B
- Grand Hall

300 LEVE

- Overlook to Exhibit Halls
- 310
- 309
- 308
- 307 B A
- 306
- 305
- 304 VIP
- 303 B A
- 302
- 301
- Food Court

BALLROOM LEVEL

- Kitchen
- Stage
- Ballroom B A
- Overlook to Grand Hall

General Information

NFT Map: 3
Address: 1101 Arch St
                Philadelphia, PA 19107
Phone: 215-418-4700
Website: www.paconvention.com

Overview

Spanning six downtown city blocks and covering 1.3 million square-feet, the Pennsylvania Convention Center is gigantic; the second largest convention center in the Northeast, as a matter of fact. This would be wonderful indeed if conventioneers packed the place week after week but, because of union squabbles and poor city planning, such has not been the case. After years of bickering, the Convention Center is still not being used anywhere near its capacity which, if you're of the inclination, can work as an apt metaphor for the bureaucracy of the city at large: the party is ready to roll up in the penthouse suite, but the guests aren't allowed to use the elevator to get there. And to top it all off, there's the city's latest cockamamie plan for expansion, which will wipe out valued art spaces in the factory buildings just beyond.

Unless you are attending an event, the Convention Center is not open to the public. Ergo, it's not really a hangout. It's more, with its aimless brick rest-stop chic, a fist fight on the eyes. If you happen to be there for business, however, you will be pleased to note it has state-of-the-art meeting facilities, high-speed Internet access with gigabit LAN connections, and many of the other flashy amenities true-blue bizzers crave.

For the rest of us, it's still worth checking out the calendar of events listed on the Convention Center's website. Cool exhibits and events come along every year, including such faves as the Philadelphia Auto Show (www.phillyautoshow.com), the Wizard Comic Convention, and—for God's sake, people!—the Philadelphia Flower Show (www.theflowershow.com), to which the entire city kowtows every March.

As for eating in the area goes, it's as much a story about what to avoid as what to go to. Try as hard as possible to coax your friend into the Reading Terminal Market. It's chaotic, sure, but there's pretty much every cuisine you can think of, from fresh seafood to vegan cheesesteaks to Thai curries, and everyone can find something pleasing. We'd also recommend walking a couple of blocks to Chinatown, where there's cheap, amazing eats a-plenty.

How to Get There—Driving

From the Schuykill/76, take Exit 344/676 E. Once you're on 676 E, take the second exit, Broad Street. From the exit ramp, continue straight on Vine Street and follow all the huge signs that say "PA Convention Center." Turn right onto 12th Street and proceed two blocks to the Convention Center.

From I-95 S or N, take Exit 22/676 W. Once you're on 676 take the first exit, Broad Street. Turn right off of the exit ramp onto 15th Street. Turn left onto Vine Street (second light) then right onto 12th Street and proceed two blocks to the Convention Center.

Parking

There are 42 private lots located within a 7-block radius of the Convention Center. The only street parking in that area is at two-hour meters, with restrictions on Arch Street during rush hours (check the signs).

How to Get There—Mass Transit

All Regional Lines connect directly to the Convention Center via the Market East Station. From Market East, follow signs inside the station for the Convention Center. There's no need to go outside to get to the Convention Center, which is perfect on cold or rainy days.

The Market-Frankford line stops at the Pennsylvania Convention Center/11th Street Station for easy access to the center. If you're taking the Broad Street line, make a free transfer at City Hall for the Market-Frankford line.

Trolley routes 10, 11, 13, 34, and 36 go to the Juniper Station. Walk one block north to Arch Street and then one block east (right) to 12th Street.

Bus routes 12, 17, 23, 33, 38, 44, 48, and 121 all stop at the Convention Center.

Overview

One of Philadelphia's more overlooked limbs, the Northeast is barely noticed by locals who live in other neighborhoods. The only time they really pay attention to it is when there's another accident on Roosevelt Boulevard. As the oldest north- and south-running artery in the country, established over fifty years before I-95, the Boulevard is famous for having two of the most dangerous intersections in America.

Despite being treated as the least-favorite child by most Philadelphians, though, this area possesses just as much culture, shopping, nightlife, and restaurants as the rest of Philadelphia. Just on a more diffuse scale. Philly all around is a different kind of friendly, and the Northeast is a different kind of friendly again. With its own terms, food, and attitudes, the NE is too big and *special* to ignore.

O Landmarks

- **Burholme Park** · Cottman & Central Aves
- **Flyer's Skate Zone** · 10990 Decatur Rd
- **Knowlton Mansion** · 8001 Verree Rd
- **Nabisco Factory** · Comly Rd & Roosevelt Blvd
- **Pennypack Creek Park** · 8600 Verree Rd
- **Philadelphia International Airport** · 8000 Essington Ave
- **Theodore Roosevelt Memorial Boulevard** · Roosevelt Blvd

Farmers Markets

- **Oxford Circle** · 900 E Howell St
  Thursdays, 2 pm–6 pm, in season.

Nightlife

- **Bonk's Bar** · 3467 Richmond St
- **Chickie's and Pete's** · 11000 Roosevelt Blvd
- **The Grey Lodge** · 6235 Frankford Ave
- **Hop Angel Brauhaus** · 7980 Oxford Ave
- **Sweeney's Station Saloon** · 13639 Philmont Ave

Restaurants

- **Benny the Bum's** · 9991 Bustleton Ave
- **Bill's Deli** · 2000 Castor Ave
- **Bonk's Bar** · 3467 Richmond St
- **Chickie's and Pete's** · 4010 Robbins Ave
- **Chickie's and Pete's** · 11000 Roosevelt Blvd
- **The Dining Car** · 8826 Frankford Ave
- **Hinge Cafe** · 2652 E Somerset St
- **House of Thai** · 3520 Cottman Ave
- **Joe's Steaks & Soda Shop** · 6030 Torresdale Ave
- **Joseph's Pizza** · 7947 Oxford Ave
- **Macaroni's Restaurant** · 9315 Old Bustleton Ave
- **Mayfair Diner** · 7353 Frankford Ave
- **Moe's Deli** · 7360 Frankford Ave
- **Moonstruck** · 7955 Oxford Ave
- **Nick's Roast Beef** · 2212 Cottman Ave
- **Nifty Fifty's** · 2491 Grant Ave
- **Pho Le Lai** · 2844 St. Vincent St
- **Picanha** · 6501 Castor Ave
- **Rib Rack** · 2100 Tyson Ave
- **Santucci's Square Pizza** · 4010 Cottman Ave
- **Steve's Prince of Steaks** · 7200 Bustleton Ave
- **Sweet Lucy's Smokehouse** · 7500 State Road
- **Syrenka** · 3173 Richmond St
- **Tiffany Diner** · 9010 Roosevelt Blvd

Shopping

- **Custards Last Stand** · 7302 Rising Sun Ave
- **Dutch Country Farmers' Market** · 2031 Cottman Ave
- **Franklin Mills** · 1455 Franklin Mills Cir
- **Harry's Natural Food Store** · 1805 Cottman Ave
- **International Coins Unlimited** · 1825 Cottman Ave
- **Lipkin's Bakery** · 8013 Castor Ave
- **ReStore** · 3016 E Thompson St
- **Roosevelt Mall** · 2311 Cottman Ave

General Information

Websites: www.virtualnjshore.com
            www.shore-guide.com

Overview

Beginning in Sandy Hook in the north and extending down to Cape May in the south, the 127-mile Jersey Shore is a prime destination for weekenders and summer vacationers. People of all ages flock to the shore for its fishy-smelling waters and pebbly beaches. Some of these people may even have been known to you at one time.

There are many communities lining the shore, and each is known for its own distinct attractions, from sandy dunes and lighthouses to gambling and shopping (and a lot of other crap). Whatever their differences, all of the towns are known for their abundance of fresh seafood—by far the Shore's best asset. The Jersey Shore experience is an indispensable part of what it means to be a Philadelphian (and, no, not all memories involve fake IDs, ugly tattoos, and vomit—only most). If you're planning a trip to the shore, check out Virtual New Jersey Shore's calendar of events at www.virtualnjshore.com/events.html.

In 2012, the Jersey Shore was hit hard by Hurricane Sandy. Some communities were devastated and are still recovering. Rebuilding has been slow in some areas. Further, in 2013, a fire swept through the Jersey Shore Boardwalk (in Seaside Park and Seaside Heights), destroying much of what remained or had been rebuilt along the boardwalk after Hurricane Sandy.

Towns/Cities

Asbury Park

While efforts are being made to restore this "seaside ghost town," Asbury Park has struggled with its growing decrepitude since the July 4, 1970 race riots. In its heyday, Asbury Park was one of the most prominent and thriving seaside resorts along the Jersey Shore. The Convention Hall, designed in the 1920s, hosted The Rolling Stones, Jefferson Airplane, The Doors, The Who, and, of course, Bruce Springsteen (who adopted Asbury as his hometown). At one point, Asbury Park drew over half a million visitors to its wide tree-lined streets, swanky hotels, lively restaurants, and packed boardwalks. The beach is still beautiful, but today there are more empty lots than tourists. That may change soon. Look beneath the grit and you'll find intrepid yuppies (try Brickwall and Bistro Olé), a large LGBT community (try Georgies Bar or The Empress), and rockers of all ages (try the legendary Stone Pony, Wonder Bar, or Asbury Lanes).

Atlantic City

www.atlanticcitynj.com

Visitors expecting a Vegas-like wonderland are in for a serious surprise. Sure, Atlantic City features the same gambling and topless dancers as does Sin City, but AC doesn't shield its guests from the more distressing side of the gambling world. The winos, the bums, and the broke grandmothers are inescapable. And while the surrounding population sinks deeper into its own morass, the casinos keep getting glitzier, with additions like the swanky billion-dollar Borgata, a new convention center, and a new upscale shopping area for all the Gucci you'll want to buy with your winnings. Right.

Harrah's remains the premiere casino venue, regularly playing host to the World Series of Poker. Donald Trump himself owns two glittering casinos here, and the Atlantic Club provides a touch of old-school glam. Caesar's is one of the largest casinos in the city, while Bally's attracts a mixed clientele. When it comes to choosing a casino, you can't really go wrong—until you start dipping into Junior's college fund.

But gambling and strip joints aren't Atlantic City's only attractions. There is golf, sailing, fishing, shopping malls on boardwalks, and slums too! Plans for a new multi-billion-dollar state-of-the-art Convention Center and Grand Boulevard are currently in the works. Stay tuned.

Long Beach Island
www.longbeachisland.com
Perhaps the least-crowded and least-schlocky of all shore destinations, LBI is a family-oriented stretch of small and even smaller towns such as Beach Haven, Surf City, Loveladies, Harvey Cedars, and Barnegat. Each town has its own character (Harvey Cedars = $$$; Beach Haven = mellow) and one or two decent restaurants/attractions. However, without a boardwalk like Seaside Heights, LBI will fortunately never get hordes of teenage jerkbags cruising the main drag and puking in hotel rooms. Courses in sea kayaking, yoga, pottery, and photography are set against a panorama of waves, white sand, blue skies, and brilliant sunsets (thank you, New Jersey pollution!). Albert Music Hall (www.alberthall.org) hosts live country, folk, and bluegrass music year-round on Saturday nights. Broadway fans can take in their favorite song and dance routines at the Surflight Theatre (www.surflight.org).

Ocean City
Ocean City without the Boardwalk is like Paris without the Champs d' Elysées: so much of this Jersey Shore town's gestalt is fashioned down at the boardwalk. One of the last authentic walkways in the area, the Boardwalk is a mixture of classic and contemporary seaside attractions. The timeless 140-foot Ferris Wheel, the requisite rollercoaster, and the ubiquitous boardwalk bumper cars stand next to the newer mini-golf courses, water rides, and waterpark (Li'l Buc's Bay), where adults are admitted only with a child. It's easy to spend a packed day without leaving the ocean front, if you can subsist on a diet of soda and french fries. Boozehounds take note: this former Methodist retreat is still completely alcohol-free. Check out the Ocean City Ghost Tour, a candlelit walking tour which runs every evening between the end of May through October, where guides recount spooky tales of local folklore (www.ghosttour.com).

Cape May
www.capemay.com
Deemed worthy of historic preservation in 1976 by the National Register of Historic Places, Cape May is as distinguished as it gets at the Jersey Shore. Here you'll find the biggest collection of Victorian houses in the country; the elaborately built pastel-colored homes are on every block and run the gamut of Victorian sensibility from Mansard and Gothic style, to Colonial Revival, Queen Anne, and Italianate-influenced homes. The Mid-Atlantic Center for the Arts offers hourly walking tours explaining the history and significance of these mansions. If you'd rather trek solo, don't miss the Abbey Bed 'n Breakfast on the corner of Gurney Street and Columbia Avenue, and the 15 elaborately decorated period rooms at Emlen Physick Estate, located at 1048 Washington Street.

Point Pleasant
www.pointpleasantbeach.com
Point Pleasant offers up the archetypal beach experience: swimming, surfing, sun bathing, ice cream, Fun House, etc. The south end of the

beach is public, but has no lifeguard on duty, while Bradshaw Beach at the north end requires an entry fee. The Sinatra House (on the corner of Water Street and Boardwalk) heats things up at night with Old Blue Eyes' crooning out the window. There's no shortage of bars or dance clubs to choose from.

Sandy Hook

Think pristine white sandy beaches, old wooden boardwalks, surf fishing, historic lighthouses, bird observatories, salt marshes, and you've got a good picture of Sandy Hook. Located at the northern tip of the NJ Shore, Sandy Hook is also known as home of the Ocean Institute— the oldest working lighthouse in America.

Seaside Heights

www.seasideheights.net

This is the spot for the surfing crowd. Seaside Heights touts itself as having "some of the top lifeguards anywhere," and its public beaches are open year-round. Beyond the waves and surf, the bustling boardwalk is another attraction. Local pubs and nightclubs line the vast stretch of wooden planks. All of them are bad. If you're older than 17 ½, this isn't the place for you.

Spring Lake

This 100-year-old, quiet family resort town is comprised of tranquil coastline, a non-commercial boardwalk, and sand dune beaches. The main street is full of quaint shops, gourmet restaurants, and cozy B&Bs. If you're looking for privacy, aim for a mid-week getaway, as the four beaches get crowded on the weekends. The area is known for great scuba diving (including an off-shore ship wreck to explore), and fresh- and salt-water fishing. If you're looking for high-energy activity, this may not be your spot, but it remains a romantic getaway for couples.

The Wildwoods

www.wildwoodsnj.com

Little-known fact: the collection of three resort communities that make up the Wildwoods— including Wildwood Crest, The City of North Wildwood, and the City of Wildwood—is known as the "Mecca of the Kiting World." *Condé Nast Traveler Magazine* also chose Wildwood as the "Best Sports Beach." Activities include golfing, shopping, deep-sea fishing, kayaking, biking, beach aerobics, water-parks, and a large beach Ultimate Frisbee tournament in the summer. Well-known fact: there are neon-drenched kitschy motels galore and a massively trashy honky-tonk boardwalk, complete with a blaring motorized tram to tote your fat vacationing ass from one end to the other. Kids can't get enough of the Morey Piers Amusement Park (www.moreyspiers.com), but adults definitely will.

Attractions

Barnegat Lighthouse

609-494-2016

Once upon a time, there were actually two lighthouses built in Barnegat. The first, standing at a puny 40 feet, was built in 1835 and crumbled shortly after. The second lighthouse, which soars nearly four times taller than its predecessor, at a majestic 165 feet, was built in 1859 and still stands to this day. Located at the north end of Long Beach Island, the Barnegat Lighthouse has become the symbol of the Jersey Shore. The red and white structure, retired in 1927, is affectionately referred to by the locals as "Old Barney." Barney is open for public viewing 9 am-4:30 pm during the winter and until 9:30 pm in the summer months.

Cape May Lighthouse

609-884-5404; Hours vary: Open daily April- November; $5 adults, $1 children; Free Parking

The 157-foot tall lighthouse is actually the third built in Cape May. The first (built in 1823) and the second (built in 1847) were both destroyed by erosion. The one that shines its beacon today, located in Cape May Point State Park's Lower Township, has been standing since 1859 and was built with bricks from the 1847 version. It's worth huffing and puffing up the 199 steps for spectacular panoramic vistas of the Cape May Peninsula. The lighthouse is currently managed by the Mid-Atlantic Center for the Arts (MAC). The non-profit group sponsors cultural and artistic events and offers daily guided tours (www.capemaymac.org).

Cape May Point State Park

609-884-2159; Open sunrise to sunset

Mockingbirds, warblers, and sparrows, oh my! Located just off the southern end of the Garden State Parkway, this 253-acre no-fee park is a haven for bird-lovers. Several trails lead to ponds, marshes, dunes, and forest habitats where all sorts of migratory birds can be spotted. Following one of the three main hiking trails, the Red Trail (0.5 mile), the Yellow Trail (1.5 miles), or the Blue Trail (2 miles), is the best way to explore the park. If you're looking to spice up your vacation with education, the park hosts nature clubs and programs for children.

Edwin B. Forsythe National Wildlife Refuge

b/w Brick Township & Brigantine

This refuge encompasses over 43,000 acres and has two divisions (Brigantine and Barnegat). Bird-watching, nature walks, great views of protected wetlands, and learning about migratory bird habitats are the main deal here. For more information, go to http://forsythe.fws.gov.

Island Beach State Park

This majestic barrier island is made up of 3,000 acres of preserved land and over ten miles of pure, untainted white sand. The park is filled with historic buildings, hiking and biking trails, naturalist programs, bathhouses, and pristine bird-watching spots. This natural wonder is a must-see for outdoor enthusiasts, and in complete contrast with the crazed, crowded Seaside Heights just up the road. Highly recommended.

Lucy the Elephant

9200 Atlantic Ave, Margate, NJ, 609-823-6473;
www.lucytheelephant.org,
Summer hours Mon-Sat 10 am-8 pm,
and Sun 10 am-5 pm

The legendary 65-foot wooden elephant, which stands mid-stride overlooking the sea, is one of the Shore's oddest intrigues. Built in 1881, Lucy's stout legs serve as a 350-step stairwell linking the bottom floor with the anterior rooms and howdah. She can be seen without binoculars from up to eight miles away. The 90-ton mammoth pachyderm was added to the National Registry of Historic Places in 1971 and now offers tours for groups of ten or more. Admission is $5 for adults and $3 for children under 12. Recommended.

Rutgers University Marine Field Station/ Great Bay Boulevard

Great Bay Blvd, Tuckerton, NJ

A completely overlooked gem amidst a morass of mid-prole dreams, the drive out to Rutgers University's Marine Field Station along Great Bay Boulevard is absolutely incredible. Low wetlands, small wooden bridges, lots of wildlife, ruined canneries, amazing sunsets, and almost no people make this about as far an experience from Seaside Heights, Wildwood, or AC as you can get. You can find cheap-ass boat rentals along the Boulevard, so you can explore, go crabbing or fishing or swimming, or just be cool. The Field Station has tours occasionally, so for more information, go to: http://marine.rutgers.edu/cool/Info/directions.html.

Sea Girt Lighthouse

Beach Blvd & Ocean Ave, 732-974-0514;
Open one Sunday/month

Sea Girt, once appropriately called "Wreck Pond," earned its menacing name because of the countless shipwrecks in the Manasquan River. With the construction of the lighthouse in 1896, which warned boats of the upcoming shoreline, "Wreck Pond" traded in its ill-omened moniker for the less threatening "Sea Girt." The lighthouse closed after the Second World War, 50 years after its opening,

and has been preserved as a historic site. The site has become a popular destination for elementary school fieldtrips, and public tours are given once a month on Sundays.

Twin Lights

732-872-1814; www.twinlightslighthouse.com;
Memorial Day-Labor Day 10 am-4:30 pm daily, Rest of the year, Wed-Sun 10 am-4:30 pm.

Towering 200 feet above sea level in Highlands, the two-towered Navesink Light station has been used as the shore's primary lighthouse since 1828. The lighthouse standing today was built in 1862, and has been open as a museum since it was acquired by the state in 1967. A climb to the top offers an unbeatable ocean-view panorama and the exhibition gallery offers historical background on the site.

Wildwood Boardwalk

16th Ave to Cresse Ave; Open daily Palm Sunday weekend through Columbus Day

Wildwood is filled with more rides than Disneyland, including the East Coast's tallest and fastest wooden coaster, the Great White. There are five amusement piers to visit with a cornucopia of carnival games, souvenir shops, and food stands (rumor has it that there are more pizza joints here per square foot than anywhere else in the world). If you're lucky at Skee-Ball, you may go home with a pair of fuzzy dice for your rearview. A tram line makes transportation between venues fast and easy. Dust off your poodle skirt for DooWop '50s Night, or mingle with the other car connoisseurs at Classic Car shows. Check out the *Cape May Times* newspaper for a calendar of events.

How to Get There—Driving

From Center City, cross the Franklin Bridge into New Jersey and follow signs to Cherry Hill (Route 38) and the beaches (stay to your left). Once on Route 38, get into the right hand lane and merge onto I-70. Take I-70 until you hit the I-72 Junction East and keep right around the Circle. Follow I-72 for 26 miles and you'll end up at the Jersey Shore. If you leave on a weekday and it's not rush hour, you can make the journey in an hour and a half. At all other times, don't leave without your mix tapes, as you'll most likely be sitting in traffic.

From the northeast, go over the Tacony-Palmyra Bridge onto Route 73 S. Head to the I-70 intersection and drive east. At the I-72 Circle, take 72 E to Long Beach Island (about 26 miles). From the south, take Route 42 E to Route 35 N, which takes you to Route 70 E. Or take the 42 to the NJ Turnpike and get off at Exit 4 (Route 73 S). Follow the directions above.

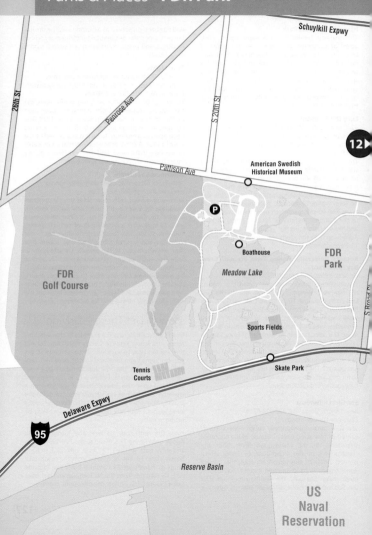

General Information

NFT Maps:	Adjacent to the west boundary of Map 12
Address:	2000 Pattison Ave Philadelphia, PA 19145
Phone:	n/a
Website:	www.phila.gov/parksandrecreation/Pages/default.aspx, www.fdrpark.org

Overview

Although thousands of fans pass through the south Philly stadiums each time there's a Phillies or Eagles game, the vast majority of them completely miss FDR Park, sitting there in plain view on the other side of Broad Street. The park offers baseball, softball, and rugby fields, tennis courts, and the infamous FDR Skate Park, which sits in the shadows directly under I-95 (more on that later). What was once a marsh is now home to the aforementioned fields and courts as well as ponds and creeks, the American Swedish Historical Museum, a gazebo and boathouse, and even a golf course, just west of the main park area.

American Swedish Historical Museum

This museum's library and various galleries are worth a visit if you're interested in Swedish history. The architecture of the building itself was intended to be a blend of Swedish and American styling; we don't know if it achieved that or not, but we will go so far as to say that it looks nice.

The Skate Park

The modern hallmark of FDR Park is the skate park. It started as a pathetic attempt on the city's part to mollify skaters barred from downtown Love Park, but has evolved into a mecca for skaters—and not just local ones. Mainly built by volunteers ("built by skaters, for skaters" is a phrase that comes up often), the shadowy collection of concrete includes installations known as the Bunker and the Minefield, among others; but regardless of the naming scheme, the park is not actually a battlefield unless BMX riders and skaters show up at the same time. Bikes are technically allowed in the park, but are generally unwelcome by the skaters, who say the bikes cause damage. Prepare to stand your ground if you show up with only two wheels.

As with many places in Philadelphia, the skate park is not for the faint of heart. It's not a terribly welcoming place in either attitude or architecture; the word "hardcore" comes to mind in describing the regulars, and this is *not* a beginner's skate park. If you're just starting out, look elsewhere. But if you're an intermediate skater looking for a challenging park in Philly, you won't do better than FDR.

How to Get There—Driving

The driving directions for FDR are essentially the same as the routes to get to the Sports Complex; you just want to end up on the west side of Broad Street instead of the east side. The most direct route is to take I-95 to Exit 17, go north on Broad Street, and make a left onto Pattison Avenue.

Parking

There's plenty of free parking inside the park.

How to Get There—Mass Transit

Take the Broad Street subway line south to the last stop-Pattison. When you come up out of the station, turn to face Broad Street. Cross Broad Street and walk to Pattison Avenue. You can enter the park just ahead on Pattison, on the left.

1. Neuropsychology Laboratories
2. Language and Communication Center
3. 3210 Cherry Street
4. Academic Building
5. 3201 Arch Street
6. Campus Security Office
7. Frederic O Hess Engineering Research Lab
8. Nesbitt Hall
9. Leonard Pearlstein Business Learning Center
10. Matheson Hall
11. Korman Center
12. Disque Hall
13. Bossone Research Enterprise Center
14. LeBow Engineering Center
15. Center for Automation Technology
16. Main Building
17. Randell Hall
18. Curtis Hall
19. Alumni Enginering Labs

Center City Campus
20. Myer Feinstein Polyclinic
21. Bobst Building
22. North Tower (Main Hospital Entrance)
23. South Tower
25. New College Building H
26. Franklin Office Center, 1427 Vine Street
27. Stiles Alumni Hall
28. Bellet Building
29. 221 N Broad Street
30. 219 N Broad Street
31. 207 N Broad Street

Center City Hahnemann Campus

Henry Ave/Queen Ln Campus

General Information

NFT Map: 2, 14, 23
Mailing Address: 3141 Chestnut St
Philadelphia, PA 19104
Phone: 215-895-2000
Website: www.drexel.edu

Overview

You could say that Drexel is experiencing a growth spurt. In the past decade, Drexel has amassed a medical school, a law school, and two new academic buildings with state-of-the-art technology. With change comes a bigger student body—the University is adding an additional underclassmen dorm building just to house everyone. Recently, Drexel made the US News & World Report's top ten national universities in Pennsylvania list.

The actual campus is composed of three locations, though most classes are held at the University City Main Campus. Nursing and Health students hang out at the Center City Hahnemann Campus, and students at the Drexel University College of Medicine take their classes at the Queen Lane Medical Campus.

There are many extracurricular activities to keep students occupied, including 140 different student clubs. Athletic types should head over to the John A Daskalakis Athletic Center; an impressive facility housing a swimming pool and indoor basketball/volleyball and squash courts.

Part of Drexel's uniqueness stems from its location. Instead of being a closed campus, their buildings are scattered among the streets of Philly—which also contributes to the lack of community many students feel. Drexel students spend lots of time off-campus anyway thanks to Drexel Co-op, one of the world's oldest and largest work-experience programs, allowing students up to 18 months of internships while still in school.

Tuition

Students choose between enrolling in a four- or five-year undergraduate degree program. The former will set you back around $43,135 a year, while the 5-year program costs about $26,125 a year (for tuition only, excluding fees, housing, and meal plans). Over 90% of students receive financial aid, and they actually encourage all students to apply regardless of whether they think they're eligible or not. As of yet, there are no financial aid incentives for students who can funnel beer through multiple orifices.

Sports

Calling all jocks! Drexel has 16 NCAA Division 1 teams to try out for, and they've been working on a major expansion of their athletic center. If you're not the ultra-competitive type, there are more casual activities, like the one-day bench-press or dart competitions. Various intramural sports also run year-round, such as beach volleyball and flag football. For the even less physically inclined, check out the Recreation Sports Office's fall term health and wellness program. Designed specifically to help you cope with the stress of those ruthless calculus assignments or how to manage those unyielding cheesesteak and Yuengling diets, the seminars are popular ways to help you survive your campus experience.

Culture on Campus

Like so many educational institutions, Drexel has its share of co-curricular and extra-curricular fun stuff. One particular favorite is the free Friday Night Movie Series that often showcases newly released flicks. Creative arts and progressive politics get equal time on DUTV's broadcasts, and the hipsters spinning at WKDU FM get a listen well beyond the campus. If theater sparks your interest, the Drexel Players put on one play per term, from musicals to dark comedies. And come early for the annual comedic performance, because tickets sell out early! (Past performers have included Lewis Black and Dane Cook.) Drexel has hosted cool theater companies for a full season in residence to great critical acclaim, so keep an eye out for future programs that bring pros to these stages. And due to the diverse student body, students can enjoy a cappella performances, impromptu cricket matches, and a Straight and Gay Alliance dance all in one weekend.

Departments

Log onto www.drexel.edu/contact for a more complete university directory.

Undergraduate Admissions	215-895-2400
Alumni Relations	888-DU-GRADS
Athletics	215-895-1999
Bursar, Office of Student Accounts	215-895-1445
Career Management: Steinbright Career Development (SCDC)	215-895-2185
Co-operative Education	215-895-2185
Computing Resources (IRT)	215-895-2698
Drexel Directory Assistance	215-895-2000
Facilities Management	215-895-1700
Financial Aid	215-895-2537
International Programs	215-895-1704
Institutional Advancement	215-895-2600
Library-Drexel University City Main Campus	215-895-1500
Library-Health Sciences Libraries	215-762-7631
President	215-895-2100
Provost	215-895-2200
Research Administration	215-895-5849
Sports	215-895-1999
Student Life- Drexel University City Main Campus	215-895-2506
Student Life- Center City Hahnemann Campus	215-762-1400
Student Resource Center (SRC)	215-895-2300
University Relations	215-895-1530

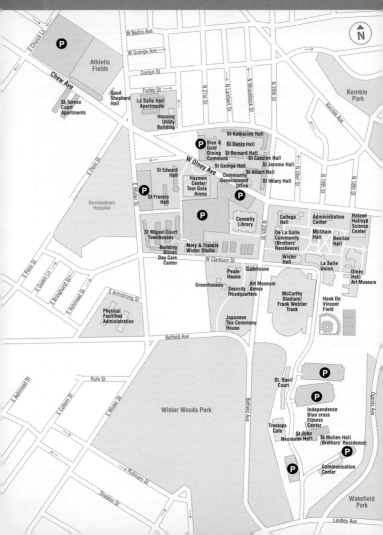

General Information

Address: 1900 W Olney Ave
          Philadelphia, PA 19141
Phone: 215-951-1000
Website: www.lasalle.edu

Overview

Founded in 1863 by the De La Salle Christian Brothers, La Salle University is a private Roman Catholic university located on a 100-acre campus not far from Center City. Between its School of Arts & Sciences, School of Nursing, and School of Business Administration, La Salle enrolls over 6,200 students a year in 61 different undergraduate and graduate degree programs. La Salle's ongoing dedication to its Roman Catholic roots is evident in its strong focus on community service and the existence of a theology and ministry graduate program.

Tuition

La Salle's 2013–2014 tuition was $37,700, and the basic room and board costs were $12,000. Just remember these figures do not include books, supplies, lab fees, sacramental ale, or personal expenses.

Sports

La Salle's student body is extremely athletic, with more than 500 of its undergraduates participating on one or more of the twenty-three NCAA Division I varsity athletic teams (not to mention the students playing intramural sports). Men's teams include baseball, basketball, crew, cross-country, golf, soccer, swimming, tennis, and indoor and outdoor track & field. Women's teams include basketball, crew, cross-country, field hockey, lacrosse, soccer, softball, swimming, tennis, volleyball, and indoor and outdoor track & field. The football team was dropped after a stellar 0-10 season. The Explorers basketball teams are also members of the Big Five; Philly's own annual basketball backyard rumble.

Culture on Campus

The La Salle University Art Museum (Lower level of Olney Hall, 1900 W Olney Ave, 215-951-1221) proudly touts itself as the only permanent collection of paintings, drawings, and sculpture from the West at any university museum in the Philadelphia region. The permanent collection focuses on European and American landscape, portraiture, still-life, and abstract paintings spanning the Middle Ages to modern times. Smaller collections include Old Master prints and drawings, illustrated rare bibles, ancient Greek terra cotta pottery, African tribal art, and Japanese prints from the 19th- and 20th-centuries. The museum is open Monday–Friday from 10 am to 4 pm on weekends by appointment, with varying hours during the summer and holidays; call ahead before planning a visit. Access to the museum is free (though donations are encouraged). Group tours are offered by appointment.

Departments

Log onto www.lasalle.edu/contact for a more complete university directory.

Undergraduate Admissions 215-951-1500
Graduate Admissions 215-951-1100
Continuing Studies Admissions...... 215-951-1655

General Information:

NFT Map: 23
Address: School House Ln & Henry Ave
             Philadelphia, PA 19144
Phone: 215-951-2700
Website: www.philau.edu

Overview

Founded in 1884 and long known as the College of Textiles & Sciences (a.k.a. "Textiles"), Philadelphia University was finally granted university status by the state of Pennsylvania in 1999 and now operates six schools—Architecture, Business Administration, Design & Media, Liberal Arts, Science & Health, and Engineering & Textiles. The University offers more than forty undergraduate and graduate degree programs to its 3,200 full- and part-time students. The school is known for its interdisciplinary approach to higher education, combining a liberal arts base with professional training. The private university is located on a 100-acre campus about twenty minutes away from Center City, and is otherwise outside of the city's consciousness, despite its name.

Tuition

For the academic year, a full-time undergraduate's tuition and fees will total around $32,990 with an additional $10,600 for room and board. For more information about extra fees, alternative board plans, or financial aid packages, call 215-951-2940.

Sports

The Philadelphia University Rams compete at the Division II level in eleven sports: men's and women's basketball, cheerleading, cross country, rowing, soccer, and tennis, men's golf and baseball, and women's field hockey, lacrosse, softball, and volleyball. The men's soccer team is a tough competitor at the Division I level. Athletic scholarships are available to students in all varsity sports. Games are free and open to the public. For scores and game highlights, call the Rams Hotline on 215-951-2852.

Philadelphia University also offers club sports and intramural teams, open to all students, staff, and faculty, that allow participants to compete in athletic events on campus at a less rigorous level than that of the varsity sports teams.

Culture on Campus

The Design Center, located in the Goldie Paley House (4200 Henry Ave, 215-951-2860; thedesigncenter. tumblr.com), is one of Philadelphia's most underrated exhibition spaces. The Hollywood rancher-style building holds over 200,000 artifacts related to textiles collected by the university over the past 125 years, from ecclesiastical attire and altar pieces to 19th-century haute-couture and a library of 19th- and 20th-century fabric. The center aims to explore the meaning of design in our everyday lives through ever-changing furniture and design exhibitions and remains a definite must-see for anyone with even a latent interest in fashion and design.

Departments

Log onto www.philau.edu/directory.asp for a more complete university directory.

Undergraduate Admissions	215-951-2800
Graduate Admissions	215-951-2943
School of Liberal Arts	215-951-2600
School of Architecture	215-951-2896
School of Design & Media	215-951-2700
School of Business Administration	215-951-2810
School of Science & Health	215-951-2870
School of Engineering & Textiles	215-951-2750

St Joseph's University

1. Lancaster Court
2. Merion Gardens
3. Wynnewood Hall
4. City Avenue
   Residence alls
5. Ashwood Hall
6. Overbrook Hall
7. Michael J Morris Quad
8. Alumni House
9. St Alphonsus House-
   Jesuit Residence
10. Tara Hall
11. Sourin Hall
12. LaFarge Hall
13. Quirk Hall
14. Power Plant
15. Simpson Hall-University Bookstore
16. Chapel of St Joseph
17. Wolfington Hall-Campus Ministry
18. Campion Hall
19. Science Center
20. Francis A Drexel Library
21. Bellermine Hall
22. Barblin/Lonergan Hall
23. Post Hall
24. Mandeville Hall
25. Barry Annex-Center
    for International Programs
26. Barry Hall
27. Flanigan Hall
28. ELS Language Center
29. Alumni Memorial Fieldhouse
30. AFROTC Program
31. Claver House-Honors
    Department
32. St Mary's Hall
33. McShain Hall/Haub
    Executive Center
34. St Albert's Annex
35. St Albert's Hall
36. Xavier Hall
37. Bronstein Hall-Office
    of Undergraduate Admissions
38. St Thomas Hall-Office
    of Financial Assistance
39. Jordan Hall
40. Boland Hall
41. Regis Annex
42. Regis Hall-President's Office
43. Loyola Center and Carriage
    House-Jesuit Residence
44. Hogan Hall
45. Sullivan Annex
46. Sullivan Hall
47. University Press-Merion
48. Human Resources-University
    Communications
49. University Press-Bala Cynwyd
50. Office of Development-5th Floor
    (off map, at 50th St & City Ave)

St Joseph's University

General Information

Address: 5600 City Ave
            Philadelphia, PA 19131
Phone: 610-660-1000
Website: www.sju.edu

Overview

Founded in 1851, St. Joseph's University is a Catholic college located on a 65-acre campus in western Philadelphia and Montgomery County. The 7,700 students (4,500 of them traditional undergraduates) are schooled in the Jesuit tradition with a strong liberal arts-focused curriculum that fosters rigorous and open-minded inquiry and maintains high academic standards.

St. Joe's also counts itself among the 142 schools in the country with a Phi Beta Kappa chapter and AACSB business school accreditation. With 75 undergraduate and 47 graduate programs to choose from, students have a variety of academic options.

But co-eds at St. Joe's aren't *all* work and no play. Following the men's basketball team's thrilling run to the Elite Eight in the NCAA tourney a few years back, the school is suddenly garnering national attention. Romance seems to be in the air as well, as the long list of "Hawkmate" wedding announcements in the alumni newsletter and the ever-busy campus chapel can attest.

Tuition

Tuition for the 2013-2014 academic year was $38,880, and room and board was an additional $13,232. Of course, these prices exclude student fees, books, and getting the 'Benz waxed.

Sports

If you see a car with a bumper sticker that reads "Friends don't let friends go to Villanova," it's very likely headed here on game days. Even when St. Joe's isn't playing its crosstown rival, "The Hawk Will Never Die!" can be heard echoing from the Alumni Memorial Fieldhouse throughout the school year. In addtion to the championship men's and women's basketball squads, St. Joseph's fields teams in twenty varsity sports including cross-country, lacrosse, rowing, soccer, tennis, and track & field for men and women, men's baseball and golf, and women's softball and field hockey. The teams compete in Division I of the National Collegiate Athletic Association and belong to the Atlantic 10 as well as Philly's own Big Five. SJU athletics, however, extend much further than varsity competition. Hundreds of students participate in intramural and club sports; thousands, including alumni and friends of the university, make the Fieldhouse and adjoining Student/Sports Recreation Center a thriving area on campus year-round. Visit www.sjuhawks.com for news and events on Hawks of all ages.

Culture on Campus

The University Gallery at Boland Hall (www.sju.edu/int/resources/gallery, 5600 City Ave, 610-660-1840) hosts eight art shows from September through May. The first five exhibitions feature professional artists who are mostly, but not exclusively, from the area. (Anyone may submit slides for consideration.) The sixth is the Senior Arts Thesis Exhibition that highlights the year-long projects of the senior art majors. Then there's a culminating Student Arts Festival that is an all-day celebration of art, music, and theater. Finally, the year closes with the Overbrook High School displaying their students' work. The University Gallery is open and free to the public throughout the school year Monday-Friday from 9 am to 7 pm and on Saturdays from 10 am to 1 pm.

The Department of Fine & Performing Arts is also home to the Cap & Bells Dramatic Arts Society, the University Singers, and the Bluett Theatre. For specific event information call 610-660-1840 or visit www.sju.edu/research-area/fine-and-performing-arts.

Departments

Log onto www.sju.edu/academic-departments-directory for a university directory and links to division and department web pages.

Undergraduate Admissions 888-BE-A-HAWK
College of Arts & Sciences 610-660-1282
Haub School of Business 610-660-1645
University College
  (Continuing Education) 610-660-1267
Graduate Arts & Sciences............. 610-660-1289
Graduate Admissions 610-660-1101
Registrar's Office 610-660-1011

General Information

Address: 1801 N Broad St
Philadelphia, PA 19122
Phone: 215-204-7000
Website: www.temple.edu

Overview

Every Philly native's safety school, Temple has risen in national standing and prominence to a point where graduating alumni (besides the Coz, who has always shown much love for the Owl) can feel very good about the quality of education they received. The school is pretty damn huge: more than 34,000 students in seventeen separate schools and colleges crowd its lecture halls. Education at Temple spans five regional campuses, including the flagship Main Campus, Health Sciences Campus, and Center City Campus in Philadelphia, as well as Temple University at Ambler and a suburban campus—Tyler School of Art—in Elkins Park. The university also has an education center in Harrisburg as well as international campuses in Tokyo, Japan, and Rome, Italy.

Tuition

For the 2013-2014 academic year, full-time undergraduate tuition and fees for Pennsylvania residents averaged $13,406, while out-of-state residents paid an average of $23,432 (although tuition sometimes varies depending on the school). Room and board for all undergraduate students averaged $9,000. Books, lab fees, and personal expenses are in addition to these prices. Graduate student tuition, fees, and expenses vary by department.

Sports

Perhaps it's better not to speak of the once miserable football team, which lost its membership in the Big East in 2004. Alas, in 2012, the team made its way back into the the Big East, now called the American Athletic Conference, so hope abounds. On the positive side, there are the hugely successful men's and women's basketball teams, who play their games in the sparkling Liacouras Center, a 10,200-seat multi-purpose venue that also hosts a full range of concerts, dramatic presentations, and exhibitions. The Center is located less than two miles from City Hall. Public bus and subway transportation can take you directly to the center. If you're driving, parking is no problem—there's a connected parking garage as well as a number of well-lighted surface lots nearby. For more information call 215-204-2400 or visit www.liacourascenter.com.

Culture on Campus

The Boyer College of Music and Dance hosts the Temple University Concert Series—over 200 recitals, concerts, master classes, and lectures presented by faculty, students, and renowned guest artists. Classical music, jazz, and dance are just a taste of the series' fare. Call 215-204-8301 for info on specific events or visit www.temple.edu/boyer.

The Tyler School of Art features public programs in many forms that are offered at various campus locations, in the galleries, and in the community. Tyler Gallery (Elkins Park, 7725 Penrose Ave, 215-782-2776) in Tyler Hall holds exhibitions each year that exhibit works from emerging area artists as well as Tyler students.

Penrose Gallery (Elkins Park, 7725 Penrose Ave, 215-782-2776) in Penrose Hall has student-curated exhibitions (known as "Produce") as well as many other student retrospectives and installations. Other informal spaces within Penrose and Tyler Halls host many more student shows each year. On Main Campus the Architecture Department installs student works regularly throughout the school year in a flexible installation space in its building. Visit tyler.temple.edu for more information.

The Temple Theater Department, which runs out of the School of Communications and Theater, puts on three to four dramatic and comedic plays during each of the fall and spring semesters. Visit www.temple.edu/theater for ticket information and dates.

Departments

Visit https://directory.temple.edu/search/ for other university phone numbers and email addresses.

College of Health Professions 215-204-7543
Tyler School of Art 215-782-2828
Fox School of Business
and Management 215-204-7676
School of Communications
and Theater 215-204-8421
School of Dentistry 215-707-2803
College of Education 215-204-8011
College of Engineering 215-204-7800
Beasley School of Law 215-204-7861
College of Liberal Arts 215-204-7743
School of Medicine 215-707-7000
School of Pharmacy 215-707-4990
College of Science and Technology 215-204-2888
School of Tourism
and Hospitality Management 215-204-8701

University of Pennsylvania

1. 3216 Chancellor
2. Pafestra
3. Hutchinson Gym
4. Ringe Squash Courts
5. Rittenhouse Laboratories
6. Dunning Coaches' Center
7. Weightman Hall
8. Moore School Building
9. Skirkanich Hall
10. Levine Hall
11. Towne Building
12. Music Building
13. Music Annex
14. Morgan Building
15. Vegalos Labs of the IAST
16. Meyerson Hall
17. Fisher Fine Arts Library
   /Duhring Wing
18. Irvine Auditorium
19. Jaffe Building
20. Van Pelt Library
21. College Hall
22. Houston Hall
23. Dietrich Graduate Library
24. Sweeten Alumni House
25. Logan Hall
26. Williams Hall
27. Silverman Hall
28. Gittis Hall
29. Pepper Hall
30. Tanenbaum Hall
31. 3401 Walnut St
32. La Terrasse
33. Franklin Building
34. 133 S 36th St
35. Penn Center for Rehabilitation & Care
36. Institute of Contemporary Art
37. Sansom Place West
38. Iron Gate Theater
   /Christian Association
39. Greenfield Intercultural Center
40. Newman Center
41. Addams Hall
42. 202 S 36th
43. The ARCH
44. Annenberg School
45. 3615/3619
46. Annenberg Center
47. Stiteler Hall
48. Graduate Education
49. Soloman Labs
51. Caster Building
52. Class of 1920 Commons
53. Clinical Research Building
56. Nursing Education Building
57. Biomedical Research Building
58. Stellar-Chance Laboratories
59. Blockley Hall
60. John Morgan Building
61. Anatomy-Chemistry Building

62. Richards Laboratories/Goddard Labs
63. Leidy Laboratories/Kaplan Wing/
   Mudd Lab
64. Lynch Laboratory
65. Rosenthal Building
66. Mabel Pew Myrin Pavlion
67. Copp Pavilion
68. Wright/Saunders Building
69. Scheie Eye Institute
70. Heart Institute/Mutch Building
71. Medical Science Research Laboratory
72. 3910 Building
73. Kelly Writers House
74. Fels Institute of Government

Wharton Business School
47. Colonial Penn Center / Locust House
52. McNeil Building
53. Lauder Fischer Hall
73. Huntsman Hall
74. Steinberg Conference Center
75. Vance Hall

General Information

NFT Map: 14
Address: 3451 Walnut St
Philadelphia, PA 19104
Phone: 215-898-5000
Website: www.upenn.edu

Overview

Ladies and gentlemen, this is Pennsylvania's Ivy League school, and don't you forget it. One of the oldest universities in the country and the first to institute a modern liberal arts curriculum, the University of Pennsylvania was established in 1749 by founding father Benjamin Franklin.

Today, with nearly 10,000 undergraduate students and 10,000 grad students enrolled in its schools, UPenn consistently ranks among the top ten universities in the annual *U.S. News & World Report* survey. The Wharton School is considered one of the country's top three business schools, and Penn's other graduate programs all rank among the top ten in their fields.

The urban campus spans a substantial 269 acres of West Philadelphia, and includes buildings by notable architects such as Frank Furness, Louis Kahn, Robert Venturi, and Denise Scott Brown. Locals once razzed UPenn students for sticking close to the campus walls, but there's no doubt that recent 'Penntrification' has changed once-decaying University City for the better. If only we could have Fresh Grocer and White Dog without the Gap and Anne Taylor. Well, you can't win them all.

Tuition

Ahem. In the 2013-2014 academic year, an undergraduate student's tuition and fees totaled $45,890, with an additional $10,000 for room and board. These figures do not include books, supplies, lab fees, furriers, therapists, polo attire, or other personal expenses. While the high tuition rate and abundance of business types has earned Penn a reputation as a "rich kids' school," in fact, about fifty-five percent of the undergraduate student body receives some form of financial aid from the university.

Sports

All twenty-eight of Penn's sports teams, nicknamed "the Quakers," compete in the NCAA Division I Ivy League conference. Men's Division I teams include baseball, basketball, fencing, football, golf, lacrosse, rowing, soccer, squash, swimming, tennis, track/cross-country, and wrestling. Women's Division I teams include basketball, fencing, field hockey, gymnastics, lacrosse, rowing, soccer, softball, squash, swimming, tennis, track/cross-country, and volleyball. All intercollegiate athletic events are free and open to the public, with the exception of football and basketball games, wrestling matches, and the famous Penn Relays, which all charge admission. Tickets to these events can be purchased at the Penn Athletic Ticket Office at 215-898-6151. Box office hours are Monday through Friday, 10 am-3 pm. You can check out the full roster of all Penn sports events at www.pennathletics.com.

Culture on Campus

The Annenberg Center is a nationally renowned non-profit multi-disciplinary performance venue that offers 170 music, theater, and dance performances every year through the program *Penn Presents*. The Annenberg Center serves as a resource not only for the immediate university community, but for the entire Delaware Valley region. Check out www.annenbergcenter.org for more details.

The Institute of Contemporary Art (118 S 36th St) exhibits the work of established and emerging contemporary visual artists. Entrance to the exhibition space is free for everyone. It wasn't always this way, so we suggest visiting before they change their minds and want your cash again. For more information, visit www.icaphila.org or call 215-898-5911.

The University of Pennsylvania Museum of Archeology and Anthropology (3260 South St, 215-898-4000) has earned international acclaim as a leading resource for anthropologists and archeologists. The permanent collection includes Egyptian, Greek, Roman, Etruscan, Buddhist, Chinese, African, Native American, and Ancient Israeli art galleries. For information on visiting exhibitions, or to take a look at art galleries online, visit www.penn.museum.

Departments

Log onto www.upenn.edu/directories for a university directory and links to division and department web pages.

Undergraduate Admissions 215-898-7507
Annenberg School for Communication 215-898-7041
Arts and Sciences, Graduate Division 215-898-5720
Law School 215-898-7400
School of Dental Medicine 215-898-8942
School of Design 215-898-3425
School of Engineering 215-898-7246
School of Medicine 215-662-4000
School of Nursing 215-898-8281
School of Social Work 215-898-5511
School of Veterinary Medicine 215-898-5434
Wharton MBA Program .215-898-6183
Wharton Undergraduate Division 215-898-7608

University of the Arts

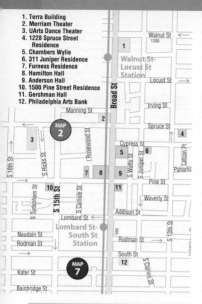

1. Terra Building
2. Merriam Theater
3. UArts Dance Theater
4. 1228 Spruce Street Residence
5. Chambers Wylie
6. 311 Juniper Residence
7. Furness Residence
8. Hamilton Hall
9. Anderson Hall
10. 1500 Pine Street Residence
11. Gershman Hall
12. Philadelphia Arts Bank

Tuition

In the 2013-2014 academic year, full-time undergraduate tuition was $36,582, with an additional $8,610 for room and board. For more information about extra fees, alternative board plans, or financial aid packages, call 215-717-6170.

Sports

Unfortunately, UArts students don't have the luxury of sports teams or even a school gym, though discounted rates are available for those who feel the need exercise more than just their paintbrush.

Culture on Campus

Where to begin. The plethora of Arts students showing off their latest work or performing in university-run shows, most often in Philadelphia Arts Bank or at the UArts dance theater are difficult to miss. The University also owns the nearby Merriam Theater, home to traveling Broadway shows and local theater productions.

In addition, The Philadelphia Museum of Art, the Rodin Museum, the Institute for Contemporary Art, and dozens of other galleries and museums are free to UArts students, encouraging all to embrace their inner starving artist.

General Information:

NFT Map: 2, 7
Address: 320 S Broad St.
    Philadelphia, PA 19102
Phone: 800-616-ARTS
Website: www.uarts.edu

Overview

Evolved from the Philadelphia College of Art (1876) and the Philadelphia College of Performing Arts (1870), University of the Arts draws hopeful actors, artists, writers, and unlabeled creative types from all over the country. Established in 1987 with the union of PCA and PCPA, UArts became the largest educational institution of its kind in the country, focusing on Art and Design, Performing Arts, Liberal Arts, and the newly established Media and Communication school. The school also has graduate and pre-college programs for budding and established artists.

Departments

Log onto www.uarts.edu/about/offices-services for a university directory and links to division and department web pages.

Admissions 215-717-6030
Division of Liberal Arts 215-717-6260
Continuing Studies 215-717-6095
Pre-College Programs 215-717-6430

Golf

Over the last few years, the majority of Philly's public courses have been taken over by Meadowbrook Golf, and the results have been mostly positive—by and large, the fairways and greens are vastly improved. In terms of accolades, **Cobb's Creek**, probably the best known of Philly's courses, has national recognition. If you fear your game is not yet up to speed, try the Karakung Course at Cobb's Creek; it's a little cheaper and much more forgiving than the regular Olde Course. **Walnut Lane**, tucked neatly into Wissahickon Park, is also a very nice run for your money—watch out for the occasional out-of-control mountain biker from the abutting Wissahickon Trail wiping out on the greens. Check out www.golfphilly.com for more information about Meadowbrook courses.

Golf Courses	Address	Phone	Rates	Par
Cobbs Creek Olde Golf Course	7400 Lansdowne Ave	215-877-8707	Regular: $33-$48; twilight: $23-$38	Par-72, 18 holes
Franklin D Roosevelt Golf Club	1954 Pattison Ave	215-462-8997	Regular: $28-43; twilight: $23-$33	Par-69, 18 holes
John F Byrne Golf Club	9550 Leon St	215-632-8666	Regular: $28-$43; twilight: $18-$33	Par-67, 18 holes
Juniata Golf Club	1363 E Cayuga St	215-743-4060	Regular: $20-$35; twilight: $15-$30	Par-66, 18 holes
Karakung Golf Course at Cobb Creek	7400 Landsdowne Ave	215-877 8707	Regular: $23-$33; twilight: $18-$28	Par-72, 18 holes
Phila Quartet Golf Club	1075 Southampton Rd	215-676-3939	$35 for associate membership fee; after Par-3, 9 holes that, $15-$17 a day.	
Walnut Lane Golf Club	700 Walnut Ln	215-482-3370	Regular: $24-$40; twilight: $12-$35	Par-62, 18 holes

Bowling

Bowling in Philadelphia is no longer limited to those who can stand the stereotypical dark and smoky alleys, although you can still hit up the no-frills BYOB **T-Bird Lanes (5830 Castor Ave)**; it's by far the most established and popular for purists of the Philadelphia bowling scene. The best modern-era alley is South Philly's **Pep Bowl (Map 7)**, and if you start a league or host a party there, it's BYOB. If you want your booze built-in, **North Bowl** in Northern Liberties **(Map 19)** oozes with neo-retro charm, plus it can fill all of your photo booth and arcade machine needs. While convenient, Center City's **Lucky Strikes (Map 2)** can be kind of a jerk parade (there's a dress code…for bowling), and the high prices reflect that.

Numerous smaller alleys are scattered throughout the city; there are too many to list, but a quick web search will give you plenty of options if the big bad boys of bowling don't interest you. (Plus a lot of the websites have coupons.) Regardless, whether you want to bowl in ripped jeans with a cigarette tucked behind your ear or hobnob with big spenders sporting Prada and their finest Dexter pro shoes downtown, you don't have to drive to Jersey to do it.

All rates are per person/per game, including shoes and tax.

Bowling Alleys	Address	Phone	Rates day/eve	Map
Lucky Strikes	1336 Chestnut St	215-665-9501	Day $4.95/game; Evening $5.95/game; Weekend Evening $6.95/game. $3.95 for shoes.	3
PEP Bowl	1200 S Broad St	215-952-BOWL	$4 per game, $3 for shoes.	7
North Bowl	909 N 2nd St	215-238-2695	Mon–Fri 5–7 pm, $3.95/game. Mon–Thurs after 7 pm, $4.95/game. After 9 pm and weekends, $5.95/game. $3 for shoes.	19
Hi Spot Lanes	3857 Pechin St	215-483-2120	$3/game, $1 for shoes.	21
Center Lanes	7550 City Line Ave	215-878-5050	Day $3.25/game, Evening $3.75/game. $2.50 for adults, $2 for children, for shoes.	n/a
Erie Lanes	1300 E Erie Ave	215-535-3500	Day $3.09/game, Evening $4.09/game. $2.49 for shoes.	n/a
Sproul Lanes	745 W Sproul Rd, Springfield	610-544-4524	Weekdays 9 am–5 pm, $3.65/game. All other times, $4.70/game. $3.40 for shoes.	n/a
T-Bird Lanes	5830 Castor Ave	215-743-2521	Day $3/game. $2.95 for shoes. They hold nightly specials. Call for details.	n/a
Thunderbird Lanes	3081 Holme Ave	215-464-7171	Day $3.50/game, Evening $4.50/game. $2.95 for shoes.	n/a
V& S Elmwood Lanes	7235 Elmwood Ave	215-365-1626	Day $2.75/game, evenings and weekends, $3.50/game. $1.50 for shoes.	n/a

Looking for a hobby to replace your increasingly frightening American Idol habit? There are plenty of clubs and organizations you can join to get yourself off the couch.

General Tips

Start with a club or league, but keep your eyes and ears open for related groups and events. If you join the Bicycle Coalition (www.bicyclecoalition.org) and are particularly interested in racing, chances are you'll eventually run into a member who can tell you more about the area's racing-focused clubs than you'd get from a web search. Word of mouth is still one of the best ways to find out about new groups and leagues in the city.

Cycling

Philadelphia is a great cycling city, and there are plenty of groups around who love to take advantage of it. Start with the Bicycle Club of Philadelphia (www.phillybikeclub.org); they offer rides for cyclists of all skill levels, and membership will get you discounts at many of the local bike shops. The Bicycle Coalition of Greater Philadelphia puts a lot of emphasis on advocacy and bike education and less on scheduled rides and events, but offers tons of great information on their website and recently began offering an Urban Cycling Course.

Running

If you sit on one of the benches along the Schuylkill River Banks every morning for a few days, you'll see familiar faces running by. But rather than springing up from your bench and running alongside the regulars hoping for an invitation to join them, why not just join one of the local clubs?

The Frontrunners (www.philadelphiafrontrunners. org) have been "running since 1983," and have regularly scheduled walks and runs. The Fairmount Running Club (www.runfairmount.org) also offers many group runs throughout the week, and no membership fees. For those interested in racing, check out the Wissahickon Wanderers (www.wanderersrunningclub.org) running club for competitive, but friendly, fun.

Sailing

The Bachelors Barge Club (www.bachelorsbargeclub.org), established in 1853, is the oldest rowing club in the country and still going strong. The Philadelphia Sailing Club (www.philadelphiasailingclub.org), based in Bala Cynwyd, is better suited for casual sailors and welcomes all skill levels.

Skating

The Landskaters (www.landskaters.org) pretty much rule the inline club scene. They offer events for all difficulty levels, including recreational skates aimed at entry-level city skaters.

Ultimate

The Philadelphia Area Disc Alliance (PADA) (www. pada.org) has the lock-down on local Ultimate leagues. The group's leagues are especially popular during the summer, but they do offer leagues during each of the four seasons, moving indoors for the winter. There are also club teams, tournaments, and PADA YO!, the organization's youth outreach program. If you're interested in disc-related events, start with these guys.

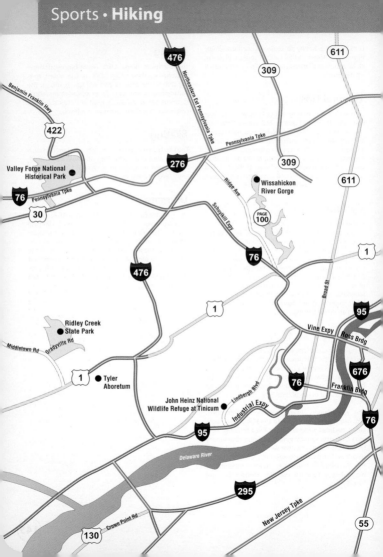

Overview

Greater Philadelphia offers plenty of potential refuge to those growing weary of buildings and asphalt. Fortunately, many of Philly's best parks are nearby and the tranquility and peace of mind that can be achieved on a hike makes a life lived in gridlock all the more bearable.

Relevant Books:
Hikes Around Philadelphia, by Boyd & Linda Newman
60 Hikes Within 60 Miles: Philadelphia, by Sandra Kear

John Heinz National Wildlife Refuge at Tinicum

www.fws.gov/heinz, 8601 Lindbergh Blvd, 215-365-3118
This 145-acre refuge just north of the Philadelphia Airport provides homes for birds (over 280 different types) and other animals, including rare endangered species such as the red-bellied turtle and southern leopard frog. Hikers and cyclists can enjoy more than ten miles of trails within the refuge, which is open from sunrise until sunset year-round. And for visual irony, you simply can't beat the view of nearby power converters and petroleum refineries over the tops of the trees.

From I-76 E, stay in the left lane and follow signs for Route 291 W/I-95 S/Airport. At the light, turn right onto Route 291 W. Follow signs to I-95 S. Traveling on I-95 S, take the Route 291/Airport Exit 10. Take the right fork, exiting for Route 291/Lester. At the first light, turn right onto Bartram Avenue. At the second light, turn left onto 84th Street, then at the second light, turn left onto Lindbergh Boulevard. SEPTA's route 37 and 108 buses both stop at 84th Street and Lindbergh Boulevard. Regional Rail stops at Eastwick Station, which is several blocks southeast of the refuge's main entrance at 86th Street and Lindbergh Boulevard.

Ridley Creek State Park

Located 16 miles outside Philadelphia, Ridley Creek State Park has an easy five-mile paved loop that accommodates wheelchairs and baby strollers. Four hiking trails (red, white, blue, yellow) through wooded terrain can be mixed and matched to form hikes of varying lengths and difficulty. The park can be reached from Gradyville Road—about 2.5 miles west of Newton Square—which can be found off either PA-352 or PA-252. Both these roads intersect Gradyville Road. You can also get there directly from PA-3 west of Newton Square.

Valley Forge National Historical Park

The 3,600-acre Valley Forge Park is a well-maintained tribute to the Revolutionary War. The main trail is a paved five-mile loop that reaches most of the major historical attractions in the park, and is good for hikers, cyclists, and rollerbladers. Trails intended solely for hiking and horseback riding include the Valley Creek Trail, Horse-Shoe Trail, and Schuylkill River Trail. Walnut Hill, an area seldom visited by tourists, also provides excellent hiking.

From Philadelphia, take the Schuylkill/76 W to Exit 327, the last exit before the tollbooth. Turn right at the first traffic light, then right onto N Gulph Road. Go north on N Gulph Road for 1.5 miles and turn left at the traffic light at the top of hill into the park entrance. If you're relying on public transportation, take SEPTA bus route 125 to the Valley Forge Visitor Center.

Wilderness Trail at Tyler Arboretum

Adjacent to Ridley Creek State Park, the Wilderness Trail is an 8.5-mile hike through the 260-hectare Tyler Arboretum. The arboretum also contains a few shorter routes—the Dogwood and Pinetum Trails—as well as unblazed trails and old roads. Spring is the best time to visit, when blooming wildflowers overtake the landscape. The $9 for adults and $5 for children (three and older) entrance fee charged by this private not-for-profit association contributes to the park's upkeep. The Tyler Arboretum is located off PA-352 about four miles north of Media. Or you can take PA-3 to PA-352 and travel south for 5.1 miles. Turn east onto Forge Road, then right onto Painter Road to reach the parking lot (www.tylerarboretum.org).

Wissahickon River Gorge

In the northernmost part of Wissahickon Park lies the steep-sided, six-mile-long Wissahickon River Gorge, referred to by locals as simply Valley Green. Forbidden Drive (the name applies to cars only), which runs mostly on the west side of the Wissahickon, is an old carriage road along the river. "Traffic" is heavy here, as many joggers, dog walkers, bicyclists, horseback riders, and anglers enjoy the trail. The eastern side of the gorge is steeper and has more rugged trails for serious hikers. Once you find Wissahickon Gorge (not the easiest place to get to by car), park in one of the three parking lots: Valley Green Inn, Kitchen's Lane, and Bell's Mill Road. Try to arrive early in the day as the lots fill quickly. The following SEPTA buses stop at the trailhead: 1, 9, 27, 35, 38, 61, 65, 124, 125, and the Manayunk/Norristown Regional Rail Line.

Rowing

The banks of Philadelphia's Schuylkill River (a.k.a. the "hidden river") possess a long and illustrious sporting history, one that many Philly residents take surprisingly seriously. Since the mid-19th century, rowers have been racing the waters along Boathouse Row. Today, this span of river is the practice course for top rowing talent in the United States—boat clubs along the Schuylkill count among their members Olympic gold medalists and World Championship winners. At the 2008 Beijing Olympic Games, the US Men's crew team included five Philadelphia-area rowers.

If the lure of Philadelphia's rowing history doesn't draw your interest, the scenery sure will. There are more than a dozen boat houses to view on Kelly Drive along the sublime Boathouse Row, all visible from I-76.

Boat Houses	Address	Phone
Bachelors Barge Club	#6 Boathouse Row, Kelly Dr	215-769-9335
College Boat Club of UPenn	#11 Boathouse Row, Kelly Dr	215-978-8918
Crescent Boat Club	#5 Boathouse Row, Kelly Dr	215-978-9816
Fairmount Rowing Association	#2 & #3 Boathouse Row, Kelly Dr	215-769-9693
Penn Athletic Club Rowing Association	#12 Boathouse Row, Kelly Dr	215-978-9458
Philadelphia Girls' Rowing Club	#14 Boathouse Row, Kelly Dr	215-978-8824
Undine Barge Club	#13 Boathouse Row, Kelly Dr	215-765-9244
University Barge Club	#7 & #8 Boathouse Row, Kelly Dr	215-232-2293
Vesper Boat Club	#9 & #10 Boathouse Row, Kelly Dr	215-769-9615

Marinas

If boating or sailing is more your speed, the Delaware River is the perfect playground. The Philadelphia Marine Center offers 338 deep-water slips with summer rates that run between $500 for personal watercraft and $5,800 for 70' craft. Winter slips are $44 per foot, $1,000 minimum. If you just want to dock your boat for a few days, the daily rate is $2.00 per foot, with a $60 minimum.

Penn's Landing Marina is another option for boat-docking but they have far fewer slips and you need to reserve one in February for the summer months. Rates depend upon the size of the boat. Up to 45 feet is $1.75 per foot, while 46-80 feet is $2.25. Penn's Landing Marina is also where you'll board river services such as the Riverboat Queen and the Spirit of Philadelphia.

The Piers Marina offers boat slips year-round for $75 per foot in the summer, and and a little less than half that in the winter. Boats can be stored year-round while full-time security staff watch out for your property.

Marinas	Address	Phone	Website	Map
Philadelphia Marine Center	Pier 12 N, Christopher Columbus Blvd & Franklin Bridge	215-931-1000	www.philamarinecenter.com	4
Penn's Landing Marina	S Columbus Blvd & Dock St	215-928-8801	www.delawareriverwaterfront.com/contact/penn-s-landing-marina	16
Piers Marina	Pier 3, 31 N Columbus Blvd b/w Market St & Race St	215-351-4101	www.thepiersmarina.com	16

Skating

Lengthy winters and cold temperatures make ice skating an ideal activity for denizens of the city. In fact, Philly is recognized for launching the first skating club in North America back in 1849—The Skater's Club of the City and County of Philadelphia. There are many beautiful outdoor settings in which to strap on your blades, including parts of the Schuylkill and Delaware Rivers and areas within the lush Fairmount and Pennypack Parks.

For a more controlled environment, check out the Blue Cross River Rink at Festival Pier (www.delawareriverwaterfront. com/places/blue-cross-riverrink). It opens from late November to early March and costs $8–$9 to skate and an additional $3 for skate rental. On particularly frigid mid winter days, indoor ice rinks are infinitely more appealing—try the Rink at Old York Road (www.rinkoyr.com).

In the warmer months, inline skating is a fun way to exercise, sightsee, or commute. Skating on all bike paths throughout the city is permitted, providing miles of traffic-free skating surfaces. On rainy days or in cold weather, hit one of Philly's indoor rinks, which also run intramural roller hockey leagues. In evenings be sure to call ahead, local rinks are popular spots for private parties and all-out roller derby brawls alike.

Ice Skating Rinks	Address	Phone	Rates	Map
Class of 1923 Ice Rink	3130 Walnut St	215-898-1923	$5–$7, $3 rental	10
Blue Cross River Rink	Columbus Blvd & Spring Garden St	215-925-7465	$8–$9, $3 rental	19
Laura Sims Skatehouse	Cobbs Creek Pkway & Walnut St	215-685-1996	$4, $2 rental	N/A
Rink at Old York Road	8116 Church Rd	215-635-0331	$7, $2 rental	N/A
Rizzo Ice Rink	1101 S Front St	215-685-1593	$4, $2 rental	11
Simons Ice Rink	Walnut Lane & Woolston St	215-685-3550	$4, $2 rental	N/A
Wissahickon Ice Skating Rink	550 W Willow Grove Ave	215-247-1907	$9, $3 rental	N/A

Roller Skating Rinks	Address	Phone	Rates	Map
Carman Roller Skating Rink	3226 Germantown Ave	215-223-2200	$7, free rental	N/A
Elmwood Roller Skating Rink	2406 S 71st St	215-492-8543	$6 weekends, $1 rental	N/A
Palace Roller Skating Center	11586 Roosevelt Blvd	215-698-8000	$3–6, $2–3 rental	N/A
JAMZ Roller Skating	7017 Roosevelt Blvd	215-335-3400	$4–$7, $3 rental	N/A

Billiards

Despite Philly's richly deserved rep as an old-school, blue-collar city, there is a decided dearth of the kind of venerated pool halls that Fast Eddie Felson prefers. This is especially true in Center City, though the welcome addition of **Buffalo Billiards (Map 16)** on Chestnut and Front at least gives stick men a place to rack 'em at an hourly rate. Dave & Busters (Map 19) is fine, as long as you don't mind wading through a sea of screaming, hopped up kids playing Super Mega Assault IV and spilling nacho cheez all over your shoes. Pool at Tattooed Mom (Map 4) is fun (and the beer is cheap), but there's only one table, so expect to, er, "queue." Then again, at least you can play Erotic Photo Hunt while you wait.

Billiard Halls	Address	Phone	Fee	Map
Buffalo Billiards	118 Chestnut St	215-574-7665	$6-$10/hr	4
Tattooed Mom	530 South St	215-238-9880	$1/game	8
Vuong Viet Pool Hall	2464 Kensington Ave	215-423-8380	$1/game	18
Dave & Buster's	325 N Columbus Blvd	214-413-1951	$8-14/hr	19

Sports • Swimming

The best thing about the city's 70 municipal pools is that they are all free. The worst thing about them is that they are often closed for repairs or due to budget issues, frequently have no lifeguards, and aren't located in the Center City area. It's surprising our government provides pools in the first place—a freak leftover from before the days of privatization pollution—so it's not surprising it ain't perfect. Open during the summer from 11 am until 7 pm (noon–5 pm weekends), the pools are much more relaxing during off-peak times. When school is out for the summer, expect thousands of children to flock to the water like some kind of crazed, freely urinating mass migration. Swimming in Center City requires a bit of renegade work, if not large sums of cash. **The Lombard Swim Club (Map 1)** is most desirable—and desired, with a multi-year wait list. And after you've graciously waited your turn, get ready to pay upward of $1000 per adult and $600 per child for a year. Some cheaper private options include the **Columbia North YMCA (Map 12)** and the **Roxborough YMCA** (7201 Ridge Ave.). YMCA memberships hover around $50 a month with a discounted "Open Doors" program for low-income families and individuals. While out in Blue Bell, Mount Airy families favor **Beachcomber Swim Club** (652 Dekalb Pk, 610-272-2870) for its huge grounds, several pools, tennis, mini-golf, classes, and community vibe. Mount Airy-ites can be found here all summer long, perched perpetually on picnic blankets. Beachcomber is a co-op, which makes it slightly less expensive; individual dues are around $400 and family memberships start at about $600.

Now for us brokies. There's **Swann Fountain in Lombard Square (Map 2)**—lean your bike against a bench anytime after midnight and dip right in—you won't be alone. There's also the most pressing option—that is, a big, salty wave. Shoot down the Atlantic City Expressway and run off the boardwalk, where they don't bother with beach tags, into one. And as far as the city's offering of water pits go, the **Marian Anderson Recreation Center (Map 1)** is actually awesome, and at 740 S 17th St it's convenient for those of us living downtown. Of course, the hotels that have pools are pretty easy to sneak into as well. Just act like you belong. If someone questions you, tell Mr. Snootypants you left your key-card in the deep end and you'll dive right in and get it.

The Philadelphia Department of Recreation (PDR) conducts aquatic programs at indoor pool locations throughout the city. The programs, many of which are free of charge, are conducted by certified Water Safety Instructors and Lifeguards. Classes include swimming lessons, team swimming, and lifeguard instruction.

* indicates indoor pool

Municipal Pools	Address	Phone	Rates	Map
Lombard Swim Club	2040 Lombard St	215-735-4144	$950/yr	1
Marian Anderson	744 S 17th St	215-685-6594		1
Ford	631 Snyder Ave	215-685-1897		2
Swan Fountain in Lombard Square	Logan Circle (After midnight–swim illegally in public fountain)			2
Stinger	S 32nd St & Dickinson St	215-685-1882		5
Chew Recreation Center	1833 Ellsworth	215-685-6596		6
O'Connor	2600 South St	215-685-6593		6
Ridgway	S 13th St & Carpenter St	215-683-1887		7
Herron	250 Reed St	215-685-1884		8
Sacks	S 4th St & Washington Ave	215-685-1889		8
39th & Olive	39th St & Olive St	215-685-7654		9
Lee	4400 Haverford Ave	215-685-7656		9
Murphy	S 4th St & W Shunk St	215-685-1874		11
Columbia North YMCA	1400 Broad St	215-235-6440	$53/mo./ $100 joiner fee	12
12th & Cambria	29 N 11th St	215-685-9780		14
*University City	37th St & Filbert St	215-685-9099		14
Francisville	1737 Francis St	215-685-2762		15
Mander	N 33rd St & W Diamond St	215-685-3894		15
East Poplar	N 9th St & Parrish St	215-685-1786		18
Northern Liberties	321 Fairmount Ave	215-686-1785		19
Fishtown	E Montgomery Ave & E Girard Ave	215-685-9885		20
Venice Island	Schuylkill Canal & Cotton St	215-685-2598		21
Hillside	201 Fountain St	215-685-2595		22
*Pickett Pool	Wayne Ave & W Chelten Ave	215-685-2230		23
Shuler	3000 Clearfield St	215-685-9750		23
Pleasant Playground	6750 Boyer St	215-685-2230		24
Ferko Sprayground	E Cayuga St & J St	215-683-3663		n/a

* indicates indoor pool

Municipal Pools	Address	Phone	Map
48th & Woodland Sprayground	48th St & Woodland Ave	215-685-2692	n/a
American Legion	Torresdale Ave & Devereaux St	215-685-8733	n/a
Amos	16th St & Berks St	215-685-2708	n/a
Baker	5431 Lansdowne Ave	215-685-0261	n/a
Barry	18th St & Bigler St	215-685-1886	n/a
Belfield	21st St & Chew Ave	215-685-2220	n/a
Bridesburg	Richmond St & Ash St	215-685-1247	n/a
Cecil B Moore	22nd St & Huntingdon St	215-685-9755	n/a
Christy Recreation Center	56th St & Christian St	215-685-1997	n/a
Cobbs Creek	280 Cobbs Creek Pkwy	215-685-1983	n/a
Cohocksink	Cedar St & E Cambria St	215-685-9884	n/a
Cruz	6th St & Master St	215-685-2759	n/a
Feltonville	Ella St & Wyoming Ave	215-685-9150	n/a
Fox Chase	Rockwell Ave & Ridgeway St	215-685-0575	n/a
Francis Myers Recreation Center	58th St & Kingsessing Ave	215-685-2698	n/a
Gathers	25th St & Diamond St	215-685-2710	n/a
Houseman	Summerdale Ave & Godfrey Ave	215-685-1240	n/a
Hunting Park	1101 W Hunting Park Ave	215-685-9153	n/a
Jacobs	4500 Linden Ave	215-685-8748	n/a
James Finnegan	S 70th St & Grovers Ave	215-685-4191	n/a
Jardel	Cottman Ave & Pennway St	215-685-0596	n/a
Junod	Mechanicsville Rd & Dunks Ferry Rd	215-685-9396	n/a
Kelly Pool	4231 N Concourse Dr	215-685-0174	n/a
Kendrick	Ridge Ave & Pensdale St	215-685-2584	n/a
Kingsessing	49th St & Kingsessing Ave	215-685-2695	n/a
Lackman	Chesworth Rd & Bartlett St	215-685-0370	n/a
Lawncrest	Rising Sun Ave & Comly St	215-685-0597	n/a
*Lincoln	Rowland Ave & Shelmire Ave	215-685-8751	n/a
Lonnie Young	E Chelten Ave & Ardleigh St	215-685-2236	n/a
*Marcus Foster	1601 W Hunting Park Ave	215-685-9154	n/a
Max Myers	Oakland St & Magee Ave	215-685-1242	n/a
McVeigh	D St & Ontario St	215-685-9896	n/a
ML King	22nd St & Cecil B Moore Ave	215-685-2733	n/a
Monkiewicz	Richmond St & E Allegheny Ave	215-685-9894	n/a
Morris Estate	16th St & Chelten Ave	215-685-2891	n/a
Penrose	12th St & Susquehanna Ave	215-685-2711	n/a
Piccoli	Castor St & Cayuga St	215-685-1249	n/a
*Rhodes Pool	29th St & Clearfield St	215-227-4907	n/a
Samuel	Gaul St & Tioga St	215-685-1245	n/a
*Sayre-Morris	59th St & Spruce St	215-685-1993	n/a
Schmidt	N Howard St & W Ontario St	215-685-9895	n/a
Shepard	57th St & Haverford Ave	215-685-1991	n/a
Simpson	Arrot St & Large St	215-685-1223	n/a
Smith Sprayground	2100 S 24th St	215-683-3663	n/a
Vogt	Cottage St & Unruh Ave	215-685-8752	n/a
Waterloo	2502 N Howard St	215-685-9891	n/a
Waterview Recreation Center	5826 McMahon St	215-685-2229	n/a

* indicates indoor pool

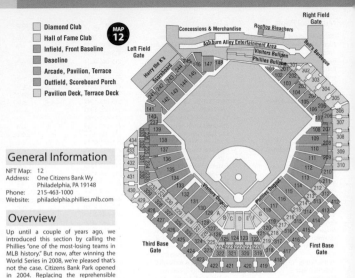

General Information

NFT Map: 12
Address: One Citizens Bank Wy
          Philadelphia, PA 19148
Phone: 215-463-1000
Website: philadelphia.phillies.mlb.com

Overview

Up until a couple of years ago, we introduced this section by calling the Phillies "one of the most-losing teams in MLB history." But now, after winning the World Series in 2008, we're pleased that's not the case. Citizens Bank Park opened in 2004. Replacing the reprehensible Veterans Stadium, the venue is an impressive collection of sporting and entertainment facilities including restaurants, stores, interactive baseball, a fine art collection, and even an engagement center. Not that we don't appreciate it, but it feels bit like the city took someone's horrifically ugly sister and draped her in Vera Wang. Still, Phillies fans have to like the new ballpark: unlike the cavernous and malodorous Vet, it has a moderate seating capacity (43,500) and maintains a real grass and dirt playing field. Grab a plastic cup of locally-brewed Yards, sit back, and get ready to boo...

How to Get There—Driving

The Stadium is conveniently located next to I-95. From the north, take I-95 to Broad Street/Exit 17 and follow signs into the park. From the south, take I-95 N to Exit 17, turn right and follow signs to the lot. The Schuylkill Expressway (I-76) will also get you there via the Sports Complex Exit #349 or the Packer Avenue Exit #350.

Parking

Affordable parking is available for $15 per car or $30 per bus in the Sports Complex—if you've got a group of four or more and an operating vehicle, it's cheaper to split parking costs than it is to have everyone pay for a round-trip SEPTA fare. Regular cash lots for Phillies games can be found in the Wells Fargo Center, in the lots located near Packer Avenue and Pattison Avenue. While early birds can snatch up Linc Parking right next to the ballpark, late-comers are relegated to the cramped lots west of 11th Street. There are handicapped parking areas surrounding the Park. Vehicles must have proper placards or license plates. But no matter where you park, be prepared to spend anywhere from fifteen minutes to an hour getting out of the complex after the game ends.

How to Get There—Mass Transit

Take the SEPTA Broad Street subway line southbound and get off at the last stop—Pattison Avenue. SEPTA Broad Street trains depart from Pattison Avenue immediately after the game ends, with Night Owl Bus service taking over after the trains stop running. Bus route C also stops at Broad Street.

How to Get Tickets

Ticket prices for Phillies games range from $17 to $65; don't worry if you're not pulling in the big bucks, because even the cheap seats at this park offer a good view of the game. For season and group sales, call 215-463-5000. (Hint: try the "six-pack" deal: you get to pick one game from a list of the toughest-ticket series-i.e. the Yankees or whoever won the World Series the previous year-and five more from the entire season schedule.) For individual games, call 215-463-1000. The ticket office is located at the First Base Gate Entrance on Pattison Avenue. For home games, ticket windows also operate at Citizens Bank Way and on Phillies Drive. Tickets can also be purchased on the website.

Lower
Club
Upper

MAP
12

General Information

NFT Map: 12
Address: 11th St & Pattison Ave
                    Philadelphia, PA 19148
Phone: 215-339-6700
Website: www.lincolnfinancialfield.com
Eagles Phone: 215-463-2500
Eagles Website: www.philadelphiaeagles.com
Ticketmaster Phone: 215-336-2000
Ticketmaster Website: www.ticketmaster.com

Overview

Fondly referred to as "The Link," this 68,532-seat sports complex is home to the fightin' Philadelphia Eagles. On game days, tailgate parties are varied and plentiful and often begin before 9 am. It is not advisable to attend a game dressed in enemy garb, but if you must, take ear plugs and a crash helmet. As a study in odd pairings, the Link is also home to the lowly Temple University Owls. The Link also plays host to a variety of other sporting and cultural events throughout the year, but the main attraction are those green and silver birds.

How to Get There—Driving

While I-95 is the most direct route, taking Broad Street is a good alternative when traffic is heavy, which it undoubtedly will be if you're heading to a Link event. From the north, take I-95 S to Broad St/Exit 17 and follow signs to stadium parking. From the south, take I-95 N past the airport and Navy Yard, to Broad Street/Exit 17 (formally exit 14). Follow signs to parking.

Parking

Unless you have a parking pass or two club seats to the game you're attending, the closest cash parking is across the street at the Wells Fargo Center. Additional spots can be found further south in the Triple 7 Lot (b/w Pattison Ave & 7th St). If all else fails, check out the Naval Hospital parking lot. Prices for public lots vary from event to event. Check www.lincolnfinancialfield.com for the most current rates.

How to Get There—Mass Transit

Take the SEPTA Broad Street subway to Pattison Avenue. Once above ground, cross the street, keep your head up, and merge into the stream of event-goers. Broad Street trains are scheduled to depart from Pattison Avenue shortly after events finish. If a game runs past midnight, the reliable shuttle buses on Broad Street replace the closed subway lines. The Route C bus also stops at Broad Street. If you're debating whether to drive or take the subway, you need your head examined.

How to Get Tickets

General events tickets are available through Ticketmaster. To book Eagles tickets, call 215-463-2500. For club seats and group tickets of ten or more, call 888-332-CLUB. Box office hours are Monday to Friday, 9 am to 5 pm at Headhouse (the pre-game/post game plaza inside Lincoln Financial Field). On event days, tickets are available at the remote ticket booth located at the 11th Street side of the main Lincoln Financial Field parking lot.

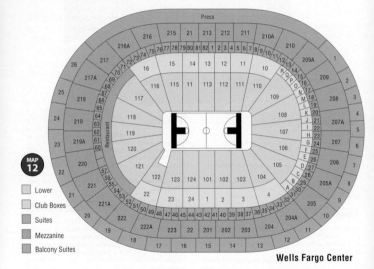

Wells Fargo Center

MAP
12

Lower
Club Boxes
Suites
Mezzanine
Balcony Suites

General Information

NFT Map:	12
Address:	3601 S Broad St
	Philadelphia, PA 19148
Phone:	215-336-3600
Websites:	www.wellsfargocenterphilly.com
Flyers:	flyers.nhl.com
Sixers:	www.nba.com/sixers
Soul:	www.philadelphiasoul.com
Wings:	www.wingslax.com

Overview

First off, don't get too accustomed to the name. In a few short years, these arenas have been named Spectrum II, Corestates Center, First Union Center, Wachovia Complex, and its present incarnation, Wells Fargo Center. Lord help us if the Wells Fargo Center ever gets bought out by Summer's Eve (inevitably: the Douche Center).

The Wells Fargo Center is home to the NBA 76ers, NHL Flyers, Indoor Football Soul, and Indoor Lacrosse Wings. The venue attracts over four million visitors each year, many of whom end up leaving drunk and dissatisfied. (Here's hoping that some of that magic that worked for the Phillies in 2008 can rub off on some of the other &*#*%$# teams.)

The Spectrum was built in 1967. In 1974, the Flyers won their first Stanley Cup on the glistening rink, and in 1976 Elvis Presley shook his hips onstage for the last time in Philadelphia. Until 2009, the Spectrum was the place to go for circus shows, traveling kiddy shows, and for the concerts of pop stars slightly less famous than Madonna or the current American Idol. It was a classic Philly old-school arena that we miss. It closed for good on Halloween night 2009 with a concert by Pearl Jam.

The somewhat fancy Wells Fargo Center, meanwhile, offers supreme spectator facilities for sporting events and concerts. With five levels and a seating capacity of 21,000, it's a prime venue for large-scale events. Check out the "in-arena" microbrewery for a pint or six (just be sure to have your credit card relatively free of debt beforehand) before the show.

How to Get There—Driving

Though directions to the Wells Fargo Center are simple, the major problem is traffic. From I-95 N/S, take the Broad Street exit and the complex is on the right.

Parking

Eight brightly lit lots with 6,100 spaces are available. You can reserve parking in advance through comcastTix or take your chances when you arrive. Patrons with disabilities can park in lot D or in the designated spots marked with the universal symbol located around the Center (call 215-389-9571 for more information). Parking rates vary from event to event. Visit www.wellsfargocenterphilly.com/parking.aspx for more information.

How to Get There—Mass Transit

Take the Broad Street subway to the last southbound stop—Pattison Avenue. Broad Street trains are scheduled to depart from Pattison Avenue shortly after events finish. If a game runs past midnight, the reliable shuttle buses on Broad Street replace the closed subway lines. The Route C bus also stops at Broad Street. Again, if you have the opportunity to avoid the snarling traffic by going the subway route, you would be wise to do so.

How to Get Tickets

All sports tickets can be obtained from the team's websites. Tickets for special events can be purchased at comcastTix.com. Tickets from the box office are available by calling 1-800-298-4200 or on location at the Broad Street side of the Wells Fargo Center. Box Office hours are Monday to Friday 12 pm-6 pm and from 10 am–4:30 pm on Saturdays and Sundays (only if there is an event on that day).

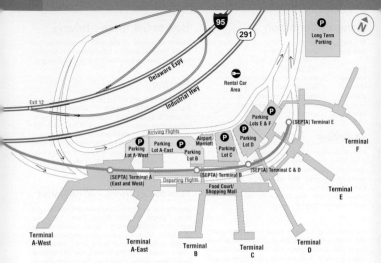

General Information

Address:	8000 Essington Ave
	Philadelphia, PA 19153
Phone:	215-937-6937
Websites:	www.phl.org
Flight/Gate Information:	800-PHL-GATE
Airport Police:	215-937-6918
Ground Transportation Hotline:	215-937-6958
Lost & Found:	215-937-6888
SEPTA (bus and rail):	215-580-7800

Overview

One of the first airports to feature such amenities as on-screen flight info and rocking chairs lining the waiting areas, Philadelphians can now gloat over one of the swankiest airports in the country. Passengers can fly to over 15 destinations in Europe and countless tropical islands to cure the winter blues. Domestic flights are still dominated by US Air and Southwest, whose fierce competition has proven beneficial for both parties.

Philly International has also added many amenities, like one of the country's first Minute Suites locations where you can rent a suite and grab a nap, local-cuisine restaurants, and a few fancy pant stores. Ain't capitalism grand? And the lauded 'street pricing' ensures buyers won't pay out the nose for a last-ditch cheesesteak. Just keep in mind, butt-heads, PHL has a 100% smoke-free environment policy.

How to Get There—Driving

Believe it or not, getting to the airport from Center City, the PA/NJ Turnpikes, or Delaware is easiest on I-95. Conveniently situated next to the PHL, this busy interstate is your best option, depending on the part of the city from which you are leaving. From CC, simply take I-95 S to the airport exit.

The other option, when leaving from Center City, is I-76 E (Schuylkill Expressway) to the airport exit. During rush hour, bumper-to-bumper, snail-paced traffic is the norm, so I-76 is not the best route if you're in a hurry. From the Pennsylvania Turnpike, take 476 S to 95. Take 95 N to the airport exit. From the NJ turnpike, take Exit 3 to the Walt Whitman Bridge and be wary of the tricky toll plaza; stay to your far right to merge onto 95 S and keep your eyes peeled for the Philadelphia Airport exit.

How to Get There—Mass Transit

If you're not carrying a lot of luggage, mass transit is the best option. From Center City, take the Airport Line, which stops at all terminals except F. The Airport Line travels from Temple University, making stops in Center City at Suburban Station and Market East Station before heading over to 30th Street Station and continuing to the airport. Trains depart every thirty minutes from the airport between approximately 5 am to midnight. For the most up-to-date schedules, call 215-580-7800 or visit www.septa.org. One-way fare is $8.75 ($10 if you buy your ticket on the train).

Navigating the buses is a little more challenging. Buses 37 and 108 have airport routes, though both are indirect and somewhat "scenic" rides. Bus 37 makes stops at Terminals B (arrivals) and E (arrivals and departures), whereas Bus 108 stops only at Terminal B (arrivals). The bus rides are both lengthy and tiresome—save yourself some pre-flight anxiety and stick with a taxi or SEPTA.

How to Get There—Really

A drop-off or pick-up buddy is a very handy resource at PHL. If that's not an option, the 24-hour taxi service is a convenient means of fleeing the hordes of travelers. Taxis charge a flat-rate of $28.50 if you're heading into or out of Center City. Flat rate hikes aren't the only way taxi drivers are gouging money out of their passengers, though. Drivers also charge $1 for each additional passenger beyond the first, not including kids under 12, for flat rate trips between the airport and Center City.

If you've a-hankerin' for some pamperin', door-to-door limousine services are also available. Limousines are an easy and luxurious way to travel, especially during peak hours or if you're with a larger group. A few mainstay services are Dave's Best Limo (215-288-1000), which is more "big-red van" than "long-stretch limo," or PHL Taxi (215-232-2000).

Parking

PHL has made way for over 6,000 brand new parking spaces in recent years. I though it's now much easier to secure a spot, the daily parking rates can be expensive, depending on where you park. If you're fortunate enough to find a space in one of the terminal garages, parking costs $20 per day. The partial rates here are $4 per 30 minutes, with prices climbing $2 for every additional half hour. The more costly ground level, short term parking is available at every baggage claim except Terminal F. Hourly rates here are the same as the garage parking, but daily rates are $40. If you're going to be gone for more than a few hours, drive up to the garages.

If you're leaving for more than a couple of days, economy parking in the remote lot past Terminal F is the best bet. Parking costs $11 per day and blue and white shuttle buses ferry passengers to and from the airport around the clock.

An even more economical parking option, especially for longer stays, is private park-and-shuttle. There are many companies to choose from, including Pacifico Airport Valet (215-492-0990), located at the Airport AutoMall. Pacifico drives you to and from the airport in your own car, so you don't have to climb into the back of some packed shuttle bus—at the reasonable cost of $9 per day. Another reputable service that uses your own car to chauffer you around is Winner Airport Valet Parking (800-978-4848) and they charge $10.99 a day plus tax. If you're not in a rush and don't mind stopping at other travelers' terminals call Colonial Airport Parking (610-521-6900), located just two miles south of PHL, for a shuttle service with rates as low as $9.00 for 24 hours.

Car Rentals   *Phone*

Alamo:	800-327-9633
Avis:	800-331-1212
Budget:	800-527-0700
Dollar:	800-800-4000
Enterprise:	800-RENTACAR
Hertz:	800-654-3131
National:	800-227-7368

Airline	Terminal	Airline	Terminal
Air Canada	D	JetBlue	E
Air Canada Jazz	D	Lufthansa Airlines	A-West
AirTran Airways	D	Southwest Airlines	E
Alaska Airlines	D	Spirit Airlines	A-East
American Airlines/American Eagle	A-East	United Airlines/United Express	D
British Airways	A-West	US Airways International	A-West
Charters	A-East	US Airways	B/C
Delta Air Lines/Delta Connection	A-East	US Airways Express	F
Frontier Airlines	A-East	Virgin America	E

General Information

Bicycle Club of Philadelphia:
www.phillybikeclub.org

Bicycle Coalition of Greater Philadelphia:
http://www.bicyclecoalition.org/

The Bicycle Network (City):
*http://www.philadelphiastreets.com/
transportation-survey_design_bureau-bicycle_
network.aspx*

Neighborhood Bike Works:
www.neighborhoodbikeworks.org

Commuting

As part of the evolving "Bicycle Network Plan," the city is currently completing a series of street-safe routes for commuting on two wheels. This plan can't happen soon enough; because of Philly's many narrow one-way streets, bikers and drivers are often at odds with one another, and you know who normally wins these little tête-à-têtes. The tiny 20-pound frame or two-ton hunk of steel? Thankfully, the car-bicycle relationship is getting better on the city streets, but bikers should still think and act defensively.

City bikers have more to worry about than just drivers' road rage—the streets themselves are not always biker-friendly. Metal grooves in the roads are the last remnants of Center City's old trolley system. Today, instead of guiding trolleys through the city, the grooves have a nasty tendency to cause bicycle crashes if they're hit at the wrong angle or when they're wet. And let's not forget about all those historic cobblestones and wooden streets...

Our best advice is to be wary of irate drivers, avoid the trolley rails at all costs, and, whatever you do, wear a helmet! A detailed map of Philadelphia's commuter bike routes can be found on the City's website philadelphiastreets. com. Check it out and plan your route before you go whizzing around town.

Recreational Riding

If inhaling exhaust fumes and dodging traffic is not your speed, venture towards Philly's more natural settings. Some of the best off-street stretches of pavement run through, or close to, the city's parks. Kelly Drive meanders through picnic areas and fishing holes along the east side of the Schuylkill River. West River Drive runs along the opposite side of the river, zipping past the zoo, the Mann Music Center, and Memorial Hall. If you feel like testing your fitness level, try Forbidden Drive; this spectacular eight-mile loop circles Wissahickon Valley Park. For off-road bikers, the granddaddy is definitely the wild and woolly Wissahickon loop; the 30-mile trail offers sufficient challenge for even experienced riders. Pennypack Creek Park also offers a diverse array of dirt and paved trails near the Delaware River in the Northeast. Along Boathouse Row, Wheel Fun Rentals (215-232-7778) has bikes you can pick up by the hour and half- or full-day to cruise through Fairmount Park and around the Philadelphia Art Museum.

Bikes on Mass Transit

Bikes are allowed on SEPTA subway lines and regional rail, though only at specific times. All SEPTA buses and trackless trolleys can now accommodate bikes, and each has a rack that can hold two bicycles.

On the Broad Street and Market-Frankford Lines, passengers may board their wheels on weekdays before 6 am, between 9 am and 3 pm, and after 6 pm. Bikes can be taken on board at all times on weekends and the following holidays: Memorial Day, Independence Day, Labor Day, Thanksgiving, Christmas, and New Year's Day. On Regional Rail, there is a limit of two bikes per carriage during off-peak hours. Up to five bikes are allowed at any time during weekends and major holidays. Bikes are not permitted during peak hours, so check www.septa.org/policy/bike.html for more details.

Independent/Underground Bicycling

Philly has a long history of underground bicycle culture, where young daredevils on track bikes (read: no gears or brakes) race through the city at breakneck speeds. The city also operates with an extensive bicycle courier system. At any hour of the day, you'll catch young girls and guys swerving around traffic, balancing bright messenger bags brimming with packages on their backs. This is because the more packages they deliver per day, the more cash they bring in.

By law, the couriers must obey traffic laws and are not allowed to ride on the sidewalk, but for these bikers some rules were made to be broken. On their breaks, many bike messengers congregate at the entrance to Clark Park, playing chess or wolfing down hoagies before pedaling off to their next destination. If nothing else, it makes for great people-watching.

To let off steam, couriers can participate in sponsored bike races. There are also events for non-couriers, including the Philadelphia Bike Party (phillybikeparty.org) and Critical Mass, a loosely-organized bike ride through the city, which gets a group of riders together one day every month to raise awareness about using bicycles as transportation, as opposed to, say, gas-guzzling SUVs.

Bike Share

In late 2012 it was announced that a bike share program would launch in Philadelphia, joining the likes of Washington DC, Boston, and New York. And we finally have an official start date: by the end of the summer 2014. The plan calls for 150 to 200 stations to be set up, starting in the City Center core, with approximately 1,500 to 2,000 sharable bikes as part of the first wave of the system. We can't wait to hop on and give it a spin! Check out www.phila.gov/bikeshare to keep up with all the latest updates.

General Information

E-ZPass Information: 800-333-TOLL
E-ZPass Website: www.ezpass.com
DMV Phone: 800-932-4600
DMV Website: www.dmv.state.pa.us
Radio Traffic Updates: 1060 KYW
                       (every 10 minutes on the 2's)
Real-Time Traffic: www.phillytraffic.com

Delaware River Crossings

Only you can answer why you want to go to New Jersey in the first place. But if you have to go, you're taking a bridge, which means you're sitting in bridge traffic. The Walt Whitman starts close to South Philly, the Ben Franklin takes you from Center City, and the Betsy Ross services most of the Northeast. None of the bridges charge you to go to New Jersey, but they all make you pay $5 to get back. E-ZPass is accepted on all three bridges but, unfortunately, there's no discount.

The I-676 or Vine Street feeds you onto the Ben Franklin, which goes to Camden. The Walt Whitman goes to Camden as well—take 10th Street down to Packer Avenue to get onto the Walt Whitman unless it's 2 am and then I-95 may be (no guarantees) your best option. As for the Betsy Ross (destination: Pennsauken), you're pretty much stuck taking I-95, although you could go from Aramingo to Castor to Richmond. As always, keep in mind that the second you cross over to Jersey, our maps are virtually useless—that's right, we're dropping you mapless in Camden. Get directions beforehand from Google Maps or someone who really knows the area. Otherwise, you're on your own—which sounds ominous because, well, it's ominous alright.

Philadelphia's Highways

Highways seem like a good idea until they turn into parking lots; which happens all too often. If you're planning on driving during the evening or on the weekend, check to see if there's a game at one of the stadiums, and devise plans accordingly, i.e. don't go. If you must, do your best to avoid I-95. Unfortunately, there's no good way to get north and south except on I-95, unless you want to go through the city. You can avoid the Schuylkill (I-76) from Center City westward by taking Kelly Drive or, better still, West River Drive. Kelly and West River have very few lights, and the scenery is nice to boot. On a weekend day and especially at night, if you're trying to get in or out of the city, sometimes what's best is to do what seems counterintuitive—ignore I-76 altogether and go straight up Broad Street. If you hit on a good timing with the lights, you can go through uninterrupted, and it's pretty exhilarating. We should probably quickly mention I-676: it's the little bit of road that connects I-76 to I-95. 'Nuff said.

Driving in Center City

Avoid Broad Street going south and take Juniper, a tiny street between Broad and 13th—it's small and not many people know about it. It has mostly stop signs instead of stop lights, which generally gets you through more quickly. Also, you have the luxury of turning left anytime you like, something you can't do on Broad from City Hall to Pine. We recommend going out to 22nd to go north. If you want to stay on the east side of Center City, take 13th. If you're going east or west, head south a little to do it (take Spruce or Pine Streets), or head north and take Arch Street. If your ultimate destination is West Philly, keep in mind that the bridges are located at Walnut, Chestnut, Market, and South Streets. For the love of God, don't ever drive up Walnut unless you absolutely have no choice. You will inevitably regret every second of the ride.

A word on traffic flow—for whatever reason, it's not in our character to switch lanes. Maybe we're freaked out by the narrow streets, or we're just so f***ing diffident. So if you're stuck behind a line of cars that don't want to move and there's a whole car's width of space next to you to maneuver down, don't think you're wrong to do it—everybody else is wrong. It can't be explained, we're just like that—and it drives the rest of us crazy!

Driving in Northwest Philadelphia

Take Kelly Drive or West River Drive to East Falls then get on Lincoln Drive to go to Mount Airy or Chestnut Hill. If you're heading to Roxborough, Henry Avenue is a much better road to take than Ridge—get off Kelly and head up Midvale Avenue to get to Henry Avenue. Unfortunately for Manayunk, Main Street is pretty much *the* street. The good news is that you can completely avoid the Schuylkill to get to Northwest Philly except on some weekends that force the simultaneous closing of West River (closed to automobiles on Saturday and Sunday from April 1 to October 31 for regattas (damn boat races). Luckily, boat racing isn't popular enough that this will inconvenience you more than a handful of times each year. Then there are always those people who run or bike for charities that close Kelly Drive, too.

Selfish bastards.

Driving in South Philly

Believe it or not, Broad Street is not the worst route to South Philly. Stay in the middle lane to avoid frequently stopping buses and/or trash trucks. If you actually stick to the speed limit, you'll find that the lights are timed and you can pretty much drive straight through. If you want to avoid Broad Street, try 13th Street going north or 12th Street going south. Buses don't run those roads, however, double parking is a recreational activity in South Philly, and you're likely to spend more time trying to navigate the parking lot than you would toughing it out on Broad. Avoid Fitzwater until the city cleans that mess up.

Driving in West Philadelphia

The lights are timed on Walnut Street (which goes west) and Chestnut Street (which goes east). It's rare that going the speed limit is in your best interest, but, in this case, grit your teeth and stick to about 23 mph. Spruce Street is always a disaster, for reasons unknown, and should be avoided at all costs. If you want to go north and south, you're pretty screwed. 38th Street has four lanes and runs in both directions starting at Lancaster to the north, ultimately becoming University Avenue and feeding into I-76 to the south.

PENNDOT & Exam Centers

To take a driving test and complete the exam, you're going to need to visit one of the following PENNDOT locations. There are other offices in Philadelphia that deal with non-road-testing requirements such as renewals, learner's permits, and photo IDs—visit the Pennsylvania DMV website at www.dmv.state.pa.us and enter your zip code and the service you require to find the PENNDOT location nearest you. Or call 800-932-4600 for customer service.

Columbus · 1530 S Columbus Blvd
Island Avenue · 2320 Island Ave
Lawndale · Oxford Levick Shopping Center,
919 - B Levick St
West Oak Lane · 7121 Ogontz Ave

DMV Registration

Registering with the DMV is easy. Visit www.dot4.state.pa.us to look up the nearest location and what documents you'll need to bring. If you just need to renew, you can do that online. Thanks Interweb.

Overview

Philadelphia is a walkable city with good public transportation, so it's feasible for denizens to live comfortably without owning a car. In fact, the freedom that comes with removing that albatross from around the neck can be quite exhilarating. Farewell to high insurance and fuel costs, the travails of big city parking, and the constant threat of mechanical breakdown--hello to the smug satisfaction of reducing one's ecological impact on the tender earth. Still, schlepping laundry, groceries, and children around the city on public transportation isn't always ideal, and sooner or later, a private conveyance becomes temporarily necessary. Hence the concept of "car sharing," which has been catching on in cities everywhere, but which was pioneered in Philly.

Enterprise CarShare

Website: www.enterprisecarshare.com
Phone: 888-989-8900

Enterprise CarShare began in 2002 as PhillyCarShare, the innovative car sharing program with dedicated parking pods throughout the city. In 2011 the car rental company Enterprise took over PhillyCarShare, and the program survives to this day in roughly the same manner. CarShare members don't pay for insurance, gas (each vehicle has its own gas card), maintenance, or cleaning--and they never have to worry about finding a parking spot since pods are reserved for PhillyCarShare throughout the city.

You can reserve cars by telephone or online, months or minutes before you plan to pick it up. You can almost always get a car on the spur of the moment, but you probably want to reserve your car at least a day in advance, especially if you want it on a weekend. Reserving cars for holidays is ultra-competitive—be prepared to drag your ass across the city for a car if you don't make reservations a month in advance. Once you've reserved a car, pick it up at your requested location, open it with your special electronic key, drive away, and do your thing. An on-board computer tracks your time and mileage and cars must be returned to the location from whence they came. Most cars in the fleet are hybrid gas-electric Toyota Prius sedans, but some bigger hatchbacks with roof racks are available, as are pick-up trucks. CarShare has also added a Mini Cooper, VW Beetle convertible, BMWs, and the super cartoony, yet efficient, Smart Car.

To be eligible for membership, you must be at least 21 years old and have a valid credit card and driver's license. University students ages 19-20 are eligible with proof of insurance and signed consent from the insurance policy holder. There are two pricing plans available. The Keystone Plan has a low annual fee and a rate of $7.50 an hour that includes 185 free miles with each rental. The Philadelphia plan has a monthly fee and a hourly charge of 25 cents. Hourly rates for both plans are lower between midnight and 7 am.

Zipcar

Website: www.zipcar.com
Phone: 866-4ZIPCAR

Zipcar also serves the Philadelphia area. If you have a Zipcar account from another city, it might be a good option, but Zipcar doesn't have as nearly as many car locations as Enterprise CarShare. Zipcar provides customers with access to a fleet of autos parked in dozens of convenient parking spots throughout the area. For an annual subscription fee, users can reserve a vehicle up to fifteen minutes in advance (via website or Zipcar app) and drive for $7.88–8.75 an hour. A membership card and a PIN unlocks the car, which is programmed to start only for the particular subscriber holding the reservation. Frequent drivers can choose various monthly packages that include pre-paid road time and reduced hourly rates. Zipcar covers gas, insurance and maintenance costs, and well over 100 cars, trucks, SUVs and hybrids are available--even a few sporty convertibles for a spontaneous joy ride.

General Information

Philadelphia Parking Authority
Phone: 215-683-9812
Website: www.philapark.org

Meters

The Philadelphia Parking Authority is so brutal and ruthless that they've been given their own reality TV show, Parking Wars. Be sure to get back to your car before the meter runs out; they will ticket you the moment it does.

The city has finally switched over to electronic meters that accept credit cards. The green boxes that line the street aren't necessarily intuitive, but they're what we've got. Pay your price, print your ticket, and place it on your dashboard. If a meter is missing or broken, parking is still allowed for the maximum time limit on the posted sign. Vehicles can still receive "Over Time Limit" tickets in spots with broken or missing meters. At night, look for parking spaces in front of loading zones that only have time limits during the day.

Residential Parking Permits

Residential parking permits cost $35 per vehicle for the first year and $20 for annual renewal. Visitor permits are available for $15 for up to fifteen days. Permits can only be used on blocks posted for permit parking, and only within the district for which they are registered. To qualify for a parking permit, a vehicle must possess Pennsylvania license plates and be registered to a home address in Philadelphia. You will also need to provide a proof of residence (and the promise of giving up your first-born child) to apply. To request an application for a residential parking permit, call 215-683-9730.

General Parking Violations

- Vehicles can be ticketed or towed (by the request of the property owner) for blocking a driveway even when there are no signs indicating "No Parking."
- Many streets in Philadelphia are narrow, making it difficult for buses to navigate their way through the city. Vehicles can be ticketed if they are observed blocking the progress of any mass transit vehicle.
- Parking over the line of a marked crosswalk will earn you a $76 ticket in Center City.
- Throughout the city, it is illegal to park within fifteen feet of a fire hydrant or within twenty feet of a curb—this ain't New York. Sometimes there will be a sign indicating the end of the legal parking area and sometimes there won't. Even in the case of the latter, you *will* get a ticket, so walk those twenty paces before leaving your car.

- Parking in a street-cleaning zone during street-cleaning times will result in a $31 ticket. Street cleanings are usually on the first and third Wednesdays and Fridays, or Tuesdays and Thursdays, of every month. Read the signs!
- School zone violations are enforced 7:30 am 3:30 pm on school days.
- Handicapped, Disabled Veteran, and People with Disabilities vehicles are granted an additional hour of parking time after the meter expires.

Vehicle Towing and Impoundment

Lost your car? Find out if it's been towed by calling 215-683-3636. Even if your car has been towed by a private towing company, it will be reported to the Philadelphia Parking Authority, and they can tell you where your vehicle has been taken.

To get your car back after it's been towed, you must pay all outstanding parking tickets and present a valid driver's license, registration, and insurance for your car. Vehicles not claimed within twenty-one days are sold at public auction.

Payment Locations

Parking Violations Branch
Address: 913 Filbert St
              Philadelphia, PA 19107
Phone: 215-561-3636
Hours: Mon–Fri: 8 am–8 pm
              Sat: 9 am–1 pm

Parking Authority Impoundment Lot
Address: 2501 Weccacoe Ave
              Philadelphia, PA 19148
Phone: 215-683-9550
Hours: Mon–Thurs: 7 am–9.30 pm
              Fri: 7 am 3 am
              Sat: 9 am–3 am
              Sun: 12 pm–3 am

Tow Pounds

- 4200 Wissahickon Ave, 215-683-9518
- 334-375 E Price St, 215-683-9521
- 4701 Bath St, 215-683-9510
- 6801 Essington Ave, 215 683-9880

Hours for all tow pounds:
Mon–Fri: 8 am–8 pm
Sat: 8 am–5 pm
Sun: 4 pm–8 pm

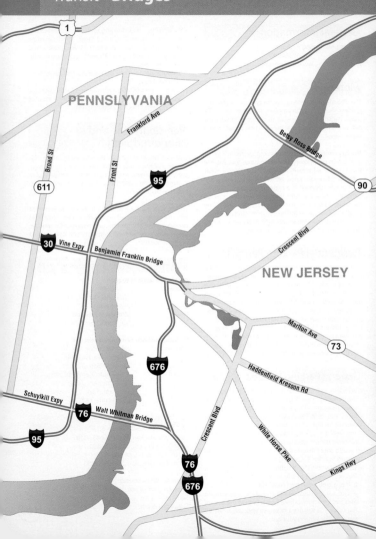

Overview

The Benjamin Franklin Bridge (Philly's answer to the Golden Gate) is an essential component to any view of the cityscape. Drive westbound over the bridge at night from Camden, New Jersey into Philadelphia's Old City and you'll get the most breathtaking sight of Philadelphia's skyline, defined by the bright red PSFS sign (once the largest neon sign in the world).

Driving eastbound on I-676, you'll see the lighted blue BF Bridge looming large on your left, the skyline rising to your right, and you will feel overwhelmed by the technological achievements of mankind. The passing commuter PATCO trains trigger a computerized lighting system in each of the bridge's cables, making it look like an ethereal dancing figure floating above the dark water. Those of the athletic persuasion can bicycle, walk, or jog on the pedestrian walkway from 6 am to 7 pm daily to experience the longest stretch of traffic-less-ness in the city.

Built in 1926, the Ben Franklin Bridge was the longest suspension bridge in the world for three years. The bridge spans the Delaware River, connecting Philadelphia and Camden, a city famous for being home to poet Walt Whitman (in his later life) and Campbell's Soup.

The Walt Whitman Bridge, meanwhile, is the Ben Franklin's Bridge's younger, uglier sibling. Opened in 1957 in order to relieve congestion on the Ben Franklin Bridge, the Walt Whitman carries with it no artistic pretense, serving a wholly utilitarian purpose.

The Walt Whitman Bridge is the best way to bypass Center City, connecting the Schuylkill Expressway (I-76) and the Delaware Expressway (I-95), as well as the North-South Freeway (I-76, I-676, and NJ 42) and US 30. However the bridge is too far south to be included in any panoramic shots of the city, and is too unattractive for anyone to be sorry about that fact. Though the Walt Whitman Bridge spans 6.2 miles, longer than the Ben Franklin, its ranking among the longest suspension bridges in the world is becoming less impressive as longer bridges are being constructed all over the world, especially in China.

The Betsy Ross Bridge, which connects the Bridesburg section of Philadelphia to Pennsuaken, New Jersey, carries the distinction of being the first bridge in the country named after a woman. Plans for the Betsy Ross Bridge began almost 20 years before the cantilever bridge opened to traffic in 1976, when officials at the Delaware River Port Authority decided it was past time to replace the Tacony-Palmyra Bridge, whose low suspension level made it an obstacle for passing ships.

The Betsy Ross follows in the footsteps of the Walt Whitman, whose function outshines its art—45,000 cars cross the Delaware on the back of the Betsy Ross Bridge everyday, making it a valuable asset to both Philadelphia and New Jersey. But the structure looks like it was fashioned out of steel remnants picked out of the scrap yard. This might be intentional, though, given that it leads to Pennsylvania. (You'll see what we mean when you get there.)

	Toll/E-ZPass	# of lanes	Pedestrians/bicyclists?	# of vehicles/day (in thousands)	Original cost (in millions)	Engineer	Main span/length	Operated by	Opened to traffic
Benjamin Franklin Bridge	5.00/5.00 (westbound only)	7	yes	100	37.1	Ralph Modjeski	1,750'	Delaware River PA	07/01/26
Betsy Ross Bridge	5.00/5.00 (westbound only)	6	no	45	103		729'	Delaware River PA	04/30/76
Walt Whitman Bridge	5.00/5.00 (westbound only)	7	no	100	90	Othmar Ammann	2,000'	Delaware River PA	05/16/57

Websites

- Ben Franklin Bridge: www.phillyroads.com/crossings/benjamin-franklin
- Betsy Ross Bridge: www.phillyroads.com/crossings/betsy-ross
- Delaware River Port Authority: www.drpa.org
- E-ZPass: www.e-zpassnj.com; www.paturnpike.com
- Traffic, weather, general transit information: http://here.com/traffic/usa/philadelphia-pa
- Walt Whitman Bridge: www.phillyroads.com/crossings/walt-whitman

SEPTA

Phone: 215-580-7800
Website: www.septa.org

Overview

The SEPTA bus system is the best public transportation the city has to offer. The massive transportation network, with its nearly 170 intercity and suburban bus transit routes, will likely get you everywhere you need to go, if not in style. For the most part, the bus routes revolve around Philadelphia and the surrounding area's main hubs. For transit to major employment centers, entertainment and sporting complexes, shopping centers, and other popular professional and recreational facilities, SEPTA is a decent choice. While the majority of buses operate between the hours of 5 am and 1 am, there are over 20 buses, known as "Owl Buses," that run 24 hours a day on the major transit routes. You just have to keep Philly bus etiquette in mind: if possible, talk loudly about your preferred method of birth control on your cell phone; never give your seat up to anyone, for any reason; and always have a bag of take-out from which you can eat as you burn through your cell minutes.

Fares & Passes

Single Ride:	$2.25 each (cash)
Token:	$1.80 (must purchase 2 or more)
One Day Convenience Pass:	$8
Weekly TransPass:	$24
Monthly TransPass:	$91
Independence Pass (Individual):	$12
Cross County Monthly Pass:	$109
Transfer fee:	$1
Seniors:	Free
Disabled Fare:	$1 ($.50 transfer fee if needed)

All passes and tokens can be purchased online. Exact change is required when paying cash. Like in most large metropolitan cities, having payment ready helps alleviate stressed searches for change and angry glares from impatient bus riders. Simply deposit the cash fare or token into the farebox, or place the transit pass through the electronic reader on top of the farebox. Be aware that some suburban routes and some city routes have additional zone charges of 50 cents.

Services

The major SEPTA terminals, where the most facilities and transfer options are available, are the Frankford Transportation Center, Olney Terminal, Wissahickon Transfer Center, 69th Street Terminal, and Norristown Transportation Center. These are also main stops on many of the bus routes. Individual route schedules are available on SEPTA's website, or can be picked up at the aforementioned terminals or other SEPTA locations including Market East Station and Suburban Station. For bike enthusiasts, front-mounted racks that accommodate two bikes are available on most routes.

Greyhound & Peter Pan

Greyhound Phone:	800- 231-2222
Greyhound Website:	www.greyhound.com
Greyhound Terminal:	1001 Filbert St Philadelphia, PA 19107 215-931-4075
Philadelphia Sigler Travel:	5608 N Broad St Philadelphia, PA 19141 215-924-1330
Peter Pan Phone:	800-343-9999
Peter Pan Website:	www.peterpanbus.com

Overview

Greyhound and Peter Pan are Philadelphia's main intercity bus services. Both are headquartered at the Greyhound terminal on Filbert Street, mere blocks from Market East Station. The Greyhound terminal and ticketing offices are open 24 hours a day. Greyhound also runs limited bus service out of Philadelphia Sigler Travel between 7:30 am and 9 pm.

Fares & Passes

Fares are comparable between the two bus companies, and booking at least seven days in advance can sometimes halve your fare. Sample fares and tickets are available on either company's website or at the terminal ticketing office. Make sure you check both websites before purchasing a ticket—sometimes they have sales like $12 one-way to NYC and $15 to Boston. A variety of student and senior discount fares are also available.

Services

Greyhound services 3,600 locations in North America and Mexico, while Peter Pan travels only to select locations in New Jersey, Connecticut, Massachusetts, Pennsylvania, New York, and New Hampshire. If you're in the mood for some high-falutin' dice-rollin' and chip-throwing, Greyhound runs a direct Philadelphia-Atlantic City Casinos line (800-231-2222). The bus leaves from both Philadelphia Greyhound locations and drops you off at the casino of your choice between 8:30 am and 11 pm daily. One of the stops in South Philly is Broad and Snyder. This is a great option if you are looking for a day in Atlantic City because you get money back! For instance on a Sunday you will pay $18.00 from the Greyhound to Bally's and once you get to Bally's Casino, you can get $15 back—that's a three-dollar trip to AC.

PHLASH Downtown Loop

Website: www.ridephillyphlash.com

Overview

The flamboyant purple trolley skittering up and down the tracks is not strictly for tourists. Though it does hit many of the city's prime attractions, such as the Philadelphia Museum of Art and Liberty Bell, and runs between major downtown hotels, the PHLASH is a quick and easy connection for locals and visitors alike.

For the affordable price of $2 per ride, the PHLASH hits 20 choice intersections and offers timely service every 12 minutes. Tickets can be purchased on the trolley, at the Independence Visitor Center (6th and Market Streets), or at the Riverlink Ferry at Penn's Landing. You can also make connections to all SEPTA and PATCO rail lines via the PHLASH. The convenient hop-on, hop-off service runs from from May to September, between 10 am and 6 pm.

Fares & Passes

The PHLASH costs $2 per ride or $12 for an all-day adult pass. Seniors (65+) and kids 4 and under ride free.

Services

The PHLASH makes stops near Market East Station and Suburban Station, as well as the PATCO Station at 8th and Market Streets. When driving into Center City, it's a good idea to park in the AutoPark at Independence Mall (5th and Market Streets), the AutoPark at Old City (2nd and Sansom Streets), or the AutoPark at the Gallery (10th and Filbert Streets). Show your PHLASH ticket here for discounted parking rates.

New Jersey Transit Buses

Phone: 973-275-5555
Website: www.NJtransit.com

Overview

New Jersey Transit offers an extensive network of 17 bus services running intrastate routes. It is an excellent travel option, offering subsidized prices for students, families, children, and frequent riders.

Fares & Passes

Monthly passes can be purchased at various New Jersey bus terminals, or at the Greyhound Bus terminal at 1001 Filbert Street. Depending on zones traveled, fares vary between $1.80 (Zone 1) and $22.75 (Zone 21). On many of the bus routes, exact coin or dollar fare is required. Monthly passes or ten-fare packages are also available. Check the website for more details.

Discount Buses

Bolt Bus: 30th St between Market & Chestnut
              1-877-BOLTBUS
              www.boltbus.com
Megabus: JFK Boulevard and 30th St,
              Market St between 6th & 7th
              877-462-634
              www.megabus.com

Overview

These relatively new discount carriers make multiple daily trips to and from New York City. Both offer free Wi-Fi on board, and Bolt Bus has outlets, just in case your phone or laptop's battery life is "the suck." If you think that makes Bolt the clear winner, hold on—If you don't need to stay ultra-connected, most Megabuses are double-decker, making for an especially freaky-fun situation traveling in one of the tunnels to/from Manhattan The Megabus also has two pick-up/drop-off spots—30th Street and Independence Mall—where the Bolt Bus just runs from 30th Street.

Fares & Passes

Both busses offer $1 tickets (plus a 50 cent service charge) if you sign up early enough. You probably won't sign up early enough. In general, if you buy a week in advance, expect to pay between $5 and $11 for a Megabus ticket and $8 and $13 for a Bolt Bus ticket. If you travel from the cheesesteak to the apple regularly, consider signing up for the Bolt Rewards program—there's no cost, and after eight rides, you'll get a free ticket.

30th Street Station

NFT Map:	14
Address:	30th St & Market St
	Philadelphia, PA 19104
Phone:	215-249-3196
Amtrak:	215-349-2153
SEPTA:	215-580-7800
NJ Transit:	800-772-2222

Overview
Architecturally, it's a marvel. Opened to the public in 1933, this eight-story concrete framed building boasts a remarkable interior laden with marble statues and skyscraper-high ceilings.

30th Street Station is a hub for SEPTA, Amtrak, and NJ Transit, accommodating 25,000 commuters each day. Amtrak's intercity trains and NJ Transit's Atlantic City line run through the station's lower level, while SEPTA Regional Rail trains serve the upper level.

Ticket Windows
Tickets for NJ Transit, Amtrak, and SEPTA are sold at the main hall ticket windows, which are accessible through the 30th Street or Market Street entrances. Amtrak's ticket window is open from 5:15 am – 9:35 pm Monday through Friday, and 6:10 am–9:35 pm on weekends. You can also purchase tickets for the NJ Transit trains at the Amtrak ticket counter, as well as at some machines. Though the station is open 24 hours a day, if you are passing through during less-active hours (10 pm-5 am), the station assumes a more ominous aura because the shops are closed and the main clientele becomes folks escaping the elements.

Parking
Finding a spot at 30th Street Station is rarely a problem. There are many parking garages, though prices are far from wallet-friendly. Parking in the new garage or underground lot (both accessible on 30th Street) costs a whopping $15 for two hours. Pricing on Arch Street's surface lot and the 29th and 30th Street surface lots are slightly more affordable. Rates are listed at $1.50 for every 20 minutes. Valet service is available at an expectedly high price of $5 per half hour. For quick pick-ups and drop-offs, the meters are the best bet; scattered around 30th, Market, and Arch Streets, meters cost 25 cents for every 7.5 minutes and $2 per hour. Unreserved monthly garage parking is available for $200 a month. Unfortunately, "unreserved" often means "unlikely availability"—there is a lengthy waiting list for these in-demand spots. For all parking inquiries, call 215-382-3567.

Services
Most of the shops and restaurants maintain 7 am to 8 pm business hours, though a select few stay open 24 hours. Among the many fast food joints and newsstands there is a post office, a flower stand, a Wells Fargo ATM, rental cars outlets, and a even few good places to grab a bite and a drink (Bridgewater's Pub has surprisingly amazing beer and food). One of the best recent additions to the station is "The Porch," complete with food trucks and a craft market.

Transit Connections
All SEPTA Regional Rail lines, the Market-Frankford line, and Trolley routes 10, 11, 13, 34, and 36 stop at 30th Street Station. Due to a recent rise in crime and loitering, the underground passageway to the Frankford line is closed; now when transferring between the stations, you must walk above ground for about a block. The NJ Transit's Atlantic City line runs from 30th Street Station to Atlantic City, while SEPTA's Trenton Line ends in Trenton and connects with NJ Transit trains to New York. If you're feeling weary from train travel, switch it up with a bus ride (Bus 30) from 30th Street Station to the 69th Street Terminal.

Suburban Station

NFT Map:	2
Address:	N 16th St & JFK Blvd
	Philadelphia, PA 19019
Phone:	215-580-6501

Overview
The fabulously ornate Suburban Station was once the shining star of Philadelphia's rail stations. That is, before the ultra-magnificent 30th Street Station came along and snatched the spotlight from its elder counterpart. Its proximity to City Hall, Love Park, and the shops at Liberty Place still make it a popular commuter station.

Built in the 1920s, with the aim of revamping Philadelphia's transportation system, the exterior of Suburban Station still stands as a glowing example of Art Deco architecture, with its gray limestone and elaborate gold and bronze gilded light fixtures. The top of Suburban Station houses an enormous 22-story office structure that spans an entire city block. From the exterior, the station is easily identifiable by the giant clothespin statue outside.

The bleak 1970s interior is disappointing in comparison to the grandiosity of its exterior. During rush hours, the station comes to life with the movement of corporate commuters and the sounds of street magicians, but when Friday evening arrives, the building becomes an empty cavern of closed stores and fast food joints.

Ticket Window

SEPTA's ticket office is on the underground's first level. The hours are Monday through Friday, 6 am-9 pm, and Saturday and Sunday, 8 am-6 pm. Service desks, public telephones, ATMs, and an abundant number of homeless folks are also available on this floor.

Parking

Unfortunately, SEPTA provides no parking at Suburban Station, though there is metered street parking in the vicinity for pick-ups and drop-offs. Honestly there is NO parking.

Services

During peak hours, the usual snack bars, fast food joints, and even a couple of sushi shops are open. There is little choice in terms of sundries on the weekends—you'll be lucky to find anything open other than Dunkin' Donuts.

Transit Connections

Dismal weekend atmosphere aside, Suburban Station is truly a connection haven. The Regional Rail lines, the Market-Frankford line, the Broad Street line, and several Trolleys all zip through this major hub. All connections are made via walkways running from Suburban Station to City Hall Station. Buses 17, 27, 31, 32, 33, 38, 44, 121, 124, 125, and C all arrive at City Hall. Bus 30 travels both east and westbound from 30th Street Station to the 69th Street Terminal, making a stop at Suburban Station. The PHLASH also has a pickup spot at 16th Street and Benjamin Franklin Parkway.

Market East Station

NFT Map: 3
Address: 12th St & Filbert St
            Philadelphia, PA 19107
Phone: 215-580-7800

Overview

Though Market East Station has little to offer visually, its location is convenient to many popular destinations including City Hall, Chinatown, Independence National Historic Park, Reading Terminal Market, and the Pennsylvania Convention Center. The station services SEPTA Regional Rail and the Market-Frankford line.

Originally labeled "the handsomest terminal passenger station of its time" after its completion in 1893, the old Reading Railroad Terminal is now the entrance to Pennsylvania's Convention Center. Also located at Market East Station is The Gallery, the first enclosed shopping mall in the US.

Ticket Window

It's best to enter the station on 12th or Filbert Streets, steering clear of The Gallery. Ticket office is open 6 am-10 pm, 8 am-9pm on Sat, 8 am-8pm on Sun.

Parking

SEPTA provides no parking, but there are some alternative parking options: two parking garages at The Gallery are nearby, as well as one at Reading Terminal Market. Metered street parking is available, however traffic in this section is among the WORST in the city, as is the parking.

Services

The range of food options at Market East Station, The Gallery, and the Reading Terminal Market is endless. Think delis overflowing with fresh produce, cafés brewing freshly roasted coffee, cheesesteak vendors simmering marinated meats, famous Italian bakeries offering fresh-baked bread—even the most picky palates will be pleased. The Gallery's stores compare to every other USA enclosed shopping mall.

Public Transportation

Beyond Regional Rail and the Market Frankford line, buses 17, 27, 31, 32, 33, 38, 44, 121, 124, 125, and C stop at City Hall, not far from Market East. If you're looking to hit up some tourist attractions, hop on the purple PHLASH bus. With stops at 12th and Market Streets, it's convenient and cheap. The PATCO from New Jersey also stops nearby, dropping passengers off at the 8th Street Station, just blocks from Market East Station.

169

General Information

Phone: 215-580-7800
Website: www.septa.org
System Map: NFT Foldout

Overview

Philly's SEPTA subway system is relatively small. It only has two lines—the Broad Street Line and the Market-Frankford Line (known to locals as the "Frankford El"). The lines are efficiently integrated into the overall SEPTA system and provide a valuable link in Philly's transit network. The subway system manages a remarkably efficient routing and connecting schedule—a noteworthy distinction from its Regional Rail cousin.

The subway is a popular transit option for commuters traveling to venues where parking is difficult, such as the Wells Fargo Center, Citizens Bank Park, or Market East Station.

It's also an efficient way to connect between regional and local rail services. It is, without question, a great alternative to the endless traffic-jams congesting the city's roadways.

Fares & Passes

A one-way subway ticket costs $2.25 cash or $1.80 token (available in packs of 2, 5, and 10). If you're going to be traveling around for the day, pick up a One Day Convenience Pass for $8. If you're a devoted subway user, the TransPass is a good investment ($24 per week and $91 per month). This card offers unlimited travel on all city transit routes, not just the subway.

The Market-Frankford Line

"You can't get to heaven on the Frankford El, because the Frankford El goes straight to Frankford"
                                    -American Dream (1970)

The Frankford Elevated Line (a.k.a. the "Blue Line") carries many Northeast commuters between the Frankford Transportation Center and the 69th Street Terminal between 5 am and midnight. Anytime after midnight, a reliable bus service replaces the Market-Frankford course, making similar stops along the route. Free transfers are available at 15th and Market Streets (City Hall) to all connecting Broad Street Line buses, which pass every 15 minutes during the morning hours.

In addition to regular trains, the Market-Frankford line is served by A and B trains during peak hours from Monday to Friday, 7:00 am-8:30 am and 3:45 pm-5:15 pm. A and B signs are displayed on the side and front of trains, so make sure you get on a train that's stopping at your destination.

Broad Street Line

Also known as the "Orange Line," the BSL is actually divided into two parts—Broad Street proper, which runs 10.1 miles, and the Broad Ridge Spur, which extends 1.9 miles. The former runs mostly underground, from the Fern Rock Transportation Center down to Pattison Avenue (near the sports and entertainment complex). Broad Ridge Spur is an eastern extension line from Fairmount down to 8th/Market (Chinatown).

Seven days a week, local trains operate every few minutes from 5:02 am to 12:30 am. A bus service takes over at night, running every 15 minutes and making a connection to all Market-Frankford Line buses at City Hall.

Between 5:50 am and 6:32 pm, express trains make stops every seven minutes (during peak hours) and every 15 minutes (non-peak hours) at Fern Rock, Olney, Girard, Spring Garden, Race-Vine, City Hall, and Walnut-Locust. The Ridge Spur service starts its weekday southbound service at 5:25 am and its northbound service at 5:45 am. On weekends, the first train travels south at 6:15 am and heads north at 6:38 am. Bikes are allowed onboard only during non-peak hours—before 6 am (for the early-birds), from 9 am to 3 pm, of after the 6 pm rush.

The Broad Street Line is absolutely your best option for attending sporting events. The local train will get you there from City Hall in 11 minutes, and you won't have to deal with the hassle of parking. Sports Express trains make stops at Fern Rock, Olney, Erie, Girard, Race-Vine, City Hall, and Walnut-Locust en route to Pattison Station. After events, there are northbound trains standing by to provide local and express service back to City Hall and Fern Rock. The line is also a great choice if you wish to travel along the Academy of the Arts, because crossing Broad Street, especially in rush hour, is akin to taking your life in your hands.

Parking

Parking during the week costs $1 at most stations and $2 at the Frankford Transportation Center, Fern Rock, and the 69th Street Terminal. There is free parking on weekends in the daily lots, while overnight and permit parking is only available at stations that also operate as Regional Rail stations. Don't forget that the parking fare boxes at SEPTA only accept change.

General Information

Phone: 215-580-7800
Website: www.septa.org
Lost & Found: 215-580-7800
Parking Information: 215-580-3400
System Map: NFT Foldout

Overview

The streets of Philadelphia are covered in trolley tracks; some of them are in current use, but many of them are no longer in operation. You'll find yourself cursing the unused portions of rail as your car twists and bumps over the tracks like a 19th-century wagon (and God help you if you are on a bike or skateboard when you hit one), but their ubiquitous remains remind us of the city's past.

At the height of service in 1911, nearly 4,000 streetcars traveled more than 86 routes. After major financial difficulties, including multiple bankruptcies and debts with other transportation companies, SEPTA finally took control of the trolley service in 1968. Today, only a few select routes continue trolley service, also known as "Subway Surface Routes." To remind riders of the days of yore, in 2004, SEPTA began running its refurbished old-fashioned trolley cars on Route 15, which travels Girard Ave.

Route 10 runs from 13th Street Station to Overbrook in West Philadelphia, while Routes 11, 13, 34, and 36 travel to points in southwest Philadelphia and Delaware County. Trolleys make stops at Suburban Station and 30th Street Station, where transfers to Amtrak, Regional Rail, and other subway lines are available. Routes 100 and 101 connect at the 69th Street Terminal and run to points south in Delaware County. Light rail Route 100 also runs northwest out to Norristown in Montgomery County.

Trolley hours vary depending on the line, but most begin service around 5 am and run until just after 1 am. Bikes are permitted on trolleys and light rail lines only during non-peak hours (before 6 am, 9 am-3 pm, and after 6 pm and anytime on weekends).

Fares & Passes

Trolley fare costs $2.25 cash or $1.80 with a token. Convenient multi-token packs are available in groups of 2, 5, or 10. Be aware that on Routes 100, 101, and 102 there is an additional charge of 50 cents for crossing suburban zones. A One Day Convenience Pass costs $8.

Like on the subways, the TransPass and TrailPass are good options for unlimited and cost-effective travel on a weekly or monthly basis. Tickets for seniors, students, and the disabled are also sold at reduced prices. Up to two children may ride free with any fare-paying adult, as long as they are less than 42 inches tall.

Parking

Finally, a place to park for free! Parking lots are available at many stations on Route 101 and 100. Visit www.septa.org for detailed listings. Most stations charge a meager $1 (in quarters!) for parking, except the 69th Street Terminal, Frankford Transportation Center, and Fern Rock which all charge $2.

General Information

Phone: 215-580-7800
Website: www.septa.org
System Map: NFT Foldout

Overview

After coming to terms with the expected rail delays and hassles (including the infamous strike season), you'll find SEPTA's Regional to be an effective, comfortable, and popular means of transportation. The eight-line service extends to the outer corners of Pennsylvania, carrying passengers to the airport and as far as Trenton, Doylestown, and Thorndale. Regional Rail also connects to Amtrak and NJ Transit services, making a trip to Washington DC, Chicago, Boston, and New York City very easy.

All SEPTA trains stop at Suburban Station, Market East Station, and 30th Street Station, and it's free to commute from one to another. All three stations connect to the Market-Frankford Line. A Broad Street Line connection can be made at Suburban Station, and Amtrak train service is available at 30th Street Station. Trolleys connect at Suburban Station and 30th Street Station.

Fares & Passes

Every Regional Rail station has a zone number, which is based on its distance from Center City. Tickets cost between $3.75 and $10 one-way. Regular riders can save some cash by purchasing 10 Trip Tickets. It's also cheaper to travel some zones off-peak. Keep in mind there is a varying surcharge for tickets bought on a train, regardless of whether or not the ticket office is open at the station where you boarded.

Zone	Peak	Off-Peak	10 Trip Tickets
1	$4.75	$3.75	$38.00
2	$4.75	$3.75	$45.00
3	$5.75	$5.00	$54.50
4	$6.50	$7.00	$62.50
NJ	$9.00	$9.00	$80.00

All fares are one way, based on advance-purchase prices. Tickets purchased on trains are between 50 cents and $1 more.

In addition to single-fare rides, fare options such as TransPass, TrailPass, Cross County Pass, and Intermediate Two Zone passes are also available for purchase on SEPTA's website and at various locations throughout the city.

TransPass is a deal that offers unlimited travel on all city transit routes and the first zone of suburban transit routes. The pass costs $24 per week and $91 per month.

TrailPass is valid for travel on Regional Rail to destinations within the zone indicated on the pass. Depending on the zones you plan to traverse, pass prices vary between $101 (Zone 1) and $191 (anywhere) per month ($27.25–$53.00 per week).

The **Cross County Pass** offers unlimited travel in three zones or more operating outside Center City, including all suburban bus routes, Routes 100, 101, 102, and Regional Rail. Passes cost $109 per month.

Regional Rail also offers discounts for persons with disabilities, seniors, students, some college students, families, and groups. Check www.septa.org for a detailed listing discounts and ticket purchase locations.

Bikes on SEPTA Regional Rail

There is a limit of two bikes per carriage during off-peak hours, and five bikes per carriage during weekends and major holidays. Bikes are never permitted during peak hours, unless they fold and can be stored out of the way.

Parking

Park-and-Ride is another cheap and efficient way to get into the city. Parking at most stations costs $1 while the Frankford Transportation Center, Fern Rock, and the 69th Street Terminal each charge $2. Be sure to take lots of loose change with you—the slot boxes only take quarters. Most SEPTA stations have numbered parking spaces next to the platform, but spots fill up quickly, so you should plan to arrive early or arrange for a drop-off buddy for the more bustling hubs like Jenkintown. Parking at smaller stations and connecting to your desired line is another option for avoiding parking congestion.

Overnight parking is also available at many stations *except* Ardmore, Bryn Mawr, Downingtown, Doylestown, Elkins Park, Haverford, Overbrook, Swarthmore, and Villanova. You need to reserve your overnight parking slot at least one day in advance and rates vary depending on location. For more information call 215-580-3400 24 hours-a-day.

General Information

Phone: 800-USA-RAIL (872-7245)
Website: www.amtrak.com
30th Street Station (PHL): 30th St & Market St
North Philadelphia (PHN): 2900 N Broad St
(& Glenwood Ave)

Overview

Two stations provide Amtrak service in Philly. 30th Street Station (PHL) is the main Amtrak station, located in the heart of Philadelphia. This massive Art Deco architectural gem is on the National Register of Historic Places and serves as a hub for both Amtrak and SEPTA. To the north is the aptly named North Philadelphia (PHN) station. It's a decrepit stop with such limited service that you're better off catching a train at the 30th Street Station. If you're a Harrison Ford fan, you might experience a little déjà vu at 30th Street Station: it was here that Peter Weir shot the beginning of his film Witness.

Acela Express

Traveling at speeds of up to 150 mph, the Acela line serves major cities along the northeastern seaboard. Philadelphia and New York City are two major stops along the Boston to Washington DC route, with several smaller stops in between. Both the Metroliner and the Regional trains run similar routes with more stops and at a slightly slower pace, but a significantly lower ticket price. Roundtrip tickets from Philadelphia to NYC on the Acela line start around $97 for a one-way ticket, but on holidays and at peak travel times, the fare rises dramatically. It's far from cheap, but if you want the quickest, least-hassle method of getting to New York, Acela is your best bet. Except, of course, when there are unexplained two hour delays.

If you're traveling to Boston, plan on paying somewhere near $200 for a one-way fare. And if you haven't maxed out your credit cards on Amtrak fares, you can head down to DC and back for a little more than $200.

Regional

The choice mode of travel for those who can afford the $54+ ticket, travelers heading from Philly to New York or Washington can reach their destination in 90 minutes for both cities. Ticket buying is generally simple on Amtrak's website or electronic kiosks (this way you can skip those painfully long lines at the station ticket booths). For longer trips, there are trains which run to destinations across the country. But comparing ticket price, travel time, and general aggravation with sleeping on the train, which can get rickety at times, other alternatives are suggested.

Baggage Check & Pet Policies

Each passenger can check up to three pieces of baggage thirty minutes before departure. You're allowed to check up to three more pieces for a $10 fee but, at that point, you'd be wiser renting a U Haul truck. You can also take two items on board with you. Electronic equipment and plastic or paper bags cannot be checked. All pets are prohibited on Amtrak trains, except for service animals.

How to Get There—Driving

The 30th Street Station is conveniently located off of I-76. Take Exit 345 and follow the signs for the station. The North Philadelphia Station can be reached from US-13.

Parking

There are five parking lots at the 30th Street Station. Two short-term lots charge $25 per 24 hours. Two long-term lots charge $20 per 24 hours. One valet lot is available for $35 per 24 hours.

How to Get There—Mass Transit

SEPTA commuter trains offer frequent service between 30th Street and Center City Philadelphia (Penn Center/Suburban Station and Market East Station). You can ride free on these trains to and from Center City with your Amtrak ticket stub. Visit www.septa.org for more information.

Transit • NJ Transit

General Information

Address:	1 Penn Plz E Newark, NJ 07105
Phone:	973-491-7000 (out of state) 800-772-2222 (in state)
Website:	www.njtransit.com

Overview

New Jersey Transit's buses, rail, and light rail services, while less luxurious than Amtrak trains, provide a far more affordable means of transportation between Philadelphia, Jersey cities, Newark International Airport, and Manhattan. Combined NJ Transit and SEPTA trains can get you to New York for less than half of what it costs to travel Amtrak. Just hop on SEPTA's Trenton Line train from Philadelphia's 30th Street Station to Trenton, NJ, then ride NJ Transit's Northeast Corridor line to New York.

Because of the low-cost fares and reliable schedules, travel during weekends and peak hours gets rather crowded—you might even find yourself standing all the way to New York on a holiday weekend. NJ Transit also provides service between Philadelphia and Atlantic City for $8 or less (and the ride takes less than an hour and a half). Just remember to buy your ticket before you get on the train, otherwise you'll be paying a five dollar surcharge (and you don't need to be wasting those five bucks before you even set foot in the casinos). The AC station is conveniently located just blocks from the boardwalk.

With fourteen bus terminals located in and around New Jersey, NJ Transit buses can take you across the river from Philadelphia to Camden, Six Flags Amusement Park, Trenton, or even to Bruce Springsteen's hometown, Asbury Park. Philadelphia's NJ Transit Bus Terminal is located at the Greyhound Bus Terminal, 1001 Filbert Street.

Fares & Passes

Bus passes must be purchased at an NJ Transit bus terminal—otherwise passengers are required to provide the driver with exact change in coins or $1 bills. Frequent riders can purchase ten trip tickets and monthly passes for reduced rates. Single-ride bus fares cost between $1.80 and $22.75, depending on the length of your trip.

Purchasing monthly passes for either the bus or train saves daily commuters about thirty percent of regular ticket costs. Monthly passes are valid for an unlimited number of trips between designated stations during the month for which they are purchased. Weekly passes, also valid for unlimited trips between designated stations, save about half of the cost of regular tickets. Check out the Quik-Tik option on the NJ Transit website to purchase passes online.

BusinessPass, offered through employers, can save commuters even more money on monthly rail and bus passes by deducting a portion of the cost from pre-tax salaries. These monthly passes are mailed directly to the work site. **PatronPass** gives businesses an opportunity to buy one-way tickets in bulk for either the bus or train in advance.

NJ Transit also offers special Family SuperSaver Fares, Student Monthly Passes, Children's Fares, and Senior Citizens packages. For more information on fare options, check out www.njtransit.com. You can also view schedules and fares online at www.njtransit.com, or can pick up a hard copy of schedules at any station.

Parking

Some train and bus stations provide free daily parking. Parking at other stations requires a permit. For parking information for each station, visit www.njtransit.com.

Baggage & Pets

Small pets are permitted on trains, but must be transported in carry-on travel cases. Service animals are always allowed to ride. On buses, each passenger is allowed to store two pieces of "conventional sized" luggage in the under-seat storage area.

Bikes Onboard

Many—but not all—NJ Transit buses carry bike racks attached to the front of the bus. The "Bike Aboard" program allows passengers to carry their bikes on NJ Transit trains for no extra charge. Most train and bus stations also offer parking facilities for up to 1,600 bicycles.

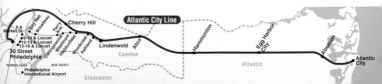

January

Mummer's Parade	Broad St	Men in dresses, drunk off their asses. www.mummers.org
MLK Jr Day of Service	Various locations	Day of action and celebration. www.campusphilly.org/mlkday

February

Philly Auto Show	Convention Center	More than 700 vehicles on show. www.phillyautoshow.com
Mardi Gras	South St	We just do the drinking part. www.southstreet.com
Chinese New Year	Chinatown	Day of the firecracker. www.phillychinatown.com
African American History Month	Various locations	City-wide events celebrate African American history. www.aampmuseum.org

March

Philly Flower Show	Convention Center	Biggest annual flower show in the country. www.theflowershow.com
St Patrick's Day Parade	City parade route	All the green beer you can stomach.

April

Cherry Blossom Festival	Various Center City locations	Japanese culture festival doused in pink.
Maya Weekend	UPenn	Mayan enthusiasts with a hankering for scholarly workshops cruise this annual event.
Penn Relays	UPenn	High-profile track meet. www.thepennrelays.com
Philadelphia International Festival of the Arts	Various locations	You have two years to gear up for the biennial, month-long arts festival offering music, dance, theater, and more. pifa.org
Philly Antiques Show	UPenn Hospital	Proceeds go to the hospital. www.thephiladelphiaantiquesshow.org
XPN Music Film Festival	Various locations	Films about all kinds of music, plus some live events too. www.xpn.org
Philadelphia Science Festival	Various locations	Ten days of brainy fun for geeks of all ages. www.philasciencefestival.org

May

Broad Street Run	Broad St	10-mile road race in early May. www.broadstreetrun.com
Police & Fire Memorial	Franklin Square Park	Honors fallen police officers and firefighters. www.phila.gov
Dad Vail Regatta	Schuylkill River	Largest collegiate rowing race in the country. www.dadvail.org
Italian Market Festival	9th St Italian Market	South Philly's 'old man' event of the year.
Philly Book Festival	Free Library of Philly	A serious series of author events mixed in with music and fun for the kids—Lyle the Crocodile is alive and well! www.philadelphiabookfestival.org
Rittenhouse Row Spring Festival	Rittenhouse Square	Indoor/outdoor street fair. www.rittenhouserow.com
Race for the Cure	Fairmount Park	5K road race to support breast cancer cure. www.komen.org
Mount Airy Day	Various locations	Performances, flea market, and games to celebrate the community. www.mtairyday.org
Philadelphia International Children's Festival	UPenn campus	Fun-filled kid fest going strong since 1984. www.annenbergcenter.org

June

FirstGlance Film Festival	Various locations	Bi-coastal indie film fest. www.firstglancefilms.com
Philly Pride Festival	Broad & Pine Sts	LGBT pride extravaganza. www.phillypride.org
Pro Cycling Championship	Ben Franklin Pkwy	Commerce Bank-sponsored bike race. www.procyclingtour.com
Bloomsday	Rosenbach Library	Reading of Joyce's *Ulysses* on the day it supposedly took place (June 16th). www.rosenbach.org
First Person Arts Festival	Various locations	Literary, film, and performance events focusing on memoir and documentary genres. www.firstpersonarts.org

| Manayunk Arts Festival | Main St in Manayunk | An impressive craft orgy. www.manayunk.com |
| Philly Beer Week | Independence Mall | Celebrate beer, Philly style. www.phillybeerweek.org |

July

Welcome America!	Various locations	Week-long birthday party for America! www.welcomeamerica.com
QFest	Various locations	A huge selection of gay and lesbian films, and lots of fun after each screening. www.qfest.com
Independence Day Regatta	Kelly Dr	Held since 1880—hope that your coxswain taught you well. www.boathouserow.org

August

Unity Day	Ben Franklin Pkwy	Celebration of Brotherly Love. www.wdasfm.com
Philly Folk Festival	Various locations	Props for not spelling "folk" with a "ph." www.pfs.org/folk-festival
GayFest!	Various locations	Theater festival exploring LGBT themes. www.quinceproductions.com/gayfest.html

September

Center City Restaurant Week	Center City	Tons of restaurants offer fixed-price menus. www.centercityphila.org
Philladelphia Live Arts Festival and Philly Fringe	Various locations	Indie theater, dance, and art performances. www.pafringe.com
Puerto Rican Festival Parade	City parade route	Puerto Rican pride celebration. www.elconcilio.net

October

Dragon Boat Races	Schuylkill River	Over 100 teams and eight lanes of action. www.philadragonboatfestival.com
Terror Behind the Walls	Eastern State Penitentiary	Jail transforms into a haunted house. http://easternstate.org
OutFest	Various locations	Coming-out block party. www.phillypride.org
Columbus Day Parade	S Broad St	Name says it all. www.phila.gov
Pulaski Day Parade	City parade route	Polish heritage celebration. www.polishamericancenter.org
215 Festival	Free Library	Showcase of established and emerging writers/musicians. www.215festival.com
Revolutionary Germantown Festival	Rittenhouse Town	Reenactments of battles and other fun for the kids. www.rittenhousetown.org
Philadelphia Film Festival	Various locations	Annual indie and foreign flicks fest. filmadelphia.org
Philadelphia Open Studio Tours	Various locations	Emerging visual artists give a sneak peak into their world. www.philaopenstudios.com

November

Philadelphia Marathon	City-wide	26.2 grueling miles. www.philadelphiamarathon.com
Thanksgiving Day Parade	Ben Franklin Pkwy	Turkey Day family fun. http://abclocal.go.com/wpvi
Philadelphia Museum of Art Contemporary Craft Show	Pennsylvania Convention Center	Top artisans sell their wares to benefit the PMA. www.pmacraftshow.org
First Person Arts Festival	Various locations	Memoir and documentary art, a la The Moth and Spalding Gray. firstpersonarts.org

December

| City Hall Tree Lighting Festival | City Hall | The usual fanfare beginning Dec 1. |
| New Year's Eve | Penn's Landing | Fireworks over the Delaware River. www.pennslandingcorp.com |

Useful Phone Numbers

Emergencies:	911
General Information:	411
Philadelphia Police Headquarters:	215-686-3220
City Hall:	215-686-3410
Comcast:	888-633-4266
Fire Department:	215-686-1300
Parking Authority:	888-591-3636
Public Defender:	215-568-3190
Tourism Information:	800-537-7676
Free Library of Philadelphia:	215-686-5332
Block Party Permits:	215-686-5560
Bucks County Board of Elections:	215-686-3943
Philadelphia Board of Elections:	215-686-3469

Essential Philadelphia Movies

The Philadelphia Story (1940)
1776 (1972)
Rocky (1976)
Blow Out (1981)
Taps (1981)
Tattoo (1981)
Trading Places (1983)
Birdy (1984)
Witness (1985)
Mannequin (1987)
Philadelphia (1993)
Twelve Monkeys (1995)
Fallen (1998)
The Sixth Sense (1999)
Unbreakable (2000)
Invincible (2006)
Rocky Balboa (2006)
Baby Mama (2008)
Law Abiding Citizen (2009)
Night Catches Us (2010)

Websites

www.citypaper.net · Online version of Philly's free weekly newspaper that tells you what to do, where to live, and more.
www.nba.com/sixers · Official website of Philly's favorite basketball team.
www.notfortourists.com · The ultimate website for everything you ever need to know about anything.
www.phawker.com · Source for under-the-radar Philadelphia news and culture commentary.
www.phila.gov · The city's official home on the web.
http://philadelphia.about.com · Tons of information on the city, from walking tours to civic issues to recommended restaurants and more.
www.philadelphiaeagles.com · Official website of Philly's favorite football team.
http://philadelphia.phillies.mlb.com · Official website of Philly's favorite baseball team.
flyers.nhl.com · This site only matters if there actually is an NHL next year, of course.
www.philadelphiaweekly.com · Online version of Philly's free weekly newspaper that tells you what to do, where to live, and more.
www.philebrity.com · Prolific gossip and local politics blog: most of it's "true."
www.philly.com · Local news, sports, jobs, cars, homes, etc.
www.philly1.com · Local news briefs and links to indie Philly-based publications.
www.phillychinatown.com · "We bring Asian market to you"
www.phillyskyline.com · The skinny on new buildings, urban landscape crises and neighborhoods uncovered via blog and photography
www.uwishunu.com · Blogging for more tourists.
hiddencityphila.org · Great Web mag from some of the folks at phillyskyline.

Essential Philadelphia Books

A House on Fire: The Rise and Fall of Philadelphia Soul (2004) by John A. Jackon
Benjamin Franklin: An American Life (2003) by Walter Isaacson
Common Sense (1776) by Thomas Paine
Diary of Independence Hall (1948) by Harold Donaldson Eberlein & Cortland Van Dyke Hubbard.
Shining Cycles of Love (1959) by Anna Coggins Dart.
The Papers of Benjamin Franklin, by Benjamin Franklin – more than 30 volumes edited and published by Yale University Press.
The Neal Pollack Anthology of American Literature (2002) by Neal Pollack

We're Number One!!!

America's first brick house: Penn House, 1682
America's first public school: Fourth & Chestnut Streets, 1698
America's first public fire engine: 1719
America's first botanical gardens: On the banks of the Schuylkill, 1728
America's first public library: Free Library of Philadelphia, 1731
America's first hospital: Philadelphia Hospital, 1732
America's first university: University of Pennsylvania, 1749
America's first anti-slavery society: 1774
America's first flag: Made in Philly by Betsy Ross, 1777
America's first Congressional meeting: Congress Hall, 1789
America's first law school: University of Pennsylvania Law School, 1790
America's first bank: Bank of North America, 1780
America's first bank robbery: $162, 821, August 31, 1798
America's first capital: Take that, Washington, 1790-1800
America's first lager: John Wagner brought lager yeast from his native Bavaria and brewed the nation's first lager beer, 1840.
America's first International Modernist skyscraper: We beat the Depression! Philadelphia Savings Fund Society Building at 12th and Market Streets, 1932.

Philadelphia Timeline—*a timeline of significant events in Philly history (by no means complete)*

1681: King Charles II grants charter of Pennsylvania.
1702: William Penn grants charter for city of Philadelphia.
1704: First Presbyterian Church erected.
1723: Benjamin Franklin arrives in Philadelphia.
1731: First Baptist Church erected.
1732: Independence Hall construction finished. Becomes home of the Liberty Bell.
1749: Ben Franklin founds the country's first university, University of Pennsylvania.
1752: Liberty Bell cracks.
1775: First Continental Congress elects Franklin as Postmaster General of colonies.
1776: Signing of the Declaration of Independence.
1777: British invade Philadelphia.
1778: American army spends cold winter in Valley Forge.
1784: Peace with England ratified by Congress.
1790: Ben Franklin dies in Philadelphia.
1803: Northern Liberties incorporated into city of Philadelphia.
1813: Spring Garden district incorporated into city of Philadelphia.
1829: Eastern State Penitentiary opened.
1829: *The Philadelphia Inquirer* founded.
1857: Academy of Music opens.
1865: City mourns Lincoln's assassination, celebrates defeat of Lee's army.
1866: Coldest night in history (18 degrees below zero): Schuylkill and Delaware freeze.
1872: Friends Meeting House (17th & Girard Sts) opened for public worship.
1874: Famous autopsy of first Siamese twins Chang and Eng completed at College of Physicians and Surgeons.
1875: South Street Bridge opened to pedestrians, 194 buildings erected throughout city.
1876: First train departs from Philadelphia to New York City.
1877: Philadelphia Museum of Art opens Memorial Hall.
1881: First African Americans join police force.
1883: Founding of the National League Team, the Phillies.
1885: City businesses closed for funeral of Ulysses S. Grant.
1889: Labor Day instituted as legal holiday in Pennsylvania.
1915: Phillies make it to the World Series with manager Pat Moran.
1922: Construction begins on the Benjamin Franklin Bridge (then the Delaware River Bridge).
1926: Benjamin Franklin Bridge opens for traffic.
1942: Phillies set club record of losing streak with 111 games.
1957: Walt Whitman Bridge opened for traffic.

1963: Philadelphia purchases Syracuse's NBA team, which becomes the 76ers.
1972: The Sixers post a 9-73 record, still the worst in NBA history.
1981: The Eagles make it to the Super Bowl. And lose to the Raiders.
1985: Infamous MOVE bombing kills 11 and burns 61 houses to the ground.
1991: Old City institutes the tradition of "First Fridays," an art community open house on the first Friday of every month.
1992: Ed Rendell begins first term as mayor of Philadelphia.
1994: Tom Ridge elected Governor of Pennsylvania.
1996: Larry Brown named coach of the 76ers.
1997: Debut of the Philadelphia Fringe Festival.
1998: Wachovia Center opens as new home of the 76ers and the Flyers.
1999: Sixers make it to the playoffs.
2000: John Street takes office as Mayor of Philadelphia.
2000: Republican National Convention held in Philadelphia.
2001: Sixers lose in the NBA finals in five games.
2002: Kimmel Center opens to rave reviews.
2003: Former mayor Ed Rendell becomes Governor of Pennsylvania.
2003: "Ride the Ducks" debuts and annoys all Philadelphians.
2003: With the purchase of "Striped Bass," Stephen Starr reaches ownership of ten restaurants in Philadelphia.
2003: Eagles open their new playing venue, Lincoln Financial Field.
2004: Eagles lose NFC Championship Game—third year in a row.
2004: Citizens Bank Park, new home of the Phillies, opens.
2004: Mayor John Street announces plans for city to become first major wireless Internet city in the country.
2005: Eagles redeem themselves (almost), making it to the Super Bowl.
2006: We celebrate Benergy!
2007: Comcast Center's giant phallus completes its erection, now the tallest building in the skyline.
2008: Philly rated America's "least attractive" and "most sedentary" city and then reveled in its First Annual Beer Week.
2008: Phils win the World Series, finally breaking the William Penn curse.
2009: Philadelphia Spectrum closes forever.
2011: Ryan Howard tears Achilles on final out of NLDS, heralding end to Phillies' brief NL East dominance.
2012: Barnes Foundation relocates to Center City.

(179)

Media

Nothing to see here! Move right along! No, those aren't a bunch of aimless ex-journalists tossed on their butts after mass lay-offs at the *Inquirer* and *Daily News*. No, Philadelphia media isn't in a state of chaos and disrepair, driving up *New York Times'* sales and down the vibrancy of real, local reportage! Oh wait, that's pretty much the case. Recent buyouts of the Inquirer (and the Daily News--a package deal) by "media companies" have left the Inquirer's wings clipped, leaving our two alt weeklies, City Paper and Philadelphia Weekly, to offer some surprisingly hard-driven reportage—paired, of course, with arts coverage, sex ads, and increasingly obsolete classifieds. *The Jewish Exponent* wants to bomb Iran and democrats. *Philadelphia City News* has ticked off the community more than once, and *Philadelphia Magazine* services the Main Line. For the real story, always rely on the hard-nosed yet compassionate Marty Moss-Coane on NPR. And Terry, we love you—keep on subtly confronting bigots in between Will Ferrell interviews.

Television

3	KYW (CBS)	philadelphia.cbslocal.com
6	WPVI (ABC)	abclocal.go.com/wpvi
10	WCAU (NBC)	www.nbcphiladelphia.com
12	WHYY (PBS)	www.whyy.org
17	WPHL	phl17.com
29	WTXF (FOX)	www.myfoxphilly.com
35	MiND TV	www.mindtv.org
51	WTVE	www.wtve.com
57	WPSG-TV	cwphilly.cbslocal.com
61	WPPX (PAX)	iontelevision.com

AM Stations

560	WFIL	Religious
610	WIP	Sports
860	WWDB	Business News
900	WURD	News
950	WPEN	Sports
990	WNTP	Conservative Talk Radio
1060	KYW	All News
1210	WPHT	Talk
1260	WNAR	Drama/Nostalgia
1480	WDAS	Gospel
1540	WNWR	Ethnic
1600	WEXP	College/Sports

FM Stations

88.1	WPEB	Student Radio
88.5	WXPN	Public/Adult Alternative
90.1	WRTI	Public/Classical/Jazz
90.7	WKPS	Student
90.9	WHYY	Public Radio/News/Talk/NPR Affiliate
91.7	WKDU	Drexel University
92.5	WXTU	Country
93.3	WMMR	Rock
94.1	WYSP	Rock
95.7	WBEN	Hot Adult Contemporary
96.5	WPTP	'80s Rock
98.1	WOGL	Oldies
98.9	WUSL	Hip Hop
101.1	WBEB	Adult Contemporary
102.1	WIOQ	Top 40
102.9	WMGK	Classic Rock
103.3	WPRB	Princeton University
104.5	WSNI	Oldies
105.3	WDAS	Urban Contemporary
106.1	WJJZ	Smooth Jazz

Print Media

Al Dia	211 N 13th St, Ste 704	215-569-4666	Latino daily.
Daily News	400 N Broad St	215-854-2000	Daily tabloid.
Daily Pennsylvanian	4015 Walnut St	215-898-6585	UPenn independent news.
Jewish Exponent	2100 Arch St	215-832-0700	Jewish weekly.
The Hawk	5600 City Avenue	610-660-1000	St. Joseph's University Weekly.
Philadelphia Metro	30 S. 15th St.	215-717-2600	National daily.
Penn Gazette	3910 Chestnut St, 3rd fl	215-898-5555	UPenn alumni magazine.
Philadelphia Business Journal	400 Market St, Ste 1200	215-238-1450	Daily business report.
Philadelphia City Paper	123 Chestnut St, 3rd fl	215-735-8444	Weekly arts & entertainment.
Philadelphia Gay News	505 S 4th St	215-625-8501	Weekly news.
Philadelphia Inquirer	400 N Broad St	215-854-2000	Daily broadsheet.
Philadelphia Magazine	1818 Market St, 36th fl	215-564-7700	City mag with "Best Of" list.
Philadelphia Observer	1520 Locust St, Ste 501	215-545-7500	Weekly African American.
Philadelphia Style	141 League St	215-468-6670	Monthly fashion/culture mag.
Philadelphia Tribune	520 S 16th St	215-893-4050	Weekly African American news.
Philadelphia Weekly	1500 Sansom St, 3rd Floor	215-563-7400	Weekly alternative.
Temple News	1755 N. 13th St, Rm 243	215-204-7416	Temple University print weekly and online daily.
The Triangle	3010 MacAlister Hall, 33rd & Chestnut Sts.	215-895-2585	Weekly Drexel University news.

Libraries

Show us a Philadelphia without budget problems, and we'll show you library locations that are always open. As it is, though, City Hall struggles to keep the city chugging forward, and many of the Free Library's 54 neighborhood locations have limited hours, or, worse, stand to be closed.

The main **Central Library** at 19th and Vine Streets **(Map 2)** is always there for you, though, and hosts a great reading series that features writers of all levels of fame, including comedians and political figures. Branch libraries also host events. Some cost money but many are free; for a schedule, go to www.freelibrary.org.

And if you can't make it to the actual library, you can always call, email or chat online with a librarian who is standing by to guide you to the information and resources you need. Hooray, hooray for the library!

Library	Address	Phone	Map
Central Library	1901 Vine St	215-686-5322	2
Charles L. Durham Branch	3320 Haverford Ave	215-685-7436	14
Charles Santore Branch	932 S 7th St	215-686-1766	8
Chestnut Hill Branch	8711 Germantown Ave	215-685-9290	27
Falls of Schuylkill Branch	3501 Midvale Ave	215-685-2093	23
Fishtown Community Branch	1217 E Montgomery Ave	215-685-9990	20
Fumo Family Branch	2437 S Broad St	215-685-1758	10
Independence Branch	18 S 7th St	215-685-1633	3
Joseph E. Coleman Northwest Regional Library	68 W Chelten Ave	215-685-2150	24
Kensington Branch	104 W Dauphin St	215-685-9996	20
Library for Blind and Physically Handicapped	919 Walnut St	215-683-3213	3
Lovett Branch	6945 Germantown Ave	215-685-2095	25
Lucien E. Blackwell West Philadelphia Regional Library	125 S 52nd St	215-685-7433	13
Philadelphia City Institute	1905 Locust St	215-685-6621	2
Queen Memorial Library	1201 S 23rd St	215-685-1899	6
Ramonita de Rodriguez Branch	600 W Girard Ave	215-686-1768	19
Roxborough Branch	6245 Ridge Ave	215-685-2550	21
South Philadelphia Branch	1700 S Broad St	215-685-1866	10
Thomas F. Donatucci, Sr. Branch	1935 Shunk St	215-685-1755	9
Walnut Street West Branch	201 S 40th St	215-685-7671	13
Whitman Branch	200 E Snyder Ave	215-685-1754	11
Widener Branch	2808 W Lehigh Ave	215-685-9799	15

Police Stations

	Address	Phone	Map
12th Police District	6448 Woodland Ave	215-686-3120	n/a
14th Police District	43 W Haines St	215-686-3140	24
15th Police District	2831 Levick St	215-686-3150	n/a
16th Police District	3900 Lancaster Ave	215-686-3160	13
17th Police District	1201 S 20th St	215-686-3170	6
18th Police District	5510 Pine St	215-686-3180	n/a
19th Police District	61st St & Thompson St	215-686-3190	n/a
1st Police District	S 24th St & Wolf St	215-686-3010	n/a
22nd Police District	17th St & Montgomery Ave	215-686-3220	n/a
24th Police District	3901 Whitaker Ave	215-686-3240	n/a
25th Police District	3901 Whitaker Ave	215-686-3250	n/a
26th Police District	Girard Ave & Montgomery Ave	215-686-3260	20
2nd Police District	2831 Levick St	215-686-3020	n/a
35th Police District	N Broad St & W Champlost Ave	215-686-3350	n/a
39th Police District	N 22nd & W Hunting Park Ave	215-686-3390	n/a
3rd Police District	11th St & Wharton St	215-686-3030	7
4th Police District	11th St & Wharton St	215-686-3040	7
5th Police District	Ridge Ave & Cinnaminson St	215-686-3050	n/a
6th Police District	235 N 11th St	215-686-3060	3
7th Police District	Bustleton Ave & Bowler St	215-686-3070	n/a
8th Police District	Academy Rd & Red Lion Rd	215-686-3080	n/a
92nd Police District	Lincoln Dr & Gypsy Ln	215-686-7292	22
9th Police District	401 N 21st St	215-686-3090	17
Center City District	660 Chestnut St	215-440-5551	3
South Street Detail (3rd District)	905 South St	215-922-6706	8

Important Phone Numbers

Life-Threatening Emergencies:	911		
Non-Emergency Police Service:	311 or 215-686-1776	Domestic Violence Hotline:	866-723-3014
Wanted Persons:	888-683-9268	Missing Persons Unit:	215-685-3257
Rape Victims Hotline:	215-985-3333	Special Victims Unit:	215-685-3251
		Noise Complaints (NET):	215-686-5819
		Complaints (Internal Affairs):	215-685-5056

Crime Statistics

	2002	2003	2004	2005	2006	2011
Murder	288	348	330	377	406	331
Rape	1,035	1,004	1,001	1,024	960	833
Robbery	8,869	9,617	9,757	10,069	10,971	8,246
Aggravated Assault	9,865	9,651	9,814	10,139	10,546	8,865
Burglary	11,244	10,656	10,536	10,960	11,542	12,057
Theft	38,789	37,864	37,808	38,039	39,413	40,113
Motor Vehicle Theft	13,302	13,934	12,587	11,420	11,655	7,447

Emergency Rooms

	Address	Phone	Map
Albert Einstein Medical Center	5501 Old York Rd	215-456-7890	n/a
Aria Health-Frankford Campus	4900 Frankford Ave	215-831-2000	n/a
Chestnut Hill	8835 Germantown Ave	215-248-8200	27
Germantown Community Health Services	1 Penn Blvd	215-951-8000	n/a
Hahnemann University Hospital	Broad St & Vine St	215-762-7000	2
Hospital of the University of Pennsylvania	3400 Spruce St	215-662-4000	14
Jeanes Hospital	7600 Central Ave	215-728-2000	n/a
Jefferson University Hospital	111 S 11th St	215-955-6000	3
Methodist Hospital	2301 S Broad St	215-952-9000	10
Nazareth Hospital	2601 Holme Ave	215-335-6000	n/a
Pennsylvania Hospital	800 Spruce St	215-829-3000	3
Penn Presbyterian Medical Center	51 N 39th St	215-662-8000	13
St Joseph's Hospital	N 16th St & W Girard Ave	215-787-9000	18
Wills Eyes	840 Walnut St	215-928-3000	3

Other Hospitals

	Address	Phone	Map
Belmont Center for Comprehensive Treatment	4200 Monument Rd	215-877-2000	n/a
The Children's Hospital of Philadelphia	34th St & Civic Ctr Blvd	215-590-1000	14
Fox Chase Cancer Center	333 Cottman Ave	215-728-6900	n/a
Magee Rehabilitation Hospital	1513 Race St	800-96-MAGEE	2
Mercy Philadelphia Hospital	501 S 54th St	215-748-9000	n/a
Penn Medicine at Rittenhouse	1800 Lombard St	215-893-5000	2
Temple University Hospital	3401 Broad St	215-707-2000	12

Part of the appeal of hanging out with kids is rediscovering the fun and frivolity of childhood. We've created a list of great stores, restaurants, and activities that you should enjoy as much as the little 'uns.

Shopping Essentials

Philadelphia is not often touted as one of the fashion capitals of the world. But with the help of these stores, your kids can be as adorably clothed and accessorized as their counterparts in London, Paris, New York, and Milan.

- **babyGap** • 160 North Gulph Rd, King of Prussia • 610-265-0620 • Timeless baby fashions at moderate prices.
- **Big Blue Marble Books** • 551 Carpenter Ln • 215-844-1870 • Progressive and multi-cultural titles for lefties in the making.
- **Born Yesterday** • 1901 Walnut St • 215-568-6556. • Up-scale kiddie clothes.
- **Burberry** • 1705 Walnut St • 215-557-7400 • The famous raincoats and plaids in miniature.
- **Children's Boutique** • 1702 Walnut St • 215-732-2661 • First floor stocked with European kids' clothes and shoes, second floor devoted to toys.
- **Gymboree** • 326 Mall Blvd, King of Prussia • 610-992-0470 • Clothing store and play center chain geared at children under the age of seven.
- **Happily Ever After** • 1010 Pine St • 215-627-5790 • Old-school toy store.
- **IKEA** • 2206 S Columbus Blvd • 215-551-4532 • Great deals on kids' furniture and accessories. And kids love playing in the showroom.
- **Karl's—Baby & Teenage Furniture & Clothing** • 724 Chestnut St • 215-627-2514 • The name says it all.
- **Little Beth Boutique** • 1540 Packer Ave • 215-468-2229 • Best christening gowns in the city.
- **Motherhood Maternity and Pea in the Pod** • 1615 Walnut St • 215-567-1425 • Maternity wear.
- **O' Doodles** • 8335 Germantown Ave • 215-247-7405 • High-quality toys and beautiful children's books.

- **SimplyCottage** • 367 W Lancaster Ave, Haverford • 610-642-2905 • Unique hand-made baby goods, from linens to bookcases, to wall hangings.
- **Supercuts** • 209 South St • 215-922-2970 • Cheap cuts for kids. No appointment necessary.
- **Toys "R" Us** • 2703 S 3rd St • 215-334-4600 • Toy superstore.
- **Worn Yesterday of Manayunk** • 4235 Main St • 215-482-3316 • Consignment shop for maternity wear, kids, and baby outfits—the place to go if you want your kid to look like one of Angie's, and at one third the cost.

Outdoor Activities

Kids cooped up are like fish out of water. Here are some outdoor activities they'll love.

- **Amish Village** • Rte 896, 717-687-8511 • Guided tours through Amish country and great souvenirs.
- **Dutch Wonderland** • 2249 Lincoln Highway E, Lancaster, 886-FUN-atDW • A lower key Disney-like experience that's really quite charming.
- **Fairmount Park** • Fairmount Ave, 215-683-0200 • Historic houses, boathouse row, running and biking paths, picnic grounds.
- **Longwood Gardens** • Rte 1, Kennett Square, 610-388-1000 • Horticultural display garden that hosts all kinds of activities for kids.
- **Lower Perkiomen Valley Park** • Oaks exit, Rte 422, Oaks, 610-666-5371 • Bike trails along the Schuylkill River, playground equipment along the way.
- **Philadelphia Zoo** • 3400 W Girard Ave 215-243-1100 • Oldest zoo in the country with a primate exhibit to write home about. Check out the Zooballoon!
- **Sesame Place** • 100 Sesame Rd, Langhorne • 215-752-7070) Sesame Street-based amusement park.

Websites

gocitykids.parentsconnect.com/region/philadelphia -pa-usa

www.phillyfunguide.com/categories/index/7/0

Rainy Day Alternatives

Nothing can really beat baking or watching movies on a rainy day. But if you're motivated to leave the house, these popular destinations never come up short:

- **Academy of Natural Sciences** • 1900 Ben Franklin Pkwy, 215-299-1000 • Four floors of activities and exhibits about the world's most fascinating species and their habitats.
- **American Historical Theatre** • 2008 Mt Vernon St, 215-232-2690 • Educational, historical theater for kids and school groups.
- **Arden Children's Theater** • 40 N 2nd St, 215-922-1122 • Resident professional children's theater.
- **Dave & Buster's** • 325 N Columbus Blvd, 215-413-1951 • Arcade games, pinball machines, laser tag, batting cage (and word on the street is that Allen Iverson hangs out here).
- **The Franklin Institute** • 222 N 20th St, 215-448-1200 • Science museum that takes learning to a new level of fun (seriously).
- **Headhouse Books** • 619 S 2nd St, 215-923-9525 • Children's story hours, Chess Club 4 Kids, and art history lessons.
- **Independence Seaport Museum** • 211 S Columbus Blvd, 215-413-8655 • All things Davy Jones, plus ongoing exhibits of other nautical phenomena.
- **Insectarium** • 8046 Frankford Ave, 215-335-9500 • All-bug museum.
- **Mütter Museum** • 19 S 22nd St, 215-563-3737 • For the future doctors of the world.
- **North Bowl** • 909 N 2nd St, 215-238-BOWL • Kid friendly before 9 p.m.
- **Philadelphia Doll Museum** • 2253 N Broad St, 212-787-0220 • Diverse dolls from around the world, character dolls, talking action figures, and vintage barbies.
- **Philadelphia Museum of Art** • 26th St & Franklin Pkwy, 215-763-8100 • Art classes for kids aged 3–12.
- **Please Touch Museum** • 4231 Avenue of the Republic, 215-963-0667 • You're supposed to touch everything. That's the point. Fake supermarkets, science rooms, barnyards, and more.
- **Walnut Street Theatre for Kids** • 825 Walnut St, 215-574-3550 • Professional theater for the young 'uns.

Kid-Friendly Restaurants

They love kids and kids love them:

- **DiNardo's Famous Crabs** • 312 Race St, 215-925-5115 • Tasty crabs. Bibs are given to everyone, so the kids won't stand out as the messy ones.
- **Fiesta Pizza** • 8339 Germantown Ave, 215-247-4141 • Caters to kids—gives you crowns and fries while you wait for the 'za.
- **Hard Rock Café** • 1113 Market St, 215-238-1000 • Average food tastes better when you're staring at a signed Elvis EP. No matter how tacky you might find it, the fact of the matter is that kids really like this place.
- **Johnny Rockets** • 443 South St, 215-829-9222 • '50s-style chain diner with standard jukebox and kids' menu.
- **Keating's River Grill** • 201 N Columbus Blvd, 215-928-1234 • Okay, it's a hotel restaurant, but it has a nice view.
- **More Than Just Ice Cream** • 1119 Locust St, 215-574-0586 • Ice cream in one room, vegetarian delights in the other.
- **Nifty Fifty's** • 2491 Grant Ave, 215-676-1950 • '50s-style diner.
- **Maron Chocolates and Scoop de Ville** • 1734 Chestnut St, 215-988-9992 • Part candy shop and part ice cream you can take to the park. How can you go wrong?

The site of some of the earliest gay rights protests in the 1960s, Philadelphia has long been a gay-friendly town. The city cultivates this image, coining the slogan "Get your history straight, and your nightlife gay" to draw LGBT tourists. The Gayborhood, stretching roughly from Walnut to Pine Streets between 11th and 13th streets, is now official! Gay marriage, it's not, but the city, since this past year, now hangs rainbow flags in the area, and even gay-ed up the street signs. It's a conglomeration of plenty of gay-owned businesses and residents, as well as the 12th Street Gym (where gay bodybuilders of Philadelphia unite). Sisters is the only full-time lesbian bar; Thursday night is the most popular evening, by far, and they serve a wonderful brunch on Sunday morning.

Health Centers and Support Organizations

- **ACT UP Philadelphia**, www.critpath.org/actup
  Political advocacy group by and for people living with HIV/AIDS.
- **Attic Youth Center**, 255 S 16th St,
  215-545-4331; www.atticyouthcenter.org
  The largest GLBT youth center in Philadelphia, the Attic provides a safe social space for queer youth, as well as counseling and psychological services for young adults between the ages of 12-23.
- **Bi-Unity Social Group**, www.biunity.org
  Social group for people who identify as bisexual.
- **City of Brotherly Love Softball League**,
  215-GO-CBLSL; www.cblsl.org
  Openly gay softball league with men's and women's divisions.
- **Critical Path AIDS Project**,www.critpath.org
  Part of Philadelphia Fight, offers treatment, referrals, advocacy information, and more to HIV-positive individuals. Their website is a resource in itself.
- **Equality Advocates Pennsylvania** ,
  1211 Chestnut St, Ste 605,
  215-731-1447; www.equalitypa.org
  Advocating equality for the LGBT community in PA.
- **Fairmount Park Women's Softball League,**
  215-508-3922
  Fairmount Park Women's Softball League has been part of the women's sports community in Philadelphia for over 25 years.
- **Frontrunners Philadelphia,**
  www.frontrunnersphila.org
  Gay and lesbian running club.
- **Gay and Lesbian Lawyers of Philadelphia**,
  215-627-9090; www.galloplaw.org.
  Call if you need a referral for a lawyer.
- **Lavender Visions,**
  www.lavendervisions.com/married.html.
  Programs for lesbian and bisexual women, with excellent resources for married women who are coming out or seeking individual or group counseling.
- **Mazzoni Center**, 1201 Chestnut St, 3rd Fl,
  215-563-0652; www.mazzonicenter.org
  Free and anonymous HIV testing and counseling.
- **PA Gay and Lesbian Alliance for Political Action**,
  610-863-0227, http://eqfed.org/pagala/home.html
  The group meets on the second Tuesday of each month at the William Way Center.·
- **PFLAG Philadelphia**,
  P.O. Box 15711, Philadelphia, PA 19103
  215-572-1833; www.pflagphila.org
  Parents, Families and Friends of Lesbians and Gays.
- **Philadelphia Family Pride**,
  www.phillyfamilypride.org
  Social events for gay and lesbian parents and their children.
- **Philadelphia Fight**, 1233 Locust St, 5thFloor
  215-985-4448, www.fight.org
  AIDS service organization focusing on research and education.
- **Philadelphia FINS**,
  267-971-7932, www.philadelphia-fins.org
  Philadelphia's LGBT Masters Swim Team.
- **Philadelphia Lesbian and Gay Task Force**,
  215-772-2000
  Works on political issues and has a hotline for violence directed at gays and lesbians. Makes use of volunteers.
- **The Safeguards Project**,
  260 S Broad St 10th Floor, 215-985-6873
  Non-profit community health organization promoting a healthy lifestyle for gay men and the LBGT community through workshops, HIV testing, community programs, and health information. www.safeguards.org
- **Sisterspace**, 215-546-4890; www.sisterspace.org
  Organizes social events for women, a volleyball league, and a women of color forum.
- **William Way Lesbian, Gay, Bisexual Transgender (GLBT) Community Center**,
  1315 Spruce St, 215-732-2220; www.waygay.org
  Home to a number of community groups and host of many regular events.
- **Women in Transition Hotline**,
  215-751-1111, www.womenintransitioninc.org
  Support for lesbians in abusive relationships.

Bookstores

- **Giovanni's Room**, 345 S 12th St, 215-923-2960; www.giovannisroom.com—One of the oldest gay bookstores in the country, this little nook offers a wide selection of gay, lesbian, and feminist texts and films. Women's book discussion group meets at 7:00 pm on the first Sunday of each month.

Publications and Media

- **Philadelphia Gay News** www.edgephiladelphia.com. Celebrating over 30 years in the gay press.
- **WXPN 88.5** www.xpn.org. Hosts two programs targeted to gays and lesbians: "Amazon Country" and "Q'zine."

Annual Events

- **Equality Forum**—Formerly PrideFest America, the GLBT conference and festival takes place every April. 215-732-FEST; www.equalityforum.com.
- **LGBT Pride Parade & Festival**—Held in June each year. 215-875-9288; www.phillypride.org.
- **OutFest**—"I'm coming out, I want the world to know, go to let it show!" www.phillypride.org/outfest.php
- **GayFest!**—Theater festival held in August each year. www.quinceproductions.com/gayfest.html
- **QFest**—Held every July, it's the biggest gay film festival on the East Coast. www.qfest.com
- **QPenn**—Penn's annual Pride Week takes place every March;

Venues—Gay

- **Bike Stop** · 206 S Quince St · 215-627-1662 · www.thebikestop.com
- **iCandy** · 254 S 12th St · 267-324-3500 · www.clubicandy.com
- **Pure Nightclub** · 1221 St James Pl · 215-735-5772 · www.purephilly.com
- **Westbury** · 261 S 13th St · 215-546-5170
- **Woody's** · 202 S 13th St · 215-545-1893 · www.woodysbar.com

Venues—Mixed

- **Tavern on Camac** · 243 S Camac St · 215-545-0900 · www.tavernoncamac.com
- **Sal's on 12th** · 200 S 12th St · 215-731-9930

Websites

- **Gay and Lesbian Yellow Pages**—www.glyp.com
- **Greater Philadelphia Tourism Bureau**—www.visitphilly.com/c/gay. Information about GLBT events, culture, and community in Philly.
- **Philadelphia Gay Singles**—http://philadelphiagaysingles.com. Online meeting place for Philly's gay and lesbians.
- **QueerConnections**— http://groups.yahoo.com/neo/groups/queerconnections/info Queer Connections (QC) is a social group for women in their twenties who are queer (lesbian, bisexual, gay, or transgendered), women who are questioning their sexuality, and friends of queers (who are straight but not narrow).
- **William Way Community Center**—www.waygay.org. Website with information on a number of community groups and gay & lesbian events.
- **Craigslist**—philadelphia.craigslist.org. General community site (for straights, gays, and everyone else) that includes local "women seeking women" and "men seeking men" personal pages.

Hotels

Philly isn't big on hotel bar and lobby culture like other Northeast cities such as New York ("sell, buy!") and DC ("vote, sell your soul!"), but there are plenty of beautiful places to stay. Especially if you have buckets of cash to burn. At the very top is the **Ritz-Carlton (Map 2)**, where you'll be pampered into pure bliss. A little further down the food chain (but still requiring an Amex Gold Card) are the boutique townhouses of **Rittenhouse 1715 (Map 2)**, the stuffy and luxurious old-school vibe of **The Rittenhouse (Map 2)**, the **Four Seasons (Map 2)**, and **Hotel Palomar (Map 2)**, where you can sip for free (after laying down hundreds of dollars of course) at the nightly wine hour.

But we're betting those are just a tad outside of your price range, so here are some more realistic options that still might not be cheap but are worth the splurge. **Loews (Map 3)** is housed in a historic bank skyscraper that now boasts modern rooms, many with sweeping city views. The **Omni Hotel at Independence Park (Map 4)**, close to the Ritz Theatres, is our top pick for anybody looking to swoop in for a film festival. The contemporary and comfortable **Sofitel (Map 2)** has a chain feel, but with a French twist. The **Hyatt at the Bellevue (Map 2)** overlooks William Penn dramatically perched on top of city hall, not a bad view for the price.

Convention goers swarm the gigantic **Marriott (Map 3)** that has little personality, unless you score a room in the Headhouse Tower. If a quaint B&B-like experience is what you're after, check-in at the **Morris House Hotel (Map 3)** or **Thomas Bond House (Map 4)**. The **Alexander Inn (Map 3)**, located in the Gayborhood, is convenient to Woody's and, well, men. Plus, it has an Art Deco cruise ship feel for a decent price.

Tourists looking to explore the heart of Old City will love the newest addition to the skyline, **Hotel Monaco (Map 4)** that overlooks the Liberty Bell, the cozy but reasonable rooms at Penn's View **(Map 4)**, and the surprisingly pleasant **Best Western Independence Park (Map 4)**.

Outlying hotel options are limited (see Airbnb below), but there's **Sheraton University City (Map 14)** and **Spruce Hill Manor (Map 14)** for Penn parents, the charming **Silverstone Bed & Breakfast (Map 27)** in an old stone house, the clean and basic **Chestnut Hill Hotel (Map 27)**, and the functional but cheap **Holiday Inn (Map 12)** near the stadiums (though sadly there is no secret tunnel).

If you're looking for a short-term apartment as a home base, Airbnb is now the official king of non-hotel accommodations. There's also Craigslist and VRBO.com, but whether you're in the mood for an affordable private room when you're traveling solo in Northern Liberties or a swank pad overlooking Rittenhouse Square to impress your latest date, Airbnb is your best bet to enjoy a neighborhood slice of Philly and sleep like a local.

Map 2 • Rittenhouse / Logan Circle

		Phone	Price
Courtyard Philadelphia Downtown	21 N Juniper St	215-496-3200	165
Crowne Plaza	1800 Market St	215-561-7500	145
DoubleTree by Hilton Hotel Philadelphia Center City	237 S Broad St	215-893-1600	247
Embassy Suites	1776 Benjamin Franklin Pkwy	215-561-1776	170
Four Seasons Hotel	1 Logan Sq	215-963-1500	400
Hyatt at the Bellevue	200 Broad St	215-893-1234	190
La Reserve	1804 Pine St	215-735-1137	125
Latham Hotel	135 S 17th St	215-563-7474	139
Radisson Plaza Warwick Hotel	1701 Locust St	215-735-6000	125
Residence Inn Philadelphia Center City	1 E Penn Sq	215-557-0005	169
Rittenhouse 1715	1715 Rittenhouse Sq	215-546-6500	239
The Rittenhouse Hotel	210 W Rittenhouse Sq	215-546-9000	285
The Ritz-Carlton Philadelphia	10 Ave of the Arts	215-523-8000	219
Sheraton Philadelphia City Center Hotel	N 17th St & Race St	215-448-2000	150
Sofitel Philadelphia	120 S 17th St	215-569-8300	175
Windsor Suites	1700 Benjamin Franklin Pkwy	215-981-5678	160
The Westin Philadelphia	99 S 17th St	215-563-1600	219

Map 3 · Center City East

		Phone	Price
Alexander Inn	Spruce St & 12th St	215-923-3535	99
Antique Row Bed & Breakfast	341 S 12th St	215-592-7802	65
Clinton St B&B	1024 Clinton St	215-802-1334	139
Hampton Inn	1301 Race St	215-665-9100	179
Hilton Garden Inn	1100 Arch St	215-923-0100	160
Holiday Inn Express	1305 Walnut St	215-735-9300	144
Loews Philadelphia Hotel	1200 Market St	215-627-1200	150
Morris House Hotel	225 S 8th St	215-922-2446	150
Parker Spruce Hotel	261 S 13th St	215-735-2300	45
Philadelphia Marriott Downtown	1201 Market St	215-625-2900	200
Trade Winds Bed & Breakfast	943 Lombard St	215-592-8644	88
Travelodge	1227 Race St	215-564-2888	112

Map 4 · Old City / Society Hill

		Phone	Price
Best Western Independence Park Hotel	235 Chestnut St	215-922-4443	225
Thomas Bond House	129 S 2nd St	215-923-8523	105
Comfort Inn Downtown/Historic Area	100 N Columbus Blvd	215-627-7900	130
Holiday Inn	400 Arch St	215-923-8660	170
Hyatt Regency	201 S Columbus Blvd	215-928-1234	160
Madame Saito Bed & Breakfast	124 Lombard St	215-922-2512	80
Omni Hotel at Independence Park	401 Chestnut St	215-925-0000	230
Penn's View Hotel	14 N Front St	215-922-7600	180
Sheraton Society Hill	1 Dock St	215-238-6000	189

Map 12 · Stadiums

		Phone	Price
Holiday Inn	900 Packer Ave	215-755-9500	120

Map 13 · West Philly

		Phone	Price
Spruce Hill Manor	331 S 46th St	215-472-2213	123

Map 14 · University City

		Phone	Price
Cornerstone Bed & Breakfast	3300 Baring St	215-387-6065	140
Hilton Inn at Penn	3600 Sansom St	215-222-0200	175
Spruce Hill Manor	3709 Baring St	215-472-2213	145
Sheraton University City Hotel	3549 Chestnut St	215-387-8000	169

Map 17 · Fairmount

		Phone	Price
Best Western City Center Hotel	501 N 22nd St	215-568-8300	125

Map 18 · Spring Garden / Francisville

		Phone	Price
Carlyle Hotel	1425 Poplar St	215-978-9934	50

Map 26 · Mt Airy

		Phone	Price
Anam Cara Bed & Breakfast	52 Wooddale Ave	215-242-4327	118

Map 27 · Chestnut Hill

		Phone	Price
Chestnut Hill Hotel	8229 Germantown Ave	215-242-5905	129
Silverstone Bed & Breakfast	8840 Stenton Ave	215-242-3333	95

Philly is essentially a city of landmarks, some obvious, some a little more esoteric. Some of the city's historic moneymakers are located on Independence Mall, which houses the **Liberty Bell (Map 4)**, the **National Constitution Center (Map 4)**, and **Independence Hall (Map 4)**, where the Declaration of Independence was first signed. They are all well worth seeing, if only so you can direct friends and family members when they visit.

Whilst in Old City, you can also check out **Christ Church (Map 4)** (founded in 1695), which has a lovely garden, free-of-charge to muse in, and **Franklin Court (Map 4)**, which has a museum o' Ben and frame replica of his original house (what happens when the city doesn't have enough insight to keep the thing up). With a great view of the city, the **William Penn Statue (Map 2)** sits high atop **City Hall (Map 2)**; from some angles he looks more excited to see you than in others (ahem).

In South Philly you can behold the **Pat's and Geno's Showdown (Map 8)**, the intersection at 9th and Passyunk where the two legendary steak shops seemingly stare down each other from across the street. Both spots are legendary. Pat's is where presidential candidate John Kerry famously asked for Swiss. The bustling dirty gem that is the **Italian Market (Map 8)** has great cheese and greater personality, while **Reading Terminal Market (Map 3)** buzzes with old-timey commerce (and don't forget the Amish!).

In the artistic realm, the well-endowed **Philadelphia Museum of Art (Map 16)** has an extensive permanent collection. The steps alone hold great fame, and are a top spot for midnight romance on the cheap. Nearby is the free **Rodin Museum (Map 17)**, where you can do your best to emulate The Thinker, ironically requiring no thought. If you have children in tow and want to reward them for trekking through art museums, they'll love The **Franklin Institute (Map 1)**, which has both an IMAX theater and planetarium—and the Giant Heart inside is a landmark all on its own.

Isaiah Zagar's mosaic murals are, literally, plastered all over the city, and most notably make up the **Magic Gardens (Map 8)** on South Street. Glistening with the chunk of yesteryear's ceramics, this garden is magic—if you only believe. Drop some money into the trashcan, believers, just beyond the gate, to help preserve this masterpiece.

Armchair athletes should check out **Lincoln Financial Field (Map 12)** and **Citizens Bank Park (Map 12)** for the Eagles and Phillies, respectively—both facilities are fifty times better than the Vet, the concrete-and-carpet multi-purpose hunk of junk they replaced, though some do miss the back-in-the-day antics of the old venue's infamous "700 Level" (the spirit of which lives on in the Philly sports website of the same name)

Branch	Address	Zip	Map
30th Street Train Station	2955 Market St	19104	14
B Free Franklin	316 Market St	19106	4
Castle Finance	1713 S Broad St	19148	10
Chestnut Hill	8227 Germantown Ave	19118	27
Continental	615 Chestnut St	19106	3
East Falls	4130 Ridge Ave	19129	23
Fairmount Finance Station	1939 Fairmount Ave	19130	17
Fairmount	900 N 19th St	19130	17
Germantown	5209 Greene St	19144	24
Girard Avenue	905 N Broad St	19123	18
John Wanamaker	1234 Market St	19107	3
Kensington	1602 Frankford Ave	19125	20
Land Title Bldg	100 S Broad St	19110	2
Manayunk	4431 Main St	19127	21
Market Square	7782 Crittenden St	19118	26
Middle City	2037 Chestnut St	19103	1
Mount Airy	6711 Germantown Ave	19119	25
Penn Center	1500 John F Kennedy Blvd	19102	2
Penns Landing Postal Store	622 S 4th St	19147	8
Philadelphia Main Office	3000 Chestnut St	19104	14
Point Breeze Postal Store	2437 S 23rd St	19145	9
Roxborough Postal Store	6184 Ridge Ave	19128	21
Schuylkill	2900 Grays Ferry Ave	19146	5
Snyder Plaza Finance Station	58 Snyder Ave	19148	11
Southwark	925 Dickinson St	19147	8
University City	228 S 40th St	19104	13
William Penn Annex	900 Market St	19107	3

Dog Runs

Websites:
www.dogfriendly.com
www.phillyfido.org
www.dogloverscompanion.com
www.bringfido.com/attraction/parks/city/philadelphia_pa_us
www.dogster.com/local/PA/Philadelphia/Dog_Parks

Overview

Despite the scarcity of dog runs and dog parks, Philly still REALLY loves its dogs. But the shortage of dog-designated areas may stem from the fact that the city is really one mammoth dog run. Dogs are welcome in many restaurants, cafés, hotels, parks, and most boutiques and clothing stores. The most fascinating place to watch dogs play is in Rittenhouse Square's fountain, a popular unleashing spot—dogs love to take a dip, and, yes, we love to watch. Pooch events include the Paws for the Cause Cancer Walk (www.fccc.edu): you can get some exercise for your pooch while you make money for a good cause.

Most dog runs prohibit aggressive dogs, and do not separate the small dogs from the larger dogs, making it a veritable doggie free-for-all. It goes without saying that you need to supervise your dog(s) at all times and pick up after them.

Dog Runs	Address	Comments
Ben Franklin Parkway	Ben Franklin Pkwy & 19th St	Beautiful downtown setting.
Carpenter Woods	Wissahickon & Mt Pleasant Aves	Woody paths, doggy swimming holes.
Chester Avenue Dog Club	48th St & Chester St	$15/year membership.
Dog Park	48th St & Chester St	Constantly in jeopardy due to UPenn expansion.
Eastern State Dog Pen	Brown St & Corinthian St	Designated fenced-in areas.
Horse & Carriage Rides	Market St & 5th St	Well-behaved dogs are welcome aboard the carriages.
Manayunk Towpath and Canal	Main St b/w Green Ln & Lock St	Two-mile path along the canal.
Mario Lanza Park	Queen St & 2nd St	Nice neighborhood vibe.
Pennypack Park	Algon Ave & Bustleton Ave	1,600 acres for leashed dogs only.
Rittenhouse Square Park	Walnut St & 18th St	Leashed dogs only.
Schuylkill River Dog Run	25th St & Spruce St	Benches for you, fences for them.
Seger Dog Park	11th St & Lombard St	Open 6 am-10 pm, daily.
SPOAC Dog Run	Passyunk St & Dickinson St	South Philly dogs unite.
Washington Square Park	Walnut St & 6th St	Leashed dogs only. (Yeah, right.)

In Center City, most of your options fall into two categories. One, the art house Bermuda triangle of **Ritz Theaters (Bourse, Five, and East) (Map 4)**. Two, the insidious, stadium-seating caverns of the Riverview multiplex **(Map** 8), which we heartily encourage you to avoid, especially on weekends, unless you truly enjoy loud audiences of fifteen-year-olds hurling gummi concessions at your head. For variety, check out the **Roxy Theatre (Map 1)**, showing independent and bigger-name fare in hugely uncomfortable seats. And if you can ignore that someone got shot out front two days after the theater opened, there's the otherwise beautiful seven-screen **Pearl Theatre** (1600 N Broad St, 215-763-7700) north o' Market.

In West Philly, the **University City Penn 6 (Map 13)** has gone through a few ownership changes, but still retains its fresh look, stadium seating, advance ticketing kiosks, and most importantly, full bar service. Generally showing blockbusters, they will sprinkle in one or two classics for the students and associated smart folk who inhabit the area. And when that's sold out, you can always see if anything's playing at the **International House** (3701 Chestnut Street, 215-387-5125), an international-student housing building with a year-round film program.

You can find plenty of big corporate theaters if you're willing to drive or take the bus a ways. In Manayunk there's the **UA Main Street (Map 22)**, and if you go to **Franklin Mills** (1149 Franklin Mills Cir), you can take advantage of suburban-style discounts—if you don't mind the bratty crowds.

Movie Theater	Address	Phone	Map
AMC Franklin Mills Mall 14	1149 Franklin Mills Cir	215-923-6699	p 123
International House Theater	3701 Chestnut St	215-387-5125	14
Roxy Theatre Philadelphia	2023 Sansom St	215-923-6699	1
Ritz at the Bourse	400 Ranstead St	215-440-1181	4
Ritz East	125 S 2nd St	215-925-4535	4
Ritz Five	214 Walnut St	215-440-1184	4
The Tuttleman IMAX Theater	222 N 20th St	215-448-1111	1
United Artists Riverview Stadium 17	1400 S Columbus Blvd	215-755-2353	8
University City Penn 6	4012 Walnut St	215-386-9800	13
United Artists Main St 6	3720 Main St	215-482-6230	22

Arts & Entertainment · **Bookstores**

Overview

The Philly bookstore scene has radically changed for the much better as of late—after all, even one or two new institutions can make a difference. With the slaying of Borders, we now only have one giant behemoth store downtown that you may have heard of that's called **Barnes & Noble (Map 2)**. But there are plenty of independents vying for your business—and, heck, they deserve it already.

General New/Used

Joseph Fox (Map 2), selling literary fiction, nonfiction, poetry, art and children's books, is an excellent place to start. Tucked several streets behind the behemoth that is Barnes & Noble, this nook o' wonder has existed for over fifty years, and the original proprietor, Madeline Fox, can be found here with her son, Michael, who now runs the place. At Joseph Fox, there is a real mind behind the selection, and the shelves are packed tightly with books you get the sense you really must read—and the booksellers employed have read that book twice already, which makes for a useful conversation—or two. Penn students flock to **House of Our Own (Map 13)** to get slightly off-campus—hell, they don't do it that often, so that's really saying something. **Head House Books (Map**

8) serves Society Hill well; proprietor Richard de Wyngaert hosts readings, a chess club for kids, story hours, and book groups. Any new literary title can be found here, plus an awesome children's selection. Head House also sells plenty of that kind of five-pounder coffee-table slab, many of which can be really quite beautiful, and make a lovely gift. Two of our favorite used spots are **Last Word Bookshop (Map 13)** and **The Book Trader (Map 4)**, where we get great satisfaction from trading in our old books for ones that are new to us.

Specialty

You can get caught up on all of your anarchy manifestos at **Wooden Shoe (Map 4)** and then learn to love one another again at **Garland of Letters (Map 8)**, which also provides a wafting aroma of fine incense. Design mavens can't get enough of **AIA (Map 2)**, which has a giant array of architecture and urban planning tomes including anything by or about our city hero, Edmund Bacon. The gay/lesbian scene is neatly served by **Giovanni's Room (Map 3)**, which also offers a hugely popular reading series. To find out who really did do it, **Whodunit? (Map 2)** has all the answers. **Big Blue Marble Books (Map 25)** in Mount Airy sells progressive and multicultural titles for both adults and children.

Map 1 • Center City West

Book Corner	311 N 20th St	215-567-0527	New, rare, and good used books in all genres.
Famulus Books	244 S 22nd St	215-732-9509	Used books.
Fat Jack's Comicrypt	2006 Sansom St	215-963-0788	Comic books.

Map 2 • Rittenhouse / Logan Circle

AIA Book Store	117 S 17th St	215-569-3188	Architecture and design.
Barnes & Noble	1805 Walnut St	215-665-0716	Chain.
Barnes & Noble	1805 Walnut St	215-665-0716	Chain.
Bauman Rare Books	1608 Walnut St	215-546-6466	Rare books.
MCP Hahnemann University Bookstore	1505 Race St	215-762-7629	Drugs, diseases & more. We challenge you to find denser reading.
Joseph Fox Book Shop	1724 Sansom St	215-563-4184	Independent.
Whodunit?	1931 Chestnut St	215-567-1478	Used, more than just mysteries & thrillers.

Map 3 • Center City East

AIA Bookstore & Design Center	1218 Arch St	215-569-3188	Architecture and design.
Atlantic Books	920 South St	215-592-1275	Bookstore chain from the shore forays into the city.
Chinese Culture & Arts	126 N 10th St	215-928-1616	Chinese books.
CLC Bookcenter	730 Chestnut St	215-922-6868	Bibles & Christian books.
Cookbook Stall	51 12th St	215-923-3170	Cookbooks.
Giovanni's Room	345 S 12th St	215-923-2960	Lesbian, gay, bisexual, and transgender.
Horizon Books	901 Market St	215-625-7955	African-American.
Jefferson Medical & Health Science Bookstore	1009 Chestnut St	215-955-7922	Medical and health science.
Russakoff's Books and Records	259 S 10th St	215-592-8380	Used Books.
WJ Bookstore	1017 Arch St	215-592-9666	Chinese book store.

Map 4 · Old City / Society Hill

The Book Trader	7 N 2nd St	215-925-2080	Discounted used, first editions, and out-of-print books.

Map 8 · Bella Vista / Queen Village

Atomic City Comics	638 South St	215-625-9613	Comics, Japanese animation, cult films and beyond.
Brickbat Books	709 S 4th St	215-592-1207	Great used books, occasionally chilly staff.
Garland of Letters	527 South St	215-923-5946	New age books, trinkets, and many, many types of candles.
Head House Books	619 S 2nd St	215-923-9525	General bookstore.
Mostly Books	529 Bainbridge St	215-592-8380	Used.
Pilothouse Charts	3 N Columbus Blvd	267-773-7858	Maritime.
Wooden Shoe Books	704 South St	215-413-0999	For those who'd call *The Nation* a conservative rag.

Map 9 · Point Breeze / West Passyunk

Prosperity Bookstore	2059 Snyder Ave	215-755-1225	General bookstore.

Map 13 · West Philly

Bindlestiff Books	4530 Baltimore Ave	215-222-2432	Tiny, cute, mostly new remainders.
House of Our Own	3920 Spruce St	215-222-1576	Politics, history, sociology, and multi-cultural topics.
Last Word Bookshop	220 S 40th St	215-386-7750	Used.
The Marvelous!	4916 Baltimore Ave	215-726-8742	Comics, graphic novels.

Map 14 · University City

Barnes & Noble Drexel University	S 33rd St & Chestnut St	215-895-2860	College bookstore.
Dolbey's Medical Bookstore	3734 Spruce St	215-222-6020	Textbooks, medical, and health and science reference.
First District Bookstore	3801 Market St	215-662-5110	General.
Penn Book Center	130 S 34th St	215-222-7600	College bookstore.
Penn Bookstore	3601 Walnut St	215-898-7595	Used and new textbooks.

Map 17 · Fairmount

Bookhaven	2202 Fairmount Ave	215-235-3226	Used.

Map 18 · Spring Garden / Francisville

Community College of Philadelphia Book Store	1700 Spring Garden St	215-751-8152	Textbooks, reference, and more.

Map 19 · Northern Liberties

Bookspace	1113 Frankford Ave	215-291-5880	An emotionally warm atmosphere within a voluminous physical space.
That's the Book	1113 Frankford Ave	215-291-5880	That's the book!

Map 25 · Germantown North

Big Blue Marble Bookstore	551 Carpenter Ln	215-844-1070	Specializing in progressive and multicultural books

Map 26 · Mt Airy

Walk a Crooked Mile Books	7423 Devon St	215-242-0854	Used.

Museums

The **Philadelphia Museum of Art (Map 17)** stands proudly as one of the five best art museums in the country; allow yourself several days to peruse their permanent collection. While you're in the area, you should definitely hit up the **Rodin Museum (Map 17)**, which is filled with sculpture from one of the 20th century's most prominent artists. The **Barnes Foundation's (Map 17)** controversial move to Center City is a fascinating story (see in particular the excellent documentary The Art of the Steal) but don't let that overshadow Albert C. Barnes' impressive collection of Impressionist and Modern works that climb the gallery's walls (you have to see it to believe it). For the literary inclined, the **Rosenbach (Map 1)** has the original manuscript of Joyce's Ulysses as well as art by Maurice Sendak, author of the beloved Where The Wild Things Are. The Rosenbach is so fond of Joyce, in fact, that every June they host a Bloomsday festival, named after Leopold Bloom, the main character in Ulysses. Local volunteers read passages from the book to onlookers throughout the day. If you're up for the weird world of science and the macabre, **Mütter Museum (Map 1)** is brimming with biological specimens. For a mental twist, the **Museum of the American Philosophical Society (Map 4)** mounts intellectual, engaging exhibits about things that maybe you never thought you'd care about (the history of natural history, anyone?), and yet you really do while you're in there. For a museum that is a museum piece on museums, go to **Franklin Court (Map 4)**, under the sculptural outline of Ben Franklin's house—there, you'll receive old-school telephone calls from even older-school ghosts. On the more modern tip, the **Institute of Contemporary Art (Map 14)**, while small, uses space inventively to show up-to-the-minute art grabbed with curatorial aplomb from an international pool. And if you're a cartographic junkie (like the entire staff of NFT), make sure to check out the largest map of Philadelphia in the world at the **Philadelphia History Museum (Map 3)**.

Museum	Address	Phone	Map
The Academy of Natural Sciences	1900 Benjamin Franklin Pkwy	215-299-1000	2
The African American Museum in Philadelphia	701 Arch St	215-574-0380	3
American Philosophical Society Museum	104 S 5th St	215-440-3400	4
American Swedish Historical Museum	1900 Pattison Ave	215-389-1776	n/a
The Athenaeum	219 S 6th St	215-925-2688	4
Barnes Foundation	2025 Benjamin Franklin Pkwy	215-278-7000	17
The Fabric Workshop and Museum	1214 Arch St	215-561-8888	3
Fairmount Water Works	640 Waterworks Dr	215-685-0723	n/a
Fireman's Hall Museum	147 N 2nd St	215-923-1438	4
The Franklin Institute	222 N 20th St	215-448-1200	1
Germantown Historical Society	5501 Germantown Ave	215-844-1683	24
Grand Army of the Republic Museum and Library	4278 Griscom St	215-289-6484	n/a
Historical Society of Pennsylvania	1300 Locust St	215-732-6200	3
Independence Seaport Museum	211 S Columbus Blvd	215-413-8655	4
Insectarium	8046 Frankford Ave	215-335-9500	n/a
Institute of Contemporary Art	118 S 36th St	215-898-7108	14
Johnson House	6306 Germantown Ave	215-438-1768	25
La Salle University Art Museum	1900 W Olney Ave	215-951-1000	n/a
Mario Lanza Museum	712 Montrose St	215-238-9691	8
Masonic Temple	1 N Broad St	215-988-1900	2
Mummers Museum	1100 S 2nd St	215-336-3050	8
The Museum of Elfreth's Alley	126 Elfreth's Aly	215-574-0560	4
Mütter Museum	19 S 22nd St	215-563-3737 ext. 211	1
National Constitution Center	525 Arch St	215-409-6600	4
National Liberty Museum	321 Chestnut St	215-925-2800	4
National Museum of American Jewish History	101 S Independence Mall East	215-923-3811	4
New Hall Military Museum	320 Chestnut St	215-965-2305	4
Philadelphia Doll Museum	2253 N Broad St	215-787-0220	n/a
Philadelphia History Museum	15 S 7th St	215-685-4830	3
Philadelphia Museum of Art	2600 Benjamin Franklin Pkwy	215-763-8100	16
Philadelphia Ship Preservation Guild	801 S Columbus Blvd	215-238-0280	4
Please Touch Museum	4231 Avenue of the Republic	215-581-3181	1
Polish American Cultural Center	308 Walnut St	215-922-1700	4
Rodin Museum	2151 Benjamin Franklin Pkwy	215-568-6026	17
Romanian Folk Art Museum	1606 Spruce St	609-216-6991	2
The Rosenbach Museum & Library	2008 DeLancey Pl	215-732-1600	1
Stenton: A Historic House Museum	4601 N 18th St	215-329-7312	n/a
Shoe Museum	810 Race St	215-625-5243	3
Shofuso Japanese House & Garden	4301 Lansdowne Dr	215-878-5097	n/a
United States Mint	151 N Independence Mall E	215-408-0110	4
University of Pennsylvania Museum of Archaeology and Anthropology	3260 South St	215-898-4000	14
The Wagner Free Institute of Science	1700 W Montgomery Ave	215-763-6529	n/a
Woodmere Art Museum	9201 Germantown Ave	215-247-0476	27

Pennsylvania Academy of the Fine Arts

General Information

NFT Map: 2
Address: 118-128 N Broad St (Galleries)
Philadelphia, PA 19102
1301 Cherry St (School)
Philadelphia, PA 19107
Phone: 215-972-7600
Website: www.pafa.org
Hours: Tues–Sat 10 am–5 pm,
Sun 11 am–5 pm,
Closed Mon and legal holidays

Overview

The Pennsylvania Academy of the Fine Arts is an old and much-venerated institution: in 2005 it celebrated its 200th anniversary. This stunning architectural space is renowned for collecting, exhibiting, teaching, and promoting American fine art. The Academy is made up of a fine arts school, a public programs facility, various art galleries, and the country's oldest museum.

School of Fine Arts

The school has nearly 300 full-time students presently enrolled. The educational program includes a certificate course (painting, sculpture, and printmaking), a Bachelor of Fine Arts program (in conjunction with UPenn), and a one-year post-baccalaureate program (that allows students to work towards the two-year Masters of Fine Arts degree). Notable alumni include Philadelphia-born photographer Charles Sheeler, master painter Thomas Eakins, and oddball filmmaker David Lynch—who was so inspired by Philly's blighted glumness in the mid-'70s, he created *Eraserhead* as an homage.

The Galleries

Throughout its history, the gallery has held over 1,000 shows of artists such as Edgar Degas, Judith Rothschild, and Andy Warhol. The gallery is also renowned for exhibiting the work of new and emerging local talents. Opening hours are Tuesday through Saturday, 10 am–5 pm, and Sunday, 11 am–5 pm. Admission to the gallery is $15 for adults, $12 for students (with ID) and seniors (60+), and $8 for youth (13-18). Kids 12 and under and military personnel are free. Museum tours are given Tuesday through Sunday at 1 pm and 2 pm, and are free with admission.

How to Get There—Driving

From I-95 S, follow signs to I-676. Take I-676 to the Broad Street exit, which will put you on 15th Street. Turn left onto Race Street, then right onto Broad Street. The Academy is one block down on the right.

From I-95 N and I-76 (Schuylkill Expressway), take I-76 W, and exit at I-676/Central Philadelphia. Follow directions above.

Parking

There are three pay lots on Academy grounds. Two are between 16th and Broad Street—one on Cherry Street and one on Race Street. The third is located at the northeast corner of Broad Street and Cherry Street.

How to Get There— Mass Transit

Ride the Market/Frankford Line to the 15th Street Station. Walk one block north to Arch Street, then one block east to Broad Street. Make a left on Broad Street. The Pennsylvania Academy is one block north.

Take the Broad Street line to the Race/Vine stop. Exit the station on Race and Broad Streets. Walk one block south (toward City Hall) on Broad Street. The Museum is at the northeast corner of Broad and Cherry Streets.

By Regional Rail, take any one of the lines to the Market East Train Station. Exit the station on Market Street and walk west (toward City Hall) until you reach Broad Street, then turn right. The Museum is one block along on the left.

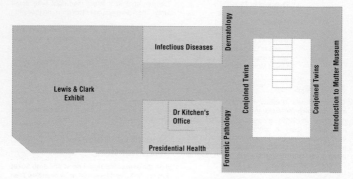

Infectious Diseases

Dermatology

Conjoined Twins

Conjoined Twins

Introduction to Mütter Museum

Lewis & Clark
Exhibit

Forensic Pathology

Dr Kitchen's
Office

Presidential Health

UPPER LEVEL

MAP
1

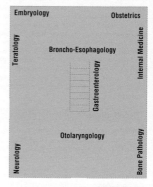

Embryology

Obstetrics

Teratology

Broncho-Esophagology

Internal Medicine

Gastroenterology

Neurology

Otolaryngology

Bone Pathology

LOWER LEVEL

General Information

NFT Map:	1
Address:	19 S 22nd St Philadelphia, PA 19103
Phone:	215-563-3737
Website:	www.collegeofphysicians.org/ mutter-museum
Hours:	Mon–Sun: 10 am–5 pm, every day of the year except for Thanksgiving, Christmas Eve, Christmas, and New Year's Day.
Admission:	Adults $15, Seniors (65+) & Military (with ID) $13, Youth (6-17) & Students (with ID) $10, Free for children 5 and under.

Overview

In the early 1800s in the US, medical students were lectured for two years then sent out to try their newly acquired knowledge on patients. In Europe at the time, medical students worked with trained physicians and surgeons throughout their education, and Thomas Mütter decided that he wanted to bring European teaching pedagogies to the US. Mütter spent $20,000 of his own money to build a teaching collection of anatomical specimens, medical instruments, and pathological models that were used by generations of medical students as part of their training. Now run by the College of Physicians of Philadelphia, the museum has become an offbeat attraction for ordinary visitors.

The most popular exhibit remains the stomach-churning five-foot long colon, which was removed from a man who lived (and died) around the turn of the century (the colon contained over forty pounds of feces when removed—grossed out yet?). Other attractions include the cast of Chang and Eng, the famous Siamese twins attached at the liver, and a collection of more than 2,000 objects that have been swallowed and removed. Did you ever wonder where Grover Cleveland's secret cheek tumor ended up? It's in a jar on the first floor.

As a warning, you'd be wise to forego that second helping of goulash before you visit, as some of the exhibited collection is definitely not for the weak-stomached. The display of diseased skin springs to mind, for example. A key goal of the museum is to provide a look at the world of health and medicine as it existed in the 19th century, some of which can be very uncomfortable for contemporary visitors to behold. But if you keep an open scientific mind, you'll likely learn a great deal about the modern history of medicine in the US.

How to Get There—Driving

Follow I-76 E (Schuylkill Expressway) to Exit 344 (I-676 E/Central Philadelphia—formerly Exit 38) and then stay in the middle lane in order to get on I-676 E. Merge right and take the first (quick) right hand exit, which is the Benjamin Franklin Parkway/23rd Street exit.

Follow the ramp to the second light and turn right on 21st Street. Stay on 21st Street for about seven blocks and then turn right on Chestnut Street and proceed one block to 22nd Street. The museum is located at 19 S 22nd Street, on the right hand side of the street.

Parking

Good luck. Trawl the streets and keep your eyes peeled!

How to Get There— Mass Transit

Take the Green Line trolley to 22nd and Market Streets. From the stop, walk down 22nd Street (against the traffic), and the museum will be on your left. Eastbound bus routes 21 and 42 stop at 22nd and Chestnut Streets. Westbound bus routes 21, 42, and 12 stop at 22nd and Walnut Streets.

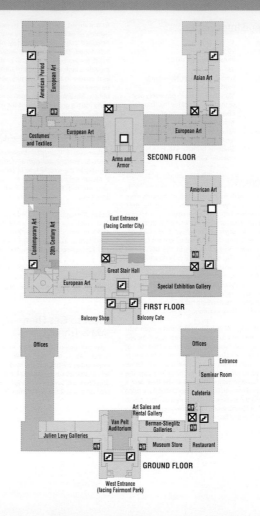

MAP 16

SECOND FLOOR

American Period European Art

Asian Art

Costumes and Textiles

European Art

European Art

Arms and Armor

FIRST FLOOR

Contemporary Art

20th Century Art

American Art

East Entrance (facing Center City)

Great Stair Hall

European Art

Special Exhibition Gallery

Balcony Shop

Balcony Cafe

GROUND FLOOR

Offices

Offices

Entrance

Seminar Room

Cafeteria

Art Sales and Rental Gallery

Van Pelt Auditorium

Berman-Stieglitz Galleries

Julien Levy Galleries

Museum Store

Restaurant

West Entrance (facing Fairmont Park)

General Information

NFT Map: 16
Address: 26th St & Benjamin Franklin Pkwy
Philadelphia, PA 19130
Phone: 215-763-8100
Recorded
Information: 215-684-7500
Website: www.philamuseum.org
Hours: Tues–Sun 10 am–5 pm, extended
hours on Wednesdays and Fridays
till 8:45 pm.
Closed Mondays, Thanksgiving,
Christmas, New Years, and July 4th.
Admission: Admission prices give access to the
main Museum building, Perelman
building, Rodin Museum, and
Historic House Mount Pleasant for
two consecutive days. Adults $20,
Seniors (65+) $18, Students (with
ID) and Youth (13–10) $14, Children
12 and under are free. First Sundays
of the month and Wednesdays after
5 pm are pay-what-you-wish.

Overview

We understand that it's difficult for tourists to resist running up the stairs in front of the Philadelphia Museum of Art and prancing around in a tight circle at the top with their fists raised in the air. Not every city has such a far-reaching pop culture icon. But as a Philly resident, you absolutely CANNOT do it (you are, however, welcome to dress the Rocky statue in pink underwear). You lose that privilege the second you move here. Besides, the main purpose of your visit to PMA should be to view the 300,000 splendid art works inside the museum.

Founded in 1876, the Philly Museum of Art is a world-renowned art institution recognized for its vast permanent collections of East Asian, American, European, and contemporary art. As with many things in this city, our museum is regularly given short shrift compared to New York's incredible facilities, but the PMA stands on its own. The impressive permanent collections are ably supplemented by the museum's visiting exhibitions in fashion, contemporary art, photography, impressionism, pop art, sculpture, and Old Masters. What's more, just down the parkway sits the fabulous Rodin Museum and its sculpture garden, which your two-day PMA ticket will get you into as well.

Special events take place throughout the week at the PMA. On Friday evenings, the austere Great Stair Hall is transformed into a pseudo-jazz club, with musicians beginning their sets at 5 pm while visitors enjoy wine and finger food to ease them into the weekend. The museum also offers lectures, classes, art classes for children, tours of the surrounding historic houses in Fairmount Park, trolley rides, and a guided Schuylkill stroll to picturesque Boathouse Row. Check the PMA website for a calendar of events.

How to Get There—Driving

From the west, take I-76 E and exit at Spring Garden Street. At end of exit ramp go left. Continue past the side of the museum, through the first traffic light and around Eakins Oval, staying in the far left lane. Turn left at the second traffic light and then bear right. Follow the sign for the Art Museum. After the sign, get in the far left lane and turn left at the first traffic light (Art Museum Drive). This will take you to the west entrance of the museum, where limited parking is available.

From I-676 (Vine Street Expressway), take the Benjamin Franklin Parkway exit on your right. At the end of the exit ramp, turn right onto 22nd Street and get into the far left lane. Turn left onto the outside lanes of the Benjamin Franklin Parkway. Follow the sign for the Art Museum. After the sign, turn left onto Art Museum Drive. This will take you to the west entrance of the museum, where limited parking is available.

Parking

The parking lot is located on the west side of the main Museum building and rates are $12 for the first four hours and $2 for each additional hour. Members receive reduced parking rates. Parking tickets must be validated inside the Museum. Limited accessible parking is available in the Upper Terrace parking area for a $12 flat rate and $8 for members (cash only). For more information call Visitor Services at (215) 763-8100.

How to Get There— Mass Transit

The PHLASH bus (215-925-TOUR) provides direct transportation from Center City and Penn's Landing to the Museum of Art between 10 am and 6 pm, May through November for only $2. SEPTA bus routes 7, 32, 38, 43, and 48 all serve the museum area.

The party is always in Philly, legally till 2 am, but usually much later. We love to drink, as evidenced by our freakish restrictions about buying booze (also known as "blue laws"). State liquor stores close by 10 pm, leaving us with two options: go to a bar or go to Jersey—and we can often be seen with swooshy fingers, taking out no-service-charge twenties at Wawa, having chosen (with all our might) to abstain from Jersey. Unfortunately, when Jersey is faced with the same dire choice, they choose not themselves, and can be spotted living—er, trashing—it up in certain special locales where spray-tans glisten with the metal sheen of the Camden side of the river. But this is just the drink talking.

Beer

In recent years, Philly's obsession with beer bars has led it to developing a massive gut becoming a premier city for beer snobs. Philly Beer Week, which takes place every June, is a veritable cavalcade of brewery tap takeovers, beer dinners, and pop up beer halls—we dare you to make it to the last day without calling out sick from work. During the other 51 weeks of the year, **Standard Tap (Map 19)**, **Royal Tavern (Map 8)**, **Devil's Den (Map 7)**, **South Philadelphia Tap Room (Map 9)**, **Bainbridge Barrel House (Map 8)**, and the granddaddy of them all, **Monk's (Map 2)**, are favorites for local beers on tap. For those who enjoy beer with your game night, head to **Barcade (Map 19)** or **Garage (Map 8)**. If you're looking more for exotic beer than a night out, try making your own six pack at **The Foodery (Map 19)**, **Hawthorne's (Map 7)**, **Bottle Bar East (Map 19)**, **The Corner Foodery (Map 2)**, or **Food & Friends (Map 2)**. For a more Irish perspective, go to **Fergie's (Map 3)**; please be aware that there really is a Fergie and he is, in fact, quite Irish. Continue your European beer tour at **The Victoria Freehouse (Map 4)**, **Frankford Hall (Map 20)**, and **Alla Spina (Map 18)**. Or stay right in your own backyard by sampling Philly's own revered breweries, **Yard's Brewing Company (Map 20)**, **Philadelphia Brewing Company (Map 20)**, and **Dock Street Brewery (Map 13)**.

Sports

If you want to watch the game(s) and be where the action is (and cross "ride a mechanical bull" off your bucket list), head to the sports-bar-to-end-all-sports-bars—**Xfinity Live (Map 12)**. Slightly less intimidating versions exist at the **Field House (Map 3)** and Chickie's and Pete's (**Northeast Philadelphia**). Alternatively, **O'Neal's (Map 8)** is relatively low-key as sports bars go, and you can even stay after the game to get your groove going. **Tir Na Nog (Map 2)**, with its league of brash devotees, continues to host athletic adventures in athletic voyeurism. We hesitate to mention it because it's both small and one of our favorite spots, but when it comes to game time, **Murph's (Map 20)** is, as the sign promises, a comfortable place to be.

Swank

The **Ritz-Carlton Rotunda (Map 2)** is the end all be all of places to be seen. Red Sky **(Map 4)** glows magenta on Market with dessert martinis. **Tria (Map 2, 3)**, from its knowledgeable servers, voluminous menu, anally chosen glassware, and artful food pairings, is wine perfect. **Ranstead Room (Map 1)**, **Franklin Mortage & Investment Co. (Map 2)**, **The Farmer's Cabinet (Map 3)** and **Hop Sing Laundromat (Map 3)** make the fanciest vintage cocktails this side of 1908, and bartenders there are walking liquor encyclopedias. **The Continental (Map 4)** in Center City is impressive for its swinging chairs and batshit roofdeck (which features terribly annoying clientele on the weekends). **The Black Sheep (Map 2)**, meanwhile, will help you wind down in style. And if you consider yourself to be a person who enjoys the finer things in life/are named Ron Swanson, make yourself at home at **Lloyd Whiskey Bar (Map 20)** and **Ashton Cigar Bar (Map 2)**.

Dive

We're not sure if a bar can still technically be a dive after being voted "Best Dive," but it takes two hands to hold **Oscars' (Map 2)** supercheap, supergigantic beers. Neighborhood obsession **Doobie's (Map 1)** is always good, especially if you like carpeting in your bar. And anything goes at **Dirty Frank's (Map 3)**. If you find yourself stuck on South Street, beeline it to **Tattooed Mom (Map 8)**, which has a smoking room and great drink specials—PBR pounders, anyone? Similarly, if you're stuck in Old City, check out **Drinker's Tavern (Map 4)** and ogle at the majesty of their frat house style basement. **Bob and Barbara's (Map 7)** will do you whiskey for cheap, and if the amazingly jazzy house band isn't putting your head back together as you systematically drink it apart, the juke box can rock, too. It seems pertinent to mention **The Dive Bar (Map 8)**, which is the zest of the neighborhood (and by zest, we mean carcinogenic) but don't miss Saturday night karaoke with a mix of dirty hipsters and old neighborhood men at **Ray's Happy Birthday Bar (Map 8)** down the street.

Dance

Most of the big clubs in Philly, including anything on Delaware Avenue, are filled with Jersey kids and suburbanites—except for **Morgan's Pier (Map 4)**, which has somehow managed to stay awesome with strong drinks, great DJs, and a view to die for. For some truer getting down during cooler months, how about **The 700 (Map 19)**? Also known as "Seven Hundies," this once-bastion of hipster dancing has lost a little of its edge, but it's still fun. If you're looking for the next big thing, though, try **The Barbary (Map 19)**. **Medusa (Map 1)** basement of rank delight is a trip alright. And five cop cars aren't pulled up beside **McFadden's (Map 19)** on a weekend for nothing—there's a party inside, and it's trashy as hell—good for a joke night that turns black-eye serious.

Gay/Lesbian

Most of the alternative bars are in roughly the same area of Center City (lovingly referred to as the "Gayborhood"). **The Bike Stop (Map 3)** is not so dainty, and has whips to boot. **Woody's (Map 3)** is the mainstay of the gay community, and is large and welcoming for all. And to venture out every once and a while (we mean from the Gayborhood, silly) check out the weekly Thursday night drag show at **Bob & Barbara's (Map 7)**.

Music Venues

Philly's music scene is as varied and wide-open as you could hope for. For Down-and-dirty indie bands, check out R5 Productions (www.r5productions.com) (occasionally all-ages) shows at the **First Unitarian Church (Map 1)**, **The Barbary (Map 19)**, and more. For the over-21 contingent, there's gigs at **Johnny Brenda's (Map 20)**, **Milkboy (Map 3)**, and **The Khyber (Map 4)**, which hosts not only music but also events like comedy shows and the like. **The Electric Factory (Map 19)** and **Union Transfer (Map 18)** are larger venues in No-Libs, but not as big (or as obnoxious) as the Wachovia Center, that's many of the big touring bands. For a more gentle vibe, the **North Star (Map 16)** and **World Cafe Live (Map 1)** are great spots to check out up-and-comers, while **TLA (Map 8)** on South Street is like a white canvas (okay, but black and a little used) where mid-level music acts make the space and crowd their own. The **Trocadero (Map 3)**, legendary for its titty show days, now hosts a wild eclectica of music acts. And finally, for the jazz set there's **Ortlieb's (Map 19)**, which was once rated as one of the top ten jazz clubs in the country by Playboy. As to whether it's funnier that Playboy did the rating or that one of the nation's top jazz cafes is in Philly, we're still not sure.

Philly has the kind of restaurant-to-person ratio we could only dream about for teacher-to-student in our public schools—the kind that allows us to sample new flavors in new seating scenarios as often as we please. And still the restaurant scene continues to grow every day. From our slew of exposed brick BYOBs, our pizza meccas and cheesesteak musts, to a whole galaxy of Starr's, there isn't one good reason to eat where you pay the rent.

Italian

Madonna mia, where to begin? Vetri (**Map 3**) lives up to its reputation and has prices to match, along with other Marc Vetri offerings like Alla Spina (**Map 18**). For purists, Villa di Roma (**Map 8**) provides absolutely kick-ass pasta dishes in an atmosphere reminiscent of the house in All in the Family. Melograno (**Map 1**), the always buzzing BYOB, provides a hip milieu some of us might require. Branzino (**Map 2**), another BYOB, serves up fine Italian dining in their breathtaking garden or mansion turned restaurant. It's tough to choose the best Italian joint in the city, but Modo Mio (**Map 19**) may top the list—and we've got the elastic waistband to prove it. Little Nonna's (**Map 3**) gets our vote for date night, with Il Pittore (**Map 2**), Bistro Romano (**Map 4**), and Osteria (**Map 18**) also earning honorable mention.

Asian

Besides the people getting on the bus to New York, everybody else is in Chinatown for the food, and with excellent reason. Vietnam (**Map 3**) is the unconquerable champion here—and its West Philly sister site, the Vietnam Cafe? (**Map 13**) is pretty wonderful as well. The best banh mi goes to QT Vietnamese Sandwich Company (**Map 3**), which combines Philly's world famous hoagie bread with lovely Vietnamese fillings.

Moving on from Vietnam (as if that were possible), other Chinatown greats include the hipster-discovered Rangoon (**Map 3**), serving Burmese food with unflinching quality, not to mention oomph—try the calamari salad. Lee How Fook (**Map 3**) has a sophisticated Chinese menu and the dishes come large enough to share. If you can't make it to Chinatown but are craving a taste of the orient, Nom Nom Ramen (**Map 2**), Han Dynasty (**Map 4, 14, 22**), and Circles (**Map 7, 19**) can fill the need.

Our sushi awards go to Hikari (**Map 19**), Vic Sushi Bar (**Map 1**), and Fat Salmon (**Map 3**)—all small, relatively inexpensive, and stocked with beautifully fresh fish. And foodies flock to Morimoto (**Map 3**), for reasons having to do with lobster.

Pizza

We don't want no trouble, we just want to share some of our favorite slices. Perhaps the most famous spot in Philly is out in Port Richmond, Tacconelli's (**Map 20**), which is so popular, they require you to reserve your dough in advance. Not good at planning in advance? Marra's (**Map 10**) is a South Philly legend, and you can't get that kind of exalted status unless you know how to twirl some dough. Lorenzo's (**Map 8**) has the Italian Market wrapped around its finger, and Mama Palma's (**Map 1**) definitely gets props for having the most variety. You want wood oven? Nomad (**Map 8**), Pizzeria Vetri (**Map 17**), Pizzera Beddia (**Map 19**), and Bufad (**Map 18**) all take the cake—or, uh, pie. Earthbread and Brewery (**Map 25**) and Dock Street Brewery (**Map 13**) put the yeast to work in both their pizzas and beer. Serious pizza enthusiasts/ninja turtles head to Pizza Brain (**Map 20**) for its creative, Brooklyn-style pies and a look-see at the world's first pizza museum.

Breakfast

For the best breakfasts in Philly, you have no choice but to buck up and wait—and the places that'll make you wait the longest, like Sam's Morning Glory Diner (Map 7), Sabrina's Cafe? (Map 8, 17), and Honey's Sit 'n' Eat (Map 6, 19), are where you should plant yourself along with the rest of us. At Morning Glory, the bright, homey feel gives way to creations no one's willing to execute at home—packed pancakes, exquisite frittatas. Sabrina's delivers similarly with a possible advantage of being in the vibrant Italian Market—or the advantage of a slightly shorter wait if you go to the Callowhill location. Honey's, meanwhile, combines Southern comfort food with Jewish fare for a result that'll leave you longing for latkes days after you've left. And a.kitchen (Map 2) is the place to be seen while nursing your Ketel One hangover. For a quieter, cheaper morning, Ida Mae's (Map 20) still has the right idea. Or you can start your day the farm-to-table way on the beautiful patio at Talula's Garden (Map 3).

Luxe

Sadly, Le Bec-Fin is no more, though Lacroix (Map 2) and Fitler Dining Room (Map 1) both provide a fine French dining experience. Guests (and gawkers) of the Four Seasons enjoy the all-encompassing luxury of Fountain (Map 2), while Sbraga (Map 2) presents the fine dining experience with a bit more modern twist. The ubiquitous Stephen Starr's ritzy meat establishment Barclay Prime (Map 2) out-steaks some of the more stern (GOP Incorporated) competition.

Vegetarian/Vegan

For a city that's built its reputation on meat sandwiches, Philly offers a surprising number of vegetarian/vegan options. In fact, Vedge (Map 3), which combines vegetables and fine dining for an amazing eating experience, is so popular among herbivores and carnivores alike, that it can often take weeks to reserve a table. Hell, our baseball stadium even offers seitan cheesesteaks from Campo's Deli (Map 4)! For the lunch crowd, there's HipCity Veg (Map 2), Maoz (Map 3, 8), Govinda's (Map 7), and Pure Fare (Map 1, 7). Other excellent (though not necessarily healthy) veg options abound at Cedar Point (Map 20), Su Xing House (Map 2), Strangelove's (Map 3), Royal Tavern (Map 8), and Blackbird Pizzeria (Map 4). And on that note, stop by Monk's (Map 2) for the best vegetarian cheesesteak in the city.

BYOB

One of Philly's most engaging traditions is its affinity for the inexpensive fine dining experience. Stop by a good wine store (say, in Jersey) and head on over to one of these beauties. **Lolita (Map 3)** shoots to the top of our list, with its sultry fusion fare—meat and tofu cooked to smoldering perfection—terribly sexy (not to mention kind) waitstaff, and house-made margarita mixes, provided you bring the tequila (which we suggest you do). Old City's **Chloe (Map 4)** continues to be a perennial favorite amongst foodies and those trying to dodge Old City in Old City. **Audrey Claire (Map 1)** is a professed favorite of the Rittenhouse crowd. Finally, what would life be like without **Dmitri's (Map 8)** loving Mediterranean fare? We shudder to think.

Hoagies and Steaks

Did you think we forgot?! Can't go wrong with Paesano's (Map 8, 19), Chickie's Italian Deli (Map 7), Pastificio (Map 12), and the old standby, Primo's Hoagies (Map 1, 9) for hoagies that would make Cliff Huxtable proud. And while Pat's King of Steaks (Map 8) and Geno's Steaks (Map 8) still crank out awesome cheesesteaks, Jim's Steaks (Map 8), Tony Luke's (Map 11), and Campo's Deli (Map 4) hit the spot.

It must be humbly admitted: We're still catching on to the fashion thing. Macy's is as good as it gets at the moment for department stores, and Walnut Street is the closest thing to any sort of "Fashion District." But you know what? Screw it. If you really want a day of big-name shopping, drive out to the King of Prussia Mall. For the funky, the used, or (fine, if you really want 'em) a $200 pair of jeans, read on!

Beauty

For sophisticates whose hair is of the utmost importance, **Giovanni & Pileggi (Map 2)** will lovingly apply their brand of follicle therapy and **Liquid (Map 2)**, also quite chic, will turn you out perfect. Other talented stylists tailor tresses at **Salon Vanity (Map 2)** and **Richard Nicholas (Map 2)**. Crave an edgy 'do from a man who makes sculptures out of human hair? Check out **Julius Scissor (Map 1)**.

Clothing

Always start with the shoes! **Head Start Shoes (Map 2)** is hands and feet down the most deliriously euro-hip place for women's shoes—starting at 200 bucks, it's okay if you want to look…or try on…or…On the flipside, **Bare Feet (Map 3, 7, 11)** is a cheap, super fun adventure in kicks and threads, while **Vagabond (Map 4)** sells elegantly artsy, flowing designs for women. The **Gap Outlet (Map 2)** is a hidden gem for deals if you don't mind the line. For the men folk only, if **Boyd's (Map 2)** is good enough for NBA 'ballers, it's probably okay for you, too. Sports fan who has (nearly) everything? **Mitchell & Ness (Map 3)** sells the unique throwback jerseys that can't go out of style. But if you need to suit up, do it in style at **Henry A. Davidson (Map 2)**. For a slightly (and just slightly) cheaper take on **Urban Outfitters (Map 2, 14)**, go by **Retrospect (Map 8)** on South Street for a chance to buy the Salvation Army's best, plucked from those racks and brought to you here. Oh, and if you crave the skintight, designed-by-a-perv look, don't worry: we have **American Apparel (Map 14)**, too.

Home and Gift

For the kitchen, **Fante's (Map 8)** offers every conceivable appliance, device, and gadget, and **Philadelphia Bar & Restaurant Supply (Map 8)** can get you all your pots, pans, and glasses for cheap. If you're a student trying to fill an empty apartment, check out **Uhuru (Map 3)**, but be prepared for Free Mumia indoctrination before, during, and after all purchases. The delightful **PHAG (Map 3)** sells hip vinyl furniture, kooky martini glasses, and more, while **Bulb (Map 1)** purveys all manner of interior lighting. Looking for something that just screams, "Hello!"? Check out **Hello World (Map 2)** and **Hello Home (Map 3)**. It's impossible to go wrong at **Open House (Map 3)**, which sells swervy furniture, geometric lamps, clever espresso cups, and even body products. If you're not quite sure what you're looking for, check out handmade grab-bag **Art Star (Map 19)**, and feel good supporting independent artists. When you're ready to dress up your outdoor space (if you're lucky enough to have one), stop by **Urban Jungle (Map 8)**, which caters to city yards. When you're done decorating, throw a party and pick up supplies at **Occassionette (Map 10)**, a Pinterest board brought to life. Finally, after a long day of hitting the pavement, stop by the **Random Tea Room (Map 19)** and score a bag of something entirely soothing.

Accessories

Chunky is in, and **De' Village (Map 3)** in Reading Terminal Market sells some pretty heavy pieces—wood, gems, or shells, there's something big and bold to be found here. Another notable place to pick up chunk is at the Philadelphia Flea Market (various locations), which comes around in the spring, summer, and fall months, and where vendors display box after box of the stuff. Not into chunk? Items of the daintier variety can be found at **Moon & Arrow (Map 8)** and **Urban Princess (Map 8)**. We'd talk about diamonds but we don't want to. Your status quo, status-driven engagement is not our problem.

Walnut Street (Map 2)

Shopping is a dangerous addiction for some. When you don't have money to make a purchase, that **Coach** print can haunt you, redundantly, in your dreams. Sometimes you just need a new necklace to make it through the day. The businesses on Walnut Street understand. They know you'll drop your last dime at **Urban Outfitters** or, for a sexy breed of biz-casual, at **Zara**—even if that means you have to eat Easy Mac every day for a week. **H&M** has most of us addicted—but if you're repulsed by cheap fashion, at least take advantage of the freon dumping zone out front during a hot day. **Anthropologie**, for the mature urban-outfit wearer, resides in a building that outshines the clothes—a 19th century mansion formerly occupied by the founder of the store. It's always amusing when a t-shirt costs $200, which is where **Ubiq**, quite unabashedly, pops in its ugly, rave-chic head. **Athleta** awards you the identity of being the best dressed gym rat in the locker room (though they do get props for their uber-liberal return policy). And then there's the **Apple Store**, for all your iNeeds.

Mall

Yep, singular. There's only one mall in the heart of the city—**The Gallery at Market East (Map 3)**. Chaotic, crowded, kids screaming on the escalators, and teenagers ruefully sucking lollipops, Market East has always seemed reminiscent of that scene in the educational film about Free Market Capitalism, shot in the eighties, that you watched in Applied Economics class. This "bustling economy" has got the usual roundup of stores like **Old Navy (Map 3)**, where consumers can choose at their leisure what they most totally need to have based on, of course, the laws of supply and demand. It also has the convenience of being a convergence of all main bus and train lines, not to mention being nice and close to the Greyhound Bus Terminal (If ever there was a sign of swank …).

Department Store

Macy's (Map 3) is Center City's only department store—unless you count K-Mart. Its window displays are more depressing than seeing somebody's run-over cat in the street and they haven't come home yet and they're about to find out. Or like Russian orphans. Sad, sad mannequins. So sad.

Vintage/Resale

You can deck yourself in Versace circa 1992 or dig for even earlier finds at stores like **Sophisticated Seconds (Map 2)** and Immortal Uncommon (Map 2) and snag some one-of-a-kind furniture for your digs at **Uhuru (Map 3)**. Shaggy chic finds can be bought and sold at **Buffalo Exchange (Map 2)**, as well as **Green Street Consignment (Map 3)** and **Philly AIDS Thrift (Map 8)**. **Retrospect (Map 8)** gets a bad rap for marking up cool stuff they found at the Salvation Army by about 1000%—but, just like on the playground, rules are rules, and they found it first!

Electronics

If you're the next Bill Gates-in-training, head over to **Bundy (Map 2)** or **Springboard Media (Map 1)** to fuel your PC needs. The **Apple Store (Map 2)** on Walnut Street means that you don't have to traipse out to King of Prussia or Cherry Hill.

Music

Whether you're a Butch Walker fan or a Lady Gaga junkie, **Sound of Market Street (Map 3)** has the biggest selection since Tower Records went out of business. The staff is incredibly knowledgeable and helpful at **AKA Music (Map 4)**, and can turn you on to underground artists. **Creep Records (Map 19)** and **Borderline Records (Map 19)** spin and sell good tunes, but you must be in-the-know to graze at **Repo (Map 8)**. Nearby **Philadelphia Record Exchange (Map 8)** is also well-worth a browse.

With each year, Philly's burgeoning art scene continues to push boundaries and make a name for itself. Between long-time traditional artists and recent graduates from the city's three highly regarded art schools, there's literally something for everyone.

A great way to become acquainted with some of the galleries, at least in Old City, is to regularly attend Philly's First Friday gatherings. On the first Friday of each month, the OC galleries stay open late, launch lots of new exhibits, and pander to guests with cheap wine and bites to eat. Check out the works at **Pentimenti (Map 4)** and **Artists' House (Map 4)**. For performance space as well as fine arts exhibits, **Painted Bride (Map 4)** has long been a Philly stalwart. In May and June, local arts students hold their senior shows

in many galleries, which results in quite a few surprisingly professional, avant-garde works. And for the younger DIY set, plenty of starving artists without access to studios make and sell their art right on the sidewalks in front of the galleries. In the warmer weather, the scene becomes a veritable open-air market, complete with live music and impromptu dancing.

There are of course also plenty of worthwhile galleries outside of the Old City boundaries. Check out **Space 1026 (Map 3)**, **The Fabric Workshop and Museum (Map 3)**, the **Highwire Gallery (Map 3)** or the **Esther Klein Gallery (Map 14)**. If you have money to burn for art, you can hit the big leagues at **Locks (Map 4)** or, for considerably less, purchase a world-class piece from **The Clay Studio (Map 4)**.

Map 1 · Center City West

Dolan/Maxwell	2046 Rittenhouse Sq	215-732-7787
The Galleries at Moore College of Art & Design	N 20th St & Benjamin Franklin Pkwy	215-965-4045
Gallery 339	339 S 21st St	215-731-1530
Sande Webster	2006 Walnut St	215-636-9003

Map 2 · Rittenhouse / Logan Circle

The Center for Emerging Visual Artists	237 S 18th St	215-546-7775
Calderwood Gallery	1622 Spruce St	215-546-5357
Fleisher/Ollman Gallery	1616 Walnut St	215-545-7562
Gross McCleaf	127 S 16th St	215-665-8138
Highwire Gallery	1315 Cherry St	215-829-1255
Makler Gallery	225 S 18th St	215-735-2540
Mangel Gallery	1714 Rittenhouse Sq	215-545-4343
Newman Galleries	1625 Walnut St	215-563-1779
Pennsylvania Academy of the Fine Arts	118 N Broad St	215-972-7600
Philadelphia Art Alliance	251 S 18th St	215-545-4302
The Print Center	1614 Latimer St	215-735-6090
Rosenwald-Wolf Gallery	333 S Broad St	215-717-6480
Schmidt/Dean Gallery	1710 Sansom St	215-569-9433
Schwarz Gallery	1806 Chestnut St	215-563-4887

Map 3 · Center City East

African American Museum in Philadelphia	701 Arch St	215-574-0380 ext. 235
Bridgette Mayer Gallery	709 Walnut St	215-413-8893
The Fabric Workshop and Museum	1222 Arch St	215-568-1111
Gallery Space 1026	1026 Arch St	215-574-7630
M Finkel and Daughter	936 Pine St	215-627-7797
The Philadelphia Sketch Club	235 S Camac St	215-545-9298
Seraphin Gallery	1108 Pine St	215-923-7000
Vox Populi	319 N 11th St	215-238-1236

Map 4 · Old City / Society Hill

3rd Street Gallery	58 N 2nd St	215-625-0993
Artists' House	57 N 2nd St	215-923-8440
ArtJaz	53 N 2nd St	215-922-4800
The Clay Studio	139 N 2nd St	215-925-3453
FAN Gallery	221 Arch St	215-922-5155
The FUEL Collection	249 Arch St	215-592-8400
Gallery Joe	302 Arch St	215-592-7752
Hot Soup	26 S Strawberry St	215-922-2332
Indigo	151 N 3rd St	215-922-4041
The Knapp Gallery	162 N 3rd St	267-455-0279
Larry Becker	43 N 2nd St	215-925-5389
Locks Gallery	600 Washington Sq S	215-629-1000
Muse Gallery	52 N 2nd St	215-627-5310
Painted Bride	230 Vine St	215-925-9914
Peng Gallery	35 S 3rd St	215-280-5753
Pentimenti	145 N 2nd St	215-625-9990
Qbix Art Gallery	211 Arch St	215-625-2521
Rodger LaPelle Galleries	122 N 3rd St	215-592-0232
Rosenfeld Gallery	113 Arch St	215-922-1376
Snyderman-Works Gallery	303 Cherry St	215-238-9576
Wexler Gallery	201 N 3rd St	215-923-7030
Wood Turning Center	501 Vine St	215-923-8000

Map 7 · Southwark West

Mew Gallery	906 Christian St	215-625-2424

Map 8 · Bella Vista / Queen Village

Da Vinci Art Alliance	704 Catharine St	215-829-0466
Eye's Gallery	402 South St	215-925-0193
Fleisher Art Memorial	719 Catharine St	215-922-3456 ext. 318
SoulPurl 77	1138 S 9th St	215-528-1367

Map 14 · University City

Arthur Ross Gallery/ University of Pennsylvania	220 S 34th St	215-898-2083
Esther M Klein Art Gallery	3701 Market St	215-966-6188
Institute of Contemporary Art	118 S 36th St	215-898-7108

Map 17 · Fairmount

Philadelphia Museum of Art	2600 Benjamin Franklin Pkwy	215-763-8100
Rodin Museum	N 22nd St & Benjamin Franklin Pkwy	215-568-6026

Map 18 · Spring Garden / Francisville

Cerulean Arts	1355 Ridge Ave	267-514-8647
Khmer Art Gallery	319 N 11th St	215-922-5600

Map 19 · Northern Liberties

Art Star Gallery	623 N 2nd St	215-238-1557
Projects Gallery	629 N 2nd St	267-303-9652
Rebekah Templeton Contemporary Art	173 W Girard Ave	267-519-3884
Tower Gallery	969 N 2nd St	215-253-9874

Map 20 · Fishtown / Port Richmond

Highwire Gallery	2040 Frankford Ave	215-426-2685

Map 27 · Chestnut Hill

The Carol Schwartz Gallery	101 Bethlehem Pike	215-242-4510
JMS Gallery	8236 Germantown Ave	215-248-4649
Woodmere Art Museum	9201 Germantown Ave	215-247-0476

General Information

NFT Map: 2
Address: 1729 Mt Vernon St
Philadelphia, PA 19130
Phone: 215-685-0750
Website: www.muralarts.org

Overview

If graffiti-covered buildings and dreary gray walls can look ominous and depressing on the most vibrant blocks, one can only imagine their effect on the psyche of poverty-stricken neighborhoods. But like concealer that hides facial blemishes, the Mural Arts Program covers up blights on the cityscape; more than 2,400 indoor and outdoor murals have been commissioned across the city since 1984. Philadelphia has quickly become the mural capital of the country, and the Mural Arts Program continues to commission up to 100 murals each year in neighborhoods that request their help.

This same public art program now offers weekly trolley tours that guide participants to some of the more obscure mural sites. Often led by mural artists, the tours explore different neighborhoods each week and provide a "behind-the-scenes" look at the making of the intricate paintings.

There's also a free Mural Arts Program map and audio guide with a walking route that you can follow at your own pace. The walking tour is approximately 2.5 miles long and takes about one hour to complete without the audio guide and two hours with it. You can access the map and audio guide via their website (www.muralarts.org).

Regular Tours

Weekly tours are mostly held on Fridays, Saturdays, and Sundays. Over the years, tour options have expanded from walking tours to a variety of options on foot and via bicycle, to trolley tours, elevated subway tours, and special themed tours. You can even hire a private "Step-On Guide" to ride around with you in your own vehicle for an intimate two-hour spin exploring Philly's murals. Tour departures vary depending on the tour, so check the website for more information. Tour tickets range from $20-30 for adults. Discounts for the Trolley Tours are available to seniors (65+) and children 3–12, and are free for children 2 and under.

Winter Tours

There are no regularly scheduled winter tours, but the Mural Arts program does offer specific programs and lectures between October and April. Check the website for events.

Sure, you don't think of us in the same league as Chicago or that rinky-dink city to our immediate north, but the truth is that Philly has a pretty vibrant theater community. Every September, the Philadelphia Live Arts Festival and Philly Fringe (separate, but concurrent) are occasions to sample the best of the local scene alongside emerging artists from around the world. You can always rely on the local Pig Iron Theatre Company (www.pigiron.org) for thought-provoking, original work. Ever since 2006's production of Killer Joe, **Theatre Exile (Map 4)** has been on a rampage, producing some of the best emotionally driven work around. And competition is good: when **Philadelphia Theatre Company (Map 2)**, moved to the Avenue of the Arts, it began rivaling the **Wilma (Map 2)** and the **Arden (Map 4)** in its caliber of performances, with, of course, its own wacky and sometimes lyrical flavoring.

History lovers will know that the venerated **Walnut Street Theatre (Map 3)** is, in fact, the oldest in the country. The **Arden Theatre (Map 4)**, in Old City, backs local playwrights Michael Hollinger and Bruce Graham, puts on Sondheim for the subscription crowd, and offers some of the most fanciful children's theatre in town. For those who enjoy the puppetry arts, there's **Spiral Q (Map 14)**, whose biggest annual event is a parade and pageant called Peoplehood. Broadway enthusiasts should head to the **Academy of Music (Map 2)**, which runs the Broadway at the Academy series, drawing touring shows of the hottest musicals to befall the great white way. The **Forrest (Map 3)** and the **Merriam (Map 2)** also provide plenty of high notes and shoe-tapping.

Philadelphia also has a small (but growing!) comedy scene. Check out **Helium Comedy Club (Map 1)**. Short form improv groups The N Crowd (www.phillyncrowd.com) and ComedySportz (www.comedysportzphilly.com) both perform weekly. The Philly Improv Theater puts on sketch and longform improv shows at the **Shubin (Map 8)**, and the **Walking Fish Theatre (Map 20)** and **Connie's Ric-Rac (Map 8)** both occasionally host comedy as well.

Theater	Address	Phone	Map
941 Theater	941 N Front St	215-235-5603	19
Academy of Music	S Broad St & Locust St	215-893-1999	2
Adrienne Theater	2030 Sansom St	215-567-2848	1
Annenberg Center for the Performing Arts	3680 Walnut St	215-898-3900	14
Arden Theatre	40 N 2nd St	215-922-1122	4
Arts Bank	601 S Broad St	215-545-0590	7
Bistro Romano Mystery Dinner Theatre	120 Lombard St	215-238-1313	4
Bushfire Theatre	224 S 52nd St	215-747-9230	13
Forrest Theatre	1114 Walnut St	215-923-1515	3
The Gershman Y	401 S Broad St	215-446-3027	2
Harold Prince Theatre	3680 Walnut St	215-898-6701	14
Harold L. Zellerbach Theatre	3680 Walnut St	215-898-6701	14
International House Theater	3701 Chestnut St	215-895-6546	14
Irvine Auditorium	3401 Spruce St	215-898-6701	14
Kimmel Center for the Performing Arts	300 S Broad St	215-790-5800	2
Merriam Theater	250 S Broad St	215-732-5997	2
Mum Puppettheatre	115 Arch St	215-925-7686	4
Philadelphia Arts Bank	601 S Broad St	215-545-0590	7
Philadelphia Theatre Company	480 S Broad St	215-985-0420	2
Plays & Players	1714 Delancey St	215-735-0630	2
Prince Music Theater	1412 Chestnut St	215-972-1000	2
Shubin Theatre	407 Bainbridge St	215-592-0119	8
Society Hill Playhouse	507 S 8th St	215-923-0210	3
Spiral Q Puppet Theater	3114 Spring Garden St	215-222-6979	14
Suzanne Roberts Theater	480 S Broad St	215-985-0420	2
Theater Catalyst	2030 Sansom St	215-563-4330	1
Theatre Exile	525 S 4th St	215-922-4462	4
Theatre of Living Arts	334 South St	215-922-2599	8
UArts Drake Dance Theater	1512 Spruce St	215-717-6110	2
Walking Fish Theatre	2509 Frankford Ave	215-427-9255	20
Walnut Street Theatre	825 Walnut St	215-574-3550	3
The Wilma Theater	265 S Broad St	215-546-7824	2

General Information

NFT Map:	2
Address:	300 S Broad St
	Philadelphia, PA 19102
Phone:	215-893-1999
Website:	www.kimmelcenter.org
Tele-charge:	215-893-1999
Hours:	Mon–Sun 10 am–6 pm, and later during evening performances.

Overview

The Kimmel Center occupies a full city block on Broad Street's southern side and is considered the crown jewel in the refurbished Avenue of the Arts. Fifteen million dollars of the $265 million project came from philanthropist Sidney Kimmel, the most generous individual donor. Playing home to the Philadelphia Orchestra, the Chamber Orchestra of Philadelphia, PHILADANCO, American Theater Arts for Youth, the Philadelphia Chamber Music Society, the Opera Company of Philadelphia, the Pennsylvania Ballet, and Philly Pops, the place oozes culture.

The 2,500-seat **Verizon Hall** was custom-built by acoustician Russell Johnson to enhance the orchestral sound of the Philadelphia Orchestra. The architectural design of the hall, with its wood paneling and curves, makes it look like the inside of a violin or cello. Despite pre-construction hoopla about the hall's planned world-class acoustics, classical music connoisseurs have found the sound to be less than exceptional; the average, untrained concertgoer will find little to complain about, though. And in May 2006, the world's largest concert hall organ was unveiled, complete with 7000 pipes, the largest of which extend 32 feet high, enough to please both size and sound queens alike.

The smaller **Perelman Theater** has 650 seats and is used for chamber music and dance performances. The 2,893-seat **Philadelphia Academy of Music** is owned by The Philadelphia Orchestra Association, managed by the Kimmel Center, and hosts performances by the Opera Company of Philadelphia, the Pennsylvania Ballet, and Philly Pops with Peter Nero. The Academy of Music also runs the Broadway at the Academy series, which features touring Broadway shows like Mamma Mia!, Jersey Boys, and The Book of Mormon, giving Philadelphians a little more breathing room in the pecking order battle with New York.

In addition to a pretty cool eatery and gift shop, the Kimmel Center has a gallery showcasing works from nearby Moore College of Art and Design.

How to Get There—Driving

From the north, follow Broad Street around City Hall and you'll find the Kimmel Center on the southwest corner of Broad and Spruce Streets. The Vine Street Expressway (I-676) will get you to Broad Street, and either I-95 or I-76 will get you to the Vine Street Expressway. From the Ben Franklin Bridge, take the first exit on 8th Street to Spruce Street and continue west to Broad Street. From the Walt Whitman Bridge, take the Broad Street exit and go north.

Parking

Entrance to the Kimmel Center parking garage is south of the Broad Street entrance to the center and can only be accessed by cars traveling south on Broad Street. Garage hours are Monday through Friday 6 am to Midnight, Saturday 8 am to 1 am, and Sunday from 8 am to Midnight. If you're in before 10 am and out by 6:30 pm, you'll pay $12 on weekdays, but if you arrive after 10 am, expect to pay $20. Staying parked in the garage after 6:30 pm will get you another $15 charge. For evening events, if you arrive after 5 pm, you'll shell out $23. Weekends are a flat rate of $20 between 8 am and 6 pm and if you arrive after 5 pm its $23 for the night. As on the weekdays, daytimers parked after 6:30 pm will incur another $15 charge. If that seems expensive, you can try your luck with street parking or check the rates of the local lots that surround the area.

How to Get There— Mass Transit

Take the subway. The Broad Street line's Walnut Locust Station is two blocks from the Kimmel Center. Make a free transfer from the Market-Frankford line and the trolleys to the Broad Street Line at the 15th & Market stop. Regional Rail is also an option, with Suburban Station a 15-minute walk away from the Kimmel Center. The PHLASH makes a stop near the Kimmel Center and bus routes C, 27, 32, 12, 9, 21 and 42 all stop at the center.

How to Get Tickets

The only way to avoid the $5 service charge per ticket is by purchasing tickets at the Kimmel Center box office, which is open daily 10 am–6 pm. Tickets are also sold online at www.kimmelcenter.org/planning/tickets.php or by phone on 215-893-1999.

If you're on a limited budget, shoot for the $10 tickets to "Kimmel Center Presents" performances. The $10 tickets are up for grabs at the box office starting at 5:30 pm for evening performances and 11:30 am for matinees. A limited number of Broadway rush tickets are available for $30 at the Academy of Music Box Office (240 S. Broad St). Tickets are available two hours before curtain time and must be paid for in cash. Student rush tickets are also available with a student ID (also $10).

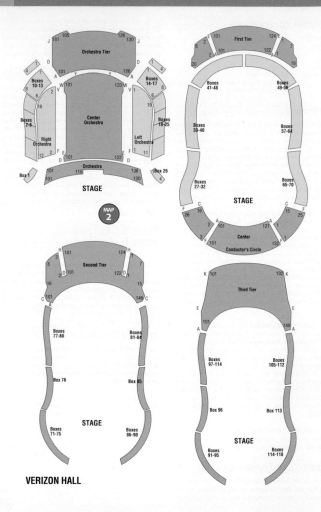

MAP 2

STAGE

VERIZON HALL

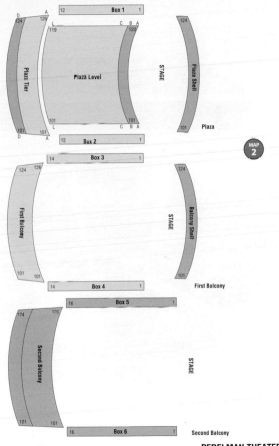

MAP
2

PERELMAN THEATER

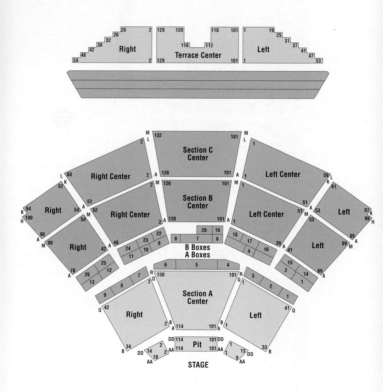

General Information

Address:	5201 Parkside Ave
	52nd St & Parkside Ave
	Philadelphia, PA 19131
Phone:	215-893-1999
Website:	www.manncenter.org

Overview

Every major city in America has a big outdoor concert space on its outskirts; the venerable Mann Center is Philly's. The venue is ideal for picnicking on the grass with family and friends while concerts serve as background music to more pertinent social activity. It's also a great place to watch the Fourth of July fireworks.

The Mann Center was originally built to serve as the summer home of the Philadelphia Orchestra. It now boasts an eclectic concert schedule including mainstream rock bands, operas, stand-up comedians, children's programs, as well as the occasional Christian Night Out.

For most events, lawn tickets are cheap and still in sight of the stage, and pavilion tickets are affordable. All tickets are non-refundable. (meaning you'll be expected to plop down on the grass, rain or shine.) You're allowed to take lawn chairs and food with you (you can also buy food there) and, depending on the event, you can also take alcohol (make sure you check before your six-pack is confiscated at the door). The formerly-confusing eating facilities have undergone a reorientation of sorts, but we recommend booking in advance if you want a sit-down meal.

How to Get There—Driving

From Center City, take the Benjamin Franklin Parkway to the Art Museum Circle. Follow the signs to West River Drive. Once you're on West River Drive, turn left at the first traffic light (Sweet Briar Cut-Off). Turn right at the stop sign to Lansdowne Drive and proceed on Lansdowne to the parking areas.

Parking

Parking costs $15 or $30 for RVs, campers, and buses. Parking areas, as well as the center itself, open two hours before any event, so you can arrive early for dinner before the show.

How to Get There—Mass Transit

SEPTA bus lines 38, 40, and 43 deliver you within walking distance of the Mann Center. The Center City Loop Bus provides service between certain stops in the city and the Mann (one-way fare is $4.50). Check the bus schedule online on the Mann Center website: www.manncenter.org

How to Get Tickets

You can purchase tickets on the Mann Center website or on the phone, but be ready to pay a service charge of $5.50 per ticket and $3 per order. Tickets purchased online can only be picked up at the Mann Center box office will-call window at 52nd Street and Parkside Drive. To avoid service charges, you can buy tickets in person from the Mann Center box office, which is open Monday-Saturday from 10 am to 5 pm. You can also purchase tickets from the Center City box office, located at the Kimmel Center (Broad St & Spruce St), for a $2 service charge per order.

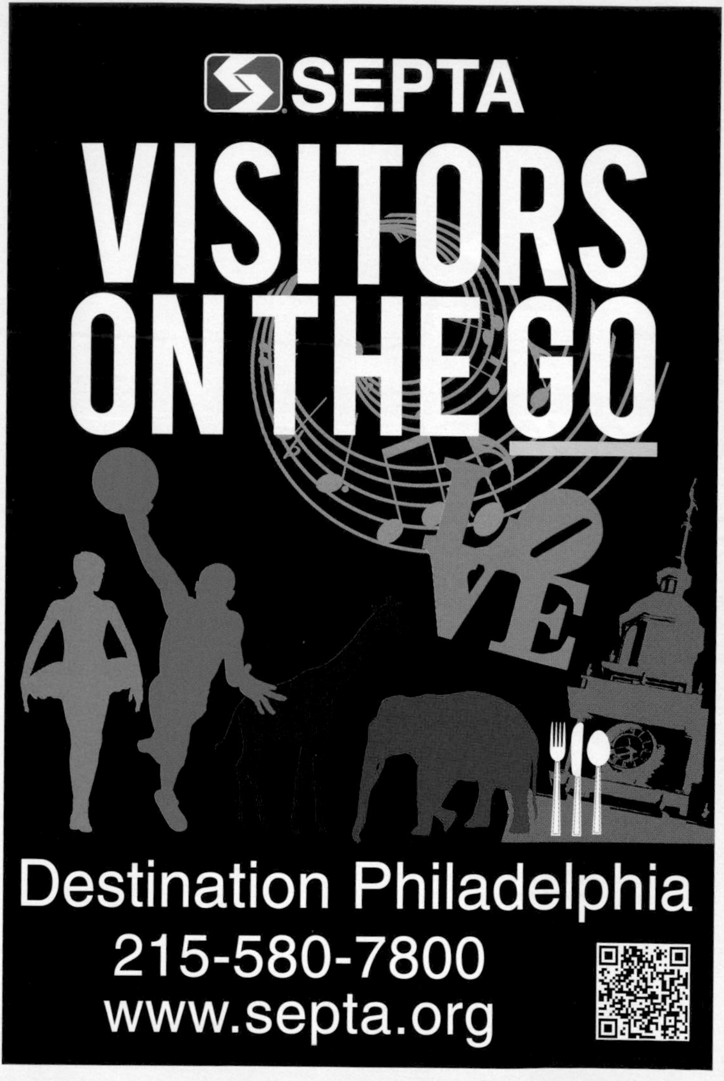
SEPTA
VISITORS
ON THE GO
LOVE
Destination Philadelphia
215-580-7800
www.septa.org

Street Index

Street Index

Street Index

Street Index

Street Index

We'll map your world.

Need a custom map?

NFT will work with you to design a custom map that promotes your company or event. NFT's team will come up with something new or put a fresh face on something you already have. We provide custom map-making and information design services to fit your needs—whether simply showing where your organization is located on one of our existing maps, or creating a completely new visual context for the information you wish to convey. NFT will help you—and your audience—make the most of the place you're in, while you're in it.

For more information, visit
www.notfortourists.com/corporatesales.aspx

NOT FOR TOURISTS™ Custom Books

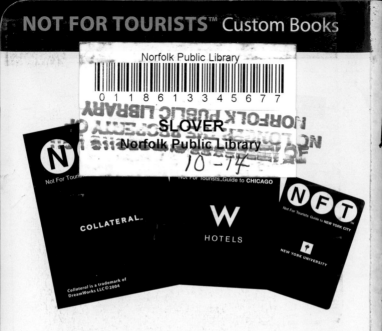

Customize your NFT.

We can put **your organization's logo or message** on NFT using custom foil stamps of your (or our) design. Not For Tourists Guidebooks make **great gifts** for employees, clients, and promotional events.

For more information, visit
www.notfortourists.com/corporatesales.aspx